FREE Test Taking Tips Video/DVD Offer

To better serve you, we created videos covering test taking tips that we want to give you for FREE. **These videos cover world-class tips that will help you succeed on your test.**

We just ask that you send us feedback about this product. Please let us know what you thought about it—whether good, bad, or indifferent.

To get your **FREE videos**, you can use the QR code below or email freevideos@studyguideteam.com with "Free Videos" in the subject line and the following information in the body of the email:

    a. The title of your product

    b. Your product rating on a scale of 1-5, with 5 being the highest

    c. Your feedback about the product

If you have any questions or concerns, please don't hesitate to contact us at info@studyguideteam.com.

Thank you!

HSPT Prep Book 2024-2025

2 Practice Tests and HSPT Study Guide for Catholic High Schools [5th Edition]

Lydia Morrison

Interested in buying more than 10 copies of our product? Contact us about bulk discounts:
bulkorders@studyguideteam.com

ISBN 13: 9781637752258

Table of Contents

Quick Overview

As you draw closer to taking your exam, effective preparation becomes more and more important. Thankfully, you have this study guide to help you get ready. Use this guide to help keep your studying on track and refer to it often.

This study guide contains several key sections that will help you be successful on your exam. The guide contains tips for what you should do the night before and the day of the test. Also included are test-taking tips. Knowing the right information is not always enough. Many well-prepared test takers struggle with exams. These tips will help equip you to accurately read, assess, and answer test questions.

A large part of the guide is devoted to showing you what content to expect on the exam and to helping you better understand that content. In this guide are practice test questions so that you can see how well you have grasped the content. Then, answer explanations are provided so that you can understand why you missed certain questions.

Don't try to cram the night before you take your exam. This is not a wise strategy for a few reasons. First, your retention of the information will be low. Your time would be better used by reviewing information you already know rather than trying to learn a lot of new information. Second, you will likely become stressed as you try to gain a large amount of knowledge in a short amount of time. Third, you will be depriving yourself of sleep. So be sure to go to bed at a reasonable time the night before. Being well-rested helps you focus and remain calm.

Be sure to eat a substantial breakfast the morning of the exam. If you are taking the exam in the afternoon, be sure to have a good lunch as well. Being hungry is distracting and can make it difficult to focus. You have hopefully spent lots of time preparing for the exam. Don't let an empty stomach get in the way of success!

When travelling to the testing center, leave earlier than needed. That way, you have a buffer in case you experience any delays. This will help you remain calm and will keep you from missing your appointment time at the testing center.

Be sure to pace yourself during the exam. Don't try to rush through the exam. There is no need to risk performing poorly on the exam just so you can leave the testing center early. Allow yourself to use all of the allotted time if needed.

Remain positive while taking the exam even if you feel like you are performing poorly. Thinking about the content you should have mastered will not help you perform better on the exam.

Once the exam is complete, take some time to relax. Even if you feel that you need to take the exam again, you will be well served by some down time before you begin studying again. It's often easier to convince yourself to study if you know that it will come with a reward!

Test-Taking Strategies

1. Predicting the Answer

When you feel confident in your preparation for a multiple-choice test, try predicting the answer before reading the answer choices. This is especially useful on questions that test objective factual knowledge. By predicting the answer before reading the available choices, you eliminate the possibility that you will be distracted or led astray by an incorrect answer choice. You will feel more confident in your selection if you read the question, predict the answer, and then find your prediction among the answer choices. After using this strategy, be sure to still read all of the answer choices carefully and completely. If you feel unprepared, you should not attempt to predict the answers. This would be a waste of time and an opportunity for your mind to wander in the wrong direction.

2. Reading the Whole Question

Too often, test takers scan a multiple-choice question, recognize a few familiar words, and immediately jump to the answer choices. Test authors are aware of this common impatience, and they will sometimes prey upon it. For instance, a test author might subtly turn the question into a negative, or he or she might redirect the focus of the question right at the end. The only way to avoid falling into these traps is to read the entirety of the question carefully before reading the answer choices.

3. Looking for Wrong Answers

Long and complicated multiple-choice questions can be intimidating. One way to simplify a difficult multiple-choice question is to eliminate all of the answer choices that are clearly wrong. In most sets of answers, there will be at least one selection that can be dismissed right away. If the test is administered on paper, the test taker could draw a line through it to indicate that it may be ignored; otherwise, the test taker will have to perform this operation mentally or on scratch paper. In either case, once the obviously incorrect answers have been eliminated, the remaining choices may be considered. Sometimes identifying the clearly wrong answers will give the test taker some information about the correct answer. For instance, if one of the remaining answer choices is a direct opposite of one of the eliminated answer choices, it may well be the correct answer. The opposite of obviously wrong is obviously right! Of course, this is not always the case. Some answers are obviously incorrect simply because they are irrelevant to the question being asked. Still, identifying and eliminating some incorrect answer choices is a good way to simplify a multiple-choice question.

4. Don't Overanalyze

Anxious test takers often overanalyze questions. When you are nervous, your brain will often run wild, causing you to make associations and discover clues that don't actually exist. If you feel that this may be a problem for you, do whatever you can to slow down during the test. Try taking a deep breath or counting to ten. As you read and consider the question, restrict yourself to the particular words used by the author. Avoid thought tangents about what the author *really* meant, or what he or she was *trying* to say. The only things that matter on a multiple-choice test are the words that are actually in the question. You must avoid reading too much into a multiple-choice question, or supposing that the writer meant something other than what he or she wrote.

5. No Need for Panic

It is wise to learn as many strategies as possible before taking a multiple-choice test, but it is likely that you will come across a few questions for which you simply don't know the answer. In this situation, avoid panicking. Because

3

most multiple-choice tests include dozens of questions, the relative value of a single wrong answer is small. As much as possible, you should compartmentalize each question on a multiple-choice test. In other words, you should not allow your feelings about one question to affect your success on the others. When you find a question that you either don't understand or don't know how to answer, just take a deep breath and do your best. Read the entire question slowly and carefully. Try rephrasing the question a couple of different ways. Then, read all of the answer choices carefully. After eliminating obviously wrong answers, make a selection and move on to the next question.

6. Confusing Answer Choices

When working on a difficult multiple-choice question, there may be a tendency to focus on the answer choices that are the easiest to understand. Many people, whether consciously or not, gravitate to the answer choices that require the least concentration, knowledge, and memory. This is a mistake. When you come across an answer

choice that is confusing, you should give it extra attention. A question might be confusing because you do not know the subject matter to which it refers. If this is the case, don't eliminate the answer before you have affirmatively settled on another. When you come across an answer choice of this type, set it aside as you look at the remaining choices. If you can confidently assert that one of the other choices is correct, you can leave the confusing answer aside. Otherwise, you will need to take a moment to try to better understand the confusing answer choice. Rephrasing is one way to tease out the sense of a confusing answer choice.

7. Your First Instinct

Many people struggle with multiple-choice tests because they overthink the questions. If you have studied sufficiently for the test, you should be prepared to trust your first instinct once you have carefully and completely read the question and all of the answer choices. There is a great deal of research suggesting that the mind can come to the correct conclusion very quickly once it has obtained all of the relevant information. At times, it may seem to you as if your intuition is working faster even than your reasoning mind. This may in fact be true. The knowledge you obtain while studying may be retrieved from your subconscious before you have a chance to work out the associations that support it. Verify your instinct by working out the reasons that it should be trusted.

8. Key Words

Many test takers struggle with multiple-choice questions because they have poor reading comprehension skills. Quickly reading and understanding a multiple-choice question requires a mixture of skill and experience. To help with this, try jotting down a few key words and phrases on a piece of scrap paper. Doing this concentrates the process of reading and forces the mind to weigh the relative importance of the question's parts. In selecting words and phrases to write down, the test taker thinks about the question more deeply and carefully. This is especially true for multiple-choice questions that are preceded by a long prompt.

4

9. Subtle Negatives

One of the oldest tricks in the multiple-choice test writer's book is to subtly reve
a word like *not* or *except*. If you are not paying attention to each word in the qu
by this trick. For instance, a common question format is, "Which of the following
instead is, "Which of the following is not...?," then the answer will be quite diffe
are aware of the potential for this mistake and will include one answer choice th
were not negated or reversed. A test taker who misses the reversal will find wha
answer and will be so confident that he or she will fail to reread the question an
only way to avoid this is to practice a wide variety of multiple-choice questions a
and every word.

10. Reading Every Answer Choice

It may seem obvious, but you should always read every one of the answer choic
habit of scanning the question and assuming that they understand the question
words. From there, they pick the first answer choice that answers the question t
takers who read all of the answer choices might discover that one of the latter a
correct. Moreover, reading all of the answer choices can remind you of facts rela
you arrive at the correct answer. Sometimes, a misstatement or incorrect detail
will trigger your memory of the subject and will enable you to find the right answ
choices is like not reading all of the items on a restaurant menu: you might miss

11. Spot the Hedges

One of the keys to success on multiple-choice tests is paying close attention to e
with words like *almost*, *most*, *some*, and *sometimes*. These words are called "hed
statement is not totally true or not true in every place and time. An absolute stat
in many subjects, the answers are not always straightforward or absolute. There

in these subjects. For this reason, you should favo
that contain hedging language. The presence of q
author is taking special care with his or her words
composing the right answer. After all, there are m
only one way to be right! For this reason, it is wis
absolute when taking a multiple-choice test. An a
things are either all one way or all another. They o
always, *best*, and *never*. If you are taking a multip
doesn't lend itself to absolute answers, be on you
words.

12. Long Answers

In many subject areas, the answers are not simple. As alrea
often requires hedges. Another common feature of the ans
question are qualifying clauses, which are groups of words
the sentence. If the question or answer choice describes a r
or the subject matter is complicated, ambiguous, or confusi
many words in order to be expressed clearly and accurately
deterred by answer choices that seem excessively long. Oft
not be able to write the correct answer without offering so

13. Restati

Sometimes, a
written. If this
important pu
question accu
words and ide
memory and

14. True St

Sometimes a
reasons why
Too often, tes
they are cont
entire questic
refer to the o
but-irrelevant

15. No Pat

One of the me
into patterns
idea that an u
pattern-seeki
unlikely that t
are scrambled
assignation o
Any attempt t
taking the tes
pattern in the

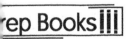

Your job is to read the answer choices thoroughly and completely and to select the one that most precisely answers the question.

g to Understand

question on a multiple-choice test is difficult not because of what it asks but because of how it is is the case, restate the question or answer choice in different words. This process serves a couple of poses. First, it forces you to concentrate on the core of the question. In order to rephrase the ately, you have to understand it well. Rephrasing the question will concentrate your mind on the key as. Second, it will present the information to your mind in a fresh way. This process may trigger your ender some useful scrap of information picked up while studying.

tements

answer choice will be true in itself, but it does not answer the question. This is one of the main is essential to read the question carefully and completely before proceeding to the answer choices. takers skip ahead to the answer choices and look for true statements. Having found one of these, nt to select it without reference to the question above. The savvy test taker will always read the n before turning to the answer choices. Then, having settled on a correct answer choice, he or she will iginal question and ensure that the selected answer is relevant. The mistake of choosing a correct-answer choice is especially common on questions related to specific pieces of objective knowledge.

erns

re dangerous ideas that circulates about multiple-choice tests is that the correct answers tend to fall These erroneous ideas range from a belief that B and C are the most common right answers, to the prepared test-taker should answer "A-B-A-C-A-D-A-B-A." It cannot be emphasized enough that g of this type is exactly the WRONG way to approach a multiple-choice test. To begin with, it is highly he test maker will plot the correct answers according to some predetermined pattern. The questions and delivered in a random order. Furthermore, even if the test maker was following a pattern in the correct answers, there is no reason why the test taker would know which pattern he or she was using. o discern a pattern in the answer choices is a waste of time and a distraction from the real work of . A test taker would be much better served by extra preparation before the test than by reliance on a answers.

Bonus Content

We host multiple bonus items online, including both practice tests in digital format. Scan the QR code or go to this link to access this content:

testprepbooks.com/bonus/hspt

The first time you access the page, you will need to register as a "new user" and verify your email address.

If you have any issues, please email support@testprepbooks.com.

Introduction to the HSPT

Function of the Test

The High School Placement Test (HSPT) is a nationally-recognized Catholic private school entrance exam used as a component of the application process. As such, the exam is intended for current eighth- and ninth-grade students only. The 3-hour exam, developed by Scholastic Testing Services (STS), includes five sections: Verbal Skills, Quantitative Skills, Reading Comprehension, Mathematics, and Language.

There is no set "passing score" on the exam. Each individual Catholic High School can set their own standards and the amount of weight given to the exam as part of the admissions process.

Test Administration

To register for the exam, students should contact the Catholic High School that they would most like to attend. Tests are administered at the prospective Catholic High Schools. In addition to their first-choice school where the exam is to be taken, test takers are able to list other schools where they would like their HSPT exam scores sent.

STS does not directly offer testing accommodations for test takers with disabilities. Accommodations might be available at the school where the student takes the exam; interested students should inquire during the registration process.

Retakes are not permitted unless special permission is granted; in these rare cases, the lower score will be accepted.

Test Format

In aggregate, the five sections of the exam contain 298 multiple-choice questions, which are to be completed in 141 minutes.

The breakdown of the sections, including the specific skills and number of questions per skill and section, is provided in the following table:

Exam Section	# of Questions
Verbal Skills	60
Quantitative Skills	52
Reading	62
Mathematics	64
Language	60

Test takers are not permitted to use calculators on the exam.

Scoring

To tabulate a test taker's raw score, each correct answer given receives one point. No points are deducted for incorrect responses, so there is no penalty for guessing. Raw scores are then converted to a scaled score from 200-800. This scaling process allows scores to be compared across various iterations of the exam. Test takers also receive a national percentile rank for each section (and a local one, in some cases), and a stanine on a $1-9$ scale, both of which give a student a way to gauge of their performance in comparison to the national cohort of test takers.

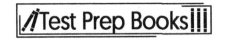

The Composite Score includes the performance on all five sections of the exam, while the Total Cognitive Skills score consists of the scores on the Verbal and Quantitative Skills subtests and the Total Basic Skills score includes the Reading, Math, and Language subtests' performances. STS also provides a Cognitive Skills Quotient (CSQ) and a Grade Equivalent (GE) Score. Somewhat akin to an IQ score, the CSQ ranges from 55 to 145, and is said to reflect the test taker's learning potential based on their test performance and age. The GE score reflects a comparison between a test taker's performance and the average performance of students at other grade levels, presented as a decimal indicating a grade level and month. A GE of 10.4, for example, represents the score of an average student in the fourth month of the 10th grade.

9

Study Prep Plan for the HSPT

1 **Schedule -** Use one of our study schedules below or come up with one of your own.

2 **Relax -** Test anxiety can hurt even the best students. There are many ways to reduce stress. Find the one that works best for you.

3 **Execute -** Once you have a good plan in place, be sure to stick to it.

One Week Study Schedule		
Day 1	Verbal Skills
Day 2	Nongeometric Comparison
Day 3	Mathematics
Day 4	Geometry
Day 5	Language
Day 6	Practice Test #1
Day 7	Take Your Exam!

Two Week Study Schedule				
Day 1	Verbal Skills	Day 8	Algebra
Day 2	Quantitative Skills	Day 9	Language
Day 3	Nongeometric Comparison	Day 10	Practice Test #1
Day 4	Reading	Day 11	Answer Explanations
Day 5	Mathematics	Day 12	Practice Test #2
Day 6	Measurements	Day 13	Answer Explanations
Day 7	Geometry	Day 14	Take Your Exam!

10

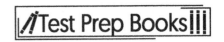

One Month Study Schedule					
Day 1	Verbal Skills	Day 11	Mathematics	Day 21	Polynomials
Day 2	Logic	Day 12	Adding and Subtracting Positive and Negative...	Day 22	Statistics and Probability
Day 3	Quantitative Skills	Day 13	Decimals	Day 23	Language
Day 4	Polygons and Solids	Day 14	Exponents	Day 24	Usage
Day 5	Effects of Changes to Dimensions on Area...	Day 15	Measurements	Day 25	Spelling
Day 6	Nongeometric Comparison	Day 16	Geometry	Day 26	Practice Test #1
Day 7	Number Manipulation	Day 17	Perimeter and Area	Day 27	Answer Explanations
Day 8	Remainders in Division Problems	Day 18	Translating Between a Geometric...	Day 28	Practice Test #2
Day 9	Reading	Day 19	Algebra	Day 29	Answer Explanations
Day 10	Vocabulary	Day 20	Linear Inequalities in One Variable	Day 30	Take Your Exam!

Build your own prep plan by visiting:
testprepbooks.com/prep

11

As you study for your test, we'd like to take the opportunity to remind you that you are capable of great things! With the right tools and dedication, you truly can do anything you set your mind to. The fact that you are holding this book right now shows how committed you are. In case no one has told you lately, you've got this! Our intention behind including this coloring page is to give you the chance to take some time to engage your creative side when you need a little brain-break from studying. As a company, we want to encourage people like you to achieve their dreams by providing good quality study materials for the tests and certifications that improve careers and change lives. As individuals, many of us have taken such tests in our careers, and we know how challenging this process can be. While we can't come alongside you and cheer you on personally, we can offer you the space to recall your purpose, reconnect with your passion, and refresh your brain through an artistic practice. We wish you every success, and happy studying!

Verbal Analogies

The verbal analogies questions on the HSPT exam test the candidate's ability to analyze words carefully and find connections in definition and/or context. The test taker must compare a selected set of words with answer choices and select the ideal word to complete the sequence. While these exercises draw upon knowledge of vocabulary, this is also a test of critical thinking and reasoning abilities. Mastering verbal analogies will help people think objectively, discern critical details, and communicate more efficiently.

Question Layout

First, two words are paired together that provide a frame for the analogy, and then there is a third word that must be found as a match in kind. It may help to think of it like this: A is to B as C is to D. Examine the breakdown below:

Apple (A) is to fruit (B) as carrot (C) is to vegetable (D).

As shown above, there are four words: the first three are given and the fourth word is the answer that must be found. The first two words are given to set up the kind of analogy that is to be replicated for the next pair. We see that apple is paired with fruit. In the first pair, a specific food item, apple, is paired to the food group category it corresponds with, which is fruit. When presented with the third word in the verbal analogy, carrot, a word must be found that best matches carrot in the way that fruit matched with apple. Again, carrot is a specific food item, so a match should be found with the appropriate food group: vegetable! Here's a sample prompt:

Morbid is to dead as jovial is to
    a. Hate.
    b. Fear.
    c. Disgust.
    d. Happiness.

As with the apple and carrot example, here is an analogy frame in the first two words: morbid and dead. Again, this will dictate how the next two words will correlate with one another. The word morbid can be defined as having a disturbing interest in unpleasant subjects, such as death and disease. In other words, morbid can mean ghastly or death-like, which is why the word dead is paired with it. Dead relates to morbid because it describes morbid. With this in mind, jovial becomes the focus. Jovial means joyful, so out of all the choices given, the closest answer describing jovial is happiness (D).

Prompts on the exam will be structured just like the one above. "A is to B as C is to ?" will be given, where the answer completes the second pair. Or sometimes, "A is to B as ? is to ?" is given, where the second pair of words must be found that replicate the relationship between the first pair. The only things that will change are the words themselves and the relationships between the words provided.

Discerning the Correct Answer

While it wouldn't hurt in test preparation to expand one's vocabulary, verbal analogies are all about delving into the words themselves and finding the right connection—the right word that will fit an analogy. People preparing for the test shouldn't think of themselves as human dictionaries, but rather as detectives. Remember, *how* the first two words are connected dictates the second pair. From there, picking the correct answer or simply eliminating the ones that aren't correct is the best strategy.

Just like a detective, a test taker needs to carefully examine the first two words of the analogy for clues. It's good to get in the habit of asking the questions: What do the two words have in common? What makes them related or unrelated? How can a similar relationship be replicated with the word I'm given and the answer choices? Here's another example:

Pillage is to steal as meander is to
    a. Stroll.
    b. Burgle.
    c. Cascade.
    d. Accelerate.

Why is pillage paired with steal? In this example, pillage and steal are synonymous: they both refer to the act of stealing. This means that the answer is a word that means the same as meander, which is stroll. In this case, the defining relationship in the whole analogy was a similar definition.

What if test takers don't know what stroll or meander mean, though? Using logic helps to eliminate choices and pick the correct answer. Looking closer into the contexts of the words pillage and steal, here are a few facts: these are things that humans do; and while they are actions, these are not necessarily types of movement. Again, pick a word that will not only match the given word, but best completes the relationship. It wouldn't make sense that burgle (B) would be the correct choice because meander doesn't have anything to do with stealing, so that eliminates burgle. Cascade (C) refers to pouring or falling, usually in the context of a waterfall and not in a reference to people, which means we can eliminate cascade as well. While people do accelerate when they move, they usually do so under additional circumstances: they accelerate while running or driving a car. All three of the words we see in the analogy are actions that can be done independently of other factors. Therefore, accelerate (D) can be eliminated, and stroll (A) should be chosen. Stroll and meander both refer to walking or wandering, so this fits perfectly.

The **process of elimination** will help rule out wrong answers. However, the best way to find the correct answer is simply to differentiate the correct answer from the other choices. For this, test takers should go back to asking questions, starting with the chief question: What's the connection? There are actually many ways that connections can be found between words. The trick is to look for the answer that is consistent with the relationship between the words given. What is the prevailing connection? Here are a few different ways verbal analogies can be formed.

Finding Connections in Word Analogies

Connections in Categories

One of the easiest ways to choose the correct answer in word analogies is simply to group words together. Ask if the words can be compartmentalized into distinct categories. Here are some examples:

Terrier is to dog as mystery is to
    a. Thriller.
    b. Murder.
    c. Detective.
    d. Novel.

This one might have been a little confusing, but when looking at the first two words in the analogy, this is clearly one in which a category is the prevailing theme. Think about it: a terrier is a type of dog. While there are several breeds of dogs that can be categorized as a terrier, in the end, all terriers are still dogs. Therefore, mystery needs to be grouped into a category. Murders and detectives can all be involved in a mystery plot, but a murder (B) and a detective (C) are not necessarily a mystery. A thriller (A) is a purely fictional concept, a kind of story or film, just like a mystery. A thriller can describe a mystery, but same issue appears as the other choices. What about novel (D)? For

16

one thing, it's distinct from all the other terms. A novel isn't a component of a mystery, but a mystery can be a type of novel. The relationship fits: a terrier is a type of dog, just like a mystery is a type of novel.

Synonym/Antonym
Some analogies are based on words meaning the same thing or expressing the same idea. Sometimes, it's the complete opposite!

Marauder is to brigand as
    a. King is to peasant.
    b. Juice is to orange.
    c. Soldier is to warrior.
    d. Engine is to engineer.

Here, soldier is to warrior (C) is the correct answer. Marauders and brigands are both thieves. They are synonyms. The only pair of words that fits this analogy is soldier and warrior because both terms describe combatants who fight.

Cap is to shoe as jacket is to
    a. Ring.
    b. Pants.
    c. Vest.
    d. Glasses.

Opposites are at play here because a cap is worn on the head/top of the person, while a shoe is worn on the foot/bottom. A jacket is worn on top of the body too, so the opposite of jacket would be pants (B) because these are worn on the bottom of the body. Often the prompts on the test provide a synonym or antonym relationship. Just consider if the sets in the prompt reflect similarity or stark difference.

Parts of a Whole
Another thing to consider when first looking at an analogy prompt is whether the words presented come together in some way. Do they express parts of the same item? Does one word complete the other? Are they connected by process or function?

Tire is to car as
    a. Wing is to bird.
    b. Oar is to boat.
    c. Box is to shelf.
    d. Hat is to head.

We know that the tire fits onto the car's wheels and this is what enables the car to drive on roads. The tire is part of the car. This is the same relationship as oar is to boat (B). The oars are attached onto a boat and enable a person to move and navigate the boat on water. At first glance, wing is to bird (A) seems to fit too, since a wing is a part of a bird that enables it to move through the air. However, since a tire and car are not alive and transport people, oar and boat fits better because they are also not alive, and they transport people. Subtle differences between answer choices should be found.

Other Relationships
There are a number of other relationships to look for when solving verbal analogies. Some relationships focus on one word being a **characteristic/NOT a characteristic** of the other word. Sometimes, the first word is the **source/comprised** of the second word. Still, other words are related by their **location**. Some analogies have

17

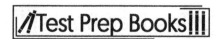

sequential relationships, and some are **cause/effect relationships**. There are analogies that show **creator/provider relationships** with the **creation/provision**. Another relationship might compare an **object with its function** or a **user with their tool**. An analogy may focus on a **change of grammar** or a **translation of language**. Finally, one word of an analogy may have a relationship to the other word in its **intensity**. The type of relationship between the first two words of the analogy should be determined before continuing to analyze the second set of words.

One effective method of determining a relationship between two words is to form a comprehensible sentence using both words and then to plug the answer choices into the same sentence. For example, consider the following analogy: *Bicycle is to handlebars as car is to steering wheel*. A sentence could be formed that says: A bicycle navigates using its handlebars; therefore, a car navigates using its steering wheel. If the second sentence makes sense, then the correct relationship has likely been found. A sentence may be more complex, depending on the relationship between the first two words in the analogy. An example of this may be: *food is to dishwasher as dirt is to carwash*. The formed sentence may be: A dishwasher cleans food off of dishes in the same way that a carwash cleans dirt off of a car.

Dealing with Multiple Connections

There are many other ways to draw connections between word sets. Several word choices might form an analogy that would fit the word set in your prompt. When this occurs, the analogy must be explored from multiple angles as, on occasion, multiple answer choices may appear to be correct. When this occurs, ask yourself: which one is an even closer match than the others? The framing word pair is another important point to consider. Can one or both words be interpreted as actions or ideas, or are they purely objects? Here's a question where words could have alternate meanings:

Hammer is to nail as saw is to
    a. Electric.
    b. Hack.
    c. Cut.
    d. Machete.

Looking at the question above, it becomes clear that the topic of the analogy involves construction tools. Hammers and nails are used in concert since the hammer is used to pound the nail. The logical first thing to do is to look for an object that a saw would be used on. Seeing that there is no such object among the answer choices, a test taker might begin to worry. After all, that seems to be the choice that would complete the analogy—but that doesn't mean it's the only choice that may fit. Encountering questions like this tests one's ability to see multiple connections between words; don't get stuck thinking that words can only be connected in a single way. The first two words given can be verbs instead of just objects. To hammer means to hit or beat; oftentimes, it refers to beating something into place. This is also what nail means when it is used as a verb. Here are the word choices that reveal the answer.

First, it's known that a saw, well, saws. It uses a steady motion to cut an object, and indeed to saw means to cut! Cut (C) is one of our answer choices, but the other options should be reviewed. While some tools are electric (A), the use of power in the tools listed in the analogy isn't a factor. Again, it's been established that these word choices are not tools in this context. Therefore, machete (D) is also ruled out because machete is also not a verb. Another important thing to consider is that while a machete is a tool that accomplishes a similar purpose as a saw, the machete is used in a slicing motion rather than a sawing/cutting motion. The verb that describes machete is hack (B), another choice that can be ruled out. A machete is used to hack at foliage. However, a saw does not hack. This leaves cut (C), which confirms that this is the word needed to complete the analogy.

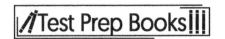

Synonyms and Antonyms

Synonyms are words that mean the same or nearly the same if given a list of words in the same language. When presented with several words and asked to choose the synonym, more than one word may be similar to the original. However, one word is generally the strongest match. Synonyms should always share the same part of speech. For instance, *shy* and *timid* are both adjectives and hold similar meanings. The words *shy* and *loner* are similar, but *shy* is an adjective, while *loner* is a noun. Another way to test for the best synonym is to reread the question with each possible word and determine which one makes the most sense. Consider the words: *adore, sweet, kind,* and *nice.*

Now consider the following sentence: *He will love you forever.*

> He will adore you forever.

> He will sweet you forever.

> He will kind you forever.

> He will nice you forever.

In the first sentence, the word *love* is used as a verb. The best synonym from the list that shares the same part of speech is *adore.* *Adore* is a verb, and when substituted in the sentence, it is the only substitution that makes grammatical and semantic sense.

Synonyms can be found for nouns, adjectives, verbs, adverbs, and prepositions. Here are some examples of synonyms from different parts of speech:

- Nouns: clothes, wardrobe, attire, apparel
- Verbs: run, spring, dash
- Adjectives: fast, quick, rapid, swift
- Adverbs: slowly, nonchalantly, leisurely
- Prepositions: near, proximal, neighboring, close

Here are several more examples of synonyms in the English language:

Word	Synonym	Meaning
smart	intelligent	having or showing a high level of intelligence
exact	specific	clearly identified
almost	nearly	not quite but very close
to annoy	to bother	to irritate
to answer	to reply	to form a written or verbal response
building	edifice	a structure that stands on its own with a roof and four walls
business	commerce	the act of purchasing, negotiating, trading, and selling
defective	faulty	when a device is not working or not working well

Antonyms are words that are complete opposites. As with synonyms, there may be several words that represent the opposite meaning of the word in question. When choosing an antonym, choose a word that represents as close to the exact opposite in meaning as the given word, and ensure it shares the same part of speech. Here are some examples of antonyms:

- Nouns: predator – prey

19

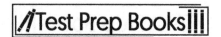
- Verbs: love – hate
- Adjectives: good – bad
- Adverbs: slowly – swiftly
- Preposition: above – below

Question Format

Synonym questions are very simple in construction. Instead of a comparison of words with an underlying connection, the prompt is just a single word. There are no special directions, alternate meanings, or analogies to work with. The objective is to analyze the given word and then choose the answer that means the same thing or <u>is closest in meaning</u> to the given word. Note the example below:

Blustery
    a. Hard
    b. Windy
    c. Mythical
    d. Stony

The synonym questions on the HSPT exam will appear exactly like the above sample. This is generally the standard layout throughout other exams, so some test takers may already be familiar with the structure. The principle remains the same: at the top of the section, clear directions will be given to choose the answer that most precisely defines the given word. In this case, the answer is windy (B), since windy and blustery are synonymous.

Pay Attention to Prefixes

The **prefix** of a word can actually reveal a lot about its definition. Many prefixes are actually Greco-Roman roots as well—but these are more familiar and a lot easier to recognize! When encountering any unfamiliar words, try looking at prefixes to discern the definition and then compare that with the choices. The prefix should be determined to help find the word's meaning. Here's an example question:

Premeditate
    a. Sporadic
    b. Calculated
    c. Interfere
    d. Determined

With premeditate, there's the common prefix *pre*. This helps draw connections to other words like prepare or preassemble. *Pre* refers to "before, already being, or having already." *Meditate* means to think or plan. *Premeditate* means to think or plan beforehand with intent. Therefore, a term that deals with thinking or planning should be found, but also something done in preparation. Among the word choices, determined (D) is an adjective with no hint of being related to something done before or in preparation. This choice is incorrect. Sporadic (A) refers to events happening in irregular patterns, so this is quite the opposite of premeditated. Interfere (C) also has nothing to do with premeditate; it goes counter to premeditate in a way similar to sporadic. Calculated (B), however, fits! A route and the cost of starting a plan can be calculated. Calculated refers to acting with a full awareness of consequences, so inherently planning is involved. In fact, calculated is synonymous with premeditated, making it the correct choice. Just by paying attention to a prefix, the doors to a meaning can open to help easily figure out which word would be the best choice. Here's another example:

20

Regain
> a. Erupt
> b. Ponder
> c. Seek
> d. Recoup

Recoup (D) is the right answer. The prefix *re-* often appears in front of words to give them the meaning of occurring again. *Regain* means to repossess something that was lost. *Recoup*, which also has the *re-* prefix, literally means to regain. In this example, both the given word and the answer share the *re-* prefix, which makes the pair easy to connect. However, don't rely only on prefixes to choose an answer. Make sure to analyze all of the options before marking an answer. Going through the other words in this sample, none of them come close to meaning regain except recoup. After checking to make sure that recoup is the best matching word, then mark it!

Word Origins and Roots

Studying a foreign language in school, particularly Latin or any of the romance languages (Latin-influenced), is advantageous. English is a language highly influenced by Latin and Greek words. The roots of much of the English vocabulary have Latin origins; these roots can bind many words together and often allude to a shared definition. Here's an example:

Fervent
> a. Lame
> b. Joyful
> c. Thorough
> d. Boiling

Fervent descends from the Latin word, *fervere*, which means "to boil or glow" and figuratively means "impassioned." The Latin root present in the word is *ferv*, which is what gives fervent the definition: showing great warmth and spirit or spirited, hot, glowing. This provides a link to boiling (D) just by root word association, but there's more to analyze. Among the other choices, none relate to fervent. The word lame (A) means crippled, disabled, weak, or inadequate. None of these match with fervent. While being fervent can reflect joy, joyful (B) directly describes "a great state of happiness," while fervent is simply expressing the idea of having very strong feelings—not necessarily joy. Thorough (C) means complete, perfect, painstaking, or with mastery; while something can be done thoroughly and fervently, none of these words match *fervent* as closely as *boiling* does. Not only does boiling connect in a linguistic way, but also in the way it is used in our language. While boiling can express being physically hot and undergoing a change, boiling is also used to reflect emotional states. People say they are "boiling over" when in heightened emotional states; "boiling mad" is another expression. Boiling, like fervent, also embodies a sense of heightened intensity. This makes boiling the best choice!

The Latin root *ferv* is seen in other words such as fervor, fervid, and even ferment. All of them are connected to and can be described by boil or glow, whether it is in a physical sense or in a metaphorical one. Such patterns can be seen in other word sets as well. Here's another example:

Gracious
> a. Fruitful
> b. Angry
> c. Grateful
> d. Understood

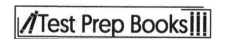

This one's a little easier; the answer is grateful (C) because both words mean thankful! Even if the meanings of both words are unknown, there's a connection found by looking at the beginnings of both words: *gra/grat*. Once again, these words are built on a root that stretches back to classical language. Both terms come from the Latin, *gratis*, which literally means "thanks."

Understanding root words can help identify the meaning in a lot of word choices, and help the test taker grasp the nature of the given word. Many dictionaries, both in book form and online, offer information on the origins of words, which highlight these roots. When studying for the test, it helps to look up an unfamiliar word for its definition and then check to see if it has a root that can be connected to any other terms.

Positive Versus Negative Sounding Words

Another tool for the mental toolbox is simply distinguishing whether a word has a positive or negative connotation. Like electrical wires, words carry energy; they are crafted to draw certain attention and to have certain strength to them. Words can be described as positive and uplifting (a stronger word) or they can be negative and scathing (a stronger word). Sometimes, they are neutral—having no particular connotation. Distinguishing how a word is supposed to be interpreted will not only help learn its definition, but also draw parallels with word choices. While it's true that words must usually be taken in the context of how they are used, word definitions have inherent meanings as well, meaning that they have a distinct vibe to pick up on. Here is an example:

Excellent
    a. Fair
    b. Optimum
    c. Reasonable
    d. Negative

As you know, *excellent* is a very positive word. It refers to something being better than good, or above average. In this sample, negative (D) can easily be eliminated because this is a word with a negative connotation. Reasonable (C) is more or less a neutral word: it's not bad but it doesn't communicate the higher quality that excellent represents. It's just, well, reasonable. This leaves the possible choices of fair (A) and optimum (B). Or does it? Fair *is* a positive word; it's used to describe things that are good, even beautiful. But in the modern context, *fair* is defined as good, but somewhat average or just decent: "You did a fairly good job." or, "That was fair." On the other hand, *optimum* is positive and a stronger word. *Optimum* describes the most favorable outcome. This makes *optimum* the best word choice that matches *excellent* in both strength and connotation. Not only are the two words positive, but they also express the same level of positivity! Here's another example:

Repulse
    a. Draw
    b. Encumber
    c. Force
    d. Disgust

Repulse just sounds negative when said aloud. It is commonly used in the context of something being repulsive, disgusting, or that which is distasteful. It's also defined as an attack that drives people away. This tells us that we need a word that also carries a negative meaning. Draw (A) and force (C) are both neutral. Encumber (B) and disgust (D) are negative. *Disgust* is a stronger negative than encumber. Of all the words given, only *disgust* directly defines a feeling of distaste and aversion that is synonymous with *repulse* and matches in both negativity and strength.

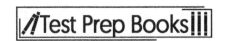

Parts of Speech

It is often very helpful to determine the part of speech of a word. Is it an adjective, adverb, noun, or verb, etc.? Oftentimes, the correct answer will also be the same part of speech as the given word. Isolate the part of speech and what it describes and look for an answer choice that also describes the same part of speech. For example: if the given word is an adverb describing an action word, then look for another adverb describing an action word.

Swiftly
    a. Fast
    b. Quickly
    c. Angry
    d. Sudden

Swiftly is an adverb that describes the speed of an action. Angry (C), fast (A), and sudden (D) can be eliminated because they are not adverbs. This leaves quickly (B), which is the correct answer. *Fast* and *sudden* may throw off some test takers because they both describe speed, but *quickly* matches more closely because it is an adverb, and *swiftly* is also an adverb.

Placing the Word in a Sentence

Often it is easier to discern the meaning of a word if it is used in a sentence. If the given word can be used in a sentence, then try replacing it with some of the answer choices to see which words seem to make sense in the same sentence. Here's an example:

Remarkable
    a. Often
    b. Capable
    c. Outstanding
    d. Shining

A sentence can be formed with the word *remarkable*. "My grade point average is remarkable." None of the examples make sense when replacing the word remarkable in the sentence other than the word outstanding (C), so outstanding is the obvious answer. Shining (D) is also a word with a positive connotation, but *outstanding* fits better in the sentence.

Looking for Relationships

Remember that all except one of the answer choices are wrong. If a close relationship between three or four of the answer choices can be found and not the fourth or fifth, then some of the choices can be eliminated. Sometimes, all of the words are related except one; the odd one out will often be the correct answer. Here is an example:

Outraged
    a. Angry
    b. Empty
    c. Forlorn
    d. Vacated

Notice that all of the answer choices have a negative connotation, but three of them are related to being alone or in low numbers. *Angry* is the best choice to match *outraged*.

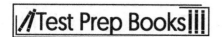

Picking the Closest Answer

As the answer choices are reviewed, two scenarios might stand out. An exact definition match might not be found for the given word among the choices, or there are several word choices that can be considered synonymous to the given word. This is intentionally done to test the ability to draw parallels between the words in order to produce an answer that best fits the prompt word. Again, the closest fitting word will be the answer. Even when facing these two circumstances, finding the one word that fits *best* is the proper strategy. Here's an example:

Insubordination
    a. Cooperative
    b. Disciplined
    c. Rebel
    d. Contagious

Insubordination refers to a defiance or utter refusal of authority. Looking over the choices, none of these terms provide definite matches to insubordination like insolence, mutiny, or misconduct would. This is fine; the answer doesn't have to be a perfect synonym. The choices don't reflect insubordination in any way, except rebel (C). After all, when *rebel* is used as a verb, it means to act against authority. It's also used as a noun: someone who goes against authority. Therefore, *rebel* is the best choice.

Playing the role of "detective" is the way to go as you may encounter two or even three answer choices that could be considered correct. However, the answer that best fits the prompt word's meaning is the best answer. Choices should be narrowed one word at a time. The least-connected word should be eliminated first and then proceed until one word is left that is the closest synonym.

Sequence
    a. List
    b. Range
    c. Series
    d. Replicate

A *sequence* reflects a particular order in which events or objects follow. The two closest options are list (A) and series (C). Both involve grouping things together, but which fits better? Consider each word more carefully. A *list* is comprised of items that fit in the same category, but that's really it. A list doesn't have to follow any particular order; it's just a list. On the other hand, a *series* is defined by events happening in a set order. A series relies on sequence, and a sequence can be described as a series. Thus, series is the correct answer!

Logic

Logic questions on this exam will give you a hypothetical scenario, and you must decide whether the answer is "uncertain," "true," or "false." The logic arguments on the test, which are often in the form of syllogisms, rely on deductive reasoning to determine the conclusion. For this portion of the test, it helps to write out the logic simulation before answering the question. Let's try an example below:

LaDonna's car can drive faster than Poppy's car. Poppy's car drives slower than Beatrice's car. Beatrice's car drives faster than LaDonna's car. If the first two statements are true, the third statement is:
    a. true
    b. false
    c. uncertain

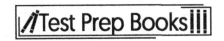

The correct answer is *C*, uncertain. Diagramming it out on a piece of paper helps a lot. Draw a circle with a "L" in it, and this represents our car. Place the "L" ahead of "P," since LaDonna's car goes faster than Poppy's car. We know this statement is true. The second statement says that Poppy's car is slower than Beatrice's car, so the "B" must go somewhere before the "P" car. But does it go in front of the "L" or behind the "L"? Given that we only know the first two statements are true, we are uncertain whether or not the "B" is placed before the "L" or behind the "L." The third statement, the fact that B's car drives faster than L's car, is uncertain at this point.

Let's look at another logic example:

All fish have scales. Some fish are pets. Some pets have scales.
    a. true
    b. false
    c. uncertain

If all fish have scales, and some of those fish are pets, then it is true that some pets have scales.

What if we said, at the end, that "all pets have scales"? Then our answer would be "uncertain." Why uncertain and why not false? That's because in the world of this simulation, we don't know whether all the pets have scales or not. If we had "All fish have scales. Some fish are pets. All pets have scales," then we don't know what other pets besides fish are included in this discussion. What if the other pets are alligators? Then all the pets would have scales. But what if the other pets were dogs? Then not all the pets would have scales. This answer is simply "uncertain."

With any of these logic questions, it is helpful to have a scratch piece of paper so that you can draw diagrams or label the objects that the questions give you. Some test takers learn visually, and so it will help to have visual objects in front, on top, or behind each other on a piece of paper so you can correctly determine where that object lies in the statement.

Verbal Classification

Preparation

In truth, there is no set way to prepare for this portion of the exam that will guarantee a perfect score. This is simply because the words used on the test are unpredictable. There is no set list provided to study from. The definition of the provided word needs to be determined on the spot. This sounds challenging, but there are still ways to prepare mentally for this portion of the test. It may help to expand your vocabulary a little each day. Several resources are available, in books and online, that collect words and definitions that tend to show up frequently on standardized tests. Knowledge of words can increase the strength of your vocabulary.

Mindset is key. The meanings of challenging words can often be found by relying on the past experiences of the test taker to help deduce the correct answer. How? Well, test takers have been talking their entire lives—knowing words and how words work. It helps to have a positive mindset from the start. It's unlikely that all definitions of words will be known immediately, but the answer can still be found. There are aspects of words that are recognizable to help discern the correct answers and eliminate the incorrect ones.

Verbal Classification

The verbal classification questions are where you are given four answer choices and asked to find the "odd one out," or the one that is unlike the others. The question will ask: "Which word does not belong with the others?" The same skills you learned to figure out Synonyms and Antonyms are the same skills you will need for this section as well. Discern the affixes and the roots of each word to see if you can derive its meaning. Pay attention to negative

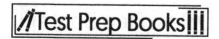

and positive connotations, as you may get one feeling from one word and similar feelings from the rest. Remember that there is one word that won't belong with the others based on its meaning. Here is an example:

Which word does *not* belong with the others?
  a. Pristine
  b. Immaculate
  c. Contaminated
  d. Sterile

Note that you don't have to know *all* of the definitions of the words in order to answer this question. We can easily use the process of elimination to answer this. Let's say you know that "pristine" and "immaculate" both mean something having to do with clean. That leaves us with "contaminated" and "sterile." One of these two answer choices does *not* mean clean, and one of them is associated with being clean. By doing this, we have a greater chance of choosing the right answer, rather than guessing outright. The correct answer is that the word "contaminated" does not belong. Contaminated means something that has become harmful or mixed with something unclean. "Sterile" means to be free of germs, so it is more like the words "pristine" and "immaculate."

Another verbal classification question could provide classification of objects or people, such as workers. Some questions will ask which object doesn't belong; like if we had three types of fruit and one vegetable, then the vegetable would be the correct answer. Let's look at the following question involving professions:

Which word does not belong with the others?
  a. Nursing
  b. Technician
  c. Social work
  d. Counselor

In the answer choices above, three of these workers are classified differently than the fourth. The terms "nursing," "social worker," and "counselor," are all considered helping professions, which are professions that address the physical, emotional, intellectual, spiritual, and psychological aspects of a person's well-being. A technician is someone who works with relevant skills in a field of technology, so this employment is in a different category altogether than the other three professions.

Quantitative Skills

Number Series

Number and Shape Patterns

Patterns within a sequence can come in 2 distinct forms: the items (shapes, numbers, etc.) either repeat in a constant order, or the items change from one step to another in some consistent way. The **core** is the smallest unit, or number of items, that repeats in a repeating pattern. For example, the pattern ∘∘▲∘∘▲∘... has a core that is ∘∘▲. Knowing only the core, the pattern can be extended. Knowing the number of steps in the core allows the identification of an item in each step without drawing/writing the entire pattern out. For example, suppose the tenth item in the previous pattern must be determined. Because the core consists of three items (∘∘▲), the core repeats in multiples of 3. In other words, steps 3, 6, 9, 12, etc. will be ▲ completing the core with the core starting over on the next step. For the above example, the 9th step will be ▲ and the 10th will be ∘.

The most common patterns in which each item changes from one step to the next are arithmetic and geometric sequences. An **arithmetic sequence** is one in which the items increase or decrease by a constant difference. In other words, the same thing is added or subtracted to each item or step to produce the next. To determine if a sequence is arithmetic, determine what must be added or subtracted to step one to produce step two. Then, check if the same thing is added/subtracted to step two to produce step three. The same thing must be added/subtracted to step three to produce step four, and so on. Consider the pattern 13, 10, 7, 4 ... To get from step one (13) to step two (10) by adding or subtracting requires subtracting by 3. The next step is checking if subtracting 3 from step two (10) will produce step three (7), and subtracting 3 from step three (7) will produce step four (4). In this case, the pattern holds true. Therefore, this is an arithmetic sequence in which each step is produced by subtracting 3 from the previous step. To extend the sequence, 3 is subtracted from the last step to produce the next. The next three numbers in the sequence are 1, -2, -5.

A **geometric sequence** is one in which each step is produced by multiplying or dividing the previous step by the same number. To determine if a sequence is geometric, decide what step one must be multiplied or divided by to produce step two. Then check if multiplying or dividing step two by the same number produces step three, and so on. Consider the pattern 2, 8, 32, 128 ... To get from step one (2) to step two (8) requires multiplication by 4. The next step determines if multiplying step two (8) by 4 produces step three (32), and multiplying step three (32) by 4 produces step four (128). In this case, the pattern holds true. Therefore, this is a geometric sequence in which each step is produced by multiplying the previous step by 4. To extend the sequence, the last step is multiplied by 4 and repeated. The next three numbers in the sequence are 512; 2,048; 8,192.

Although arithmetic and geometric sequences typically use numbers, these sequences can also be represented by shapes. For example, an arithmetic sequence could consist of shapes with three sides, four sides, and five sides (add one side to the previous step to produce the next). A geometric sequence could consist of eight blocks, four blocks, and two blocks (each step is produced by dividing the number of blocks in the previous step by 2).

Conjectures, Predictions, or Generalizations Based on Patterns

An arithmetic or geometric sequence can be written as a formula and used to determine unknown steps without writing out the entire sequence. (Note that a similar process for repeating patterns is covered in the previous section.) An arithmetic sequence progresses by a **common difference**. To determine the common difference, any step is subtracted by the step that precedes it. In the sequence 4, 9, 14, 19 ... the common difference, or d, is 5. By

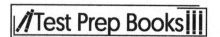

expressing each step as a_1, a_2, a_3, etc., a formula can be written to represent the sequence. a_1 is the first step. To produce step two, step 1 (a_1) is added to the common difference (d):

$$a_2 = a_1 + d$$

To produce step three, the common difference (d) is added twice to a_1:

$$a_3 = a_1 + 2d$$

To produce step four, the common difference (d) is added three times to a_1:

$$a_4 = a_1 + 3d$$

Following this pattern allows a general rule for arithmetic sequences to be written. For any term of the sequence (a_n), the first step (a_1) is added to the product of the common difference (d) and one less than the step of the term ($n - 1$):

$$a_n = a_1 + (n - 1)d$$

Suppose the 8th term (a_8) is to be found in the previous sequence. By knowing the first step (a_1) is 4 and the common difference (d) is 5, the formula can be used:

$$a_n = a_1 + (n - 1)d$$

$$a_8 = 4 + (7)5 \rightarrow a_8 = 39$$

In a geometric sequence, each step is produced by multiplying or dividing the previous step by the same number. The *common ratio*, or (r), can be determined by dividing any step by the previous step. In the sequence 1, 3, 9, 27 ... the common ratio (r) is 3($\frac{3}{1} = 3$ or $\frac{9}{3} = 3$ or $\frac{27}{9} = 3$). Each successive step can be expressed as a product of the first step (a_1) and the common ratio (r) to some power. For example:

$$a_2 = a_1 \times r$$

$$a_3 = a_1 \times r \times r \text{ or } a_3 = a_1 \times r^2$$

$$a_4 = a_1 \times r \times r \times r \text{ or } a_4 = a_1 \times r^3$$

Following this pattern, a general rule for geometric sequences can be written. For any term of the sequence (a_n), the first step (a_1) is multiplied by the common ratio (r) raised to the power one less than the step of the term ($n - 1$):

$$a_n = a_1 \times r^{(n-1)}$$

Suppose for the previous sequence, the 7th term (a_7) is to be found. Knowing the first step (a_1) is one, and the common ratio (r) is 3, the formula can be used:

$$a_n = a_1 \times r^{(n-1)} \rightarrow a_7 = (1) \times 3^6 \rightarrow a_7 = 729$$

Corresponding Terms of Two Numerical Patterns

When given two numerical patterns, the corresponding terms should be examined to determine if a relationship exists between them. Corresponding terms between patterns are the pairs of numbers that appear in the same step of the two sequences. Consider the following patterns 1, 2, 3, 4 ... and 3, 6, 9, 12 ... The corresponding terms are: 1

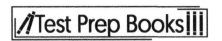

and 3; 2 and 6; 3 and 9; and 4 and 12. To identify the relationship, each pair of corresponding terms is examined and the possibilities of performing an operation (+, −, ×, ÷) to the term from the first sequence to produce the corresponding term in the second sequence are determined. In this case:

$$1 + 2 = 3 \quad \text{or} \quad 1 \times 3 = 3$$

$$2 + 4 = 6 \quad \text{or} \quad 2 \times 3 = 6$$

$$3 + 6 = 9 \quad \text{or} \quad 3 \times 3 = 9$$

$$4 + 8 = 12 \quad \text{or} \quad 4 \times 3 = 12$$

The consistent pattern is that the number from the first sequence multiplied by 3 equals its corresponding term in the second sequence. By assigning each sequence a label (input and output) or variable (x and y), the relationship can be written as an equation. If the first sequence represents the inputs, or x, and the second sequence represents the outputs, or y, the relationship can be expressed as: $y = 3x$.

Consider the following sets of numbers:

a	2	4	6	8
b	6	8	10	12

To write a rule for the relationship between the values for a and the values for b, the corresponding terms (2 and 6; 4 and 8; 6 and 10; 8 and 12) are examined. The possibilities for producing b from a are:

$2 + 4 = 6 \quad \text{or} \quad 2 \times 3 = 6$

$4 + 4 = 8 \quad \text{or} \quad 4 \times 2 = 8$

$6 + 4 = 10$

$8 + 4 = 12 \quad \text{or} \quad 8 \times 1.5 = 12$

The consistent pattern is that adding 4 to the value of a produces the value of b. The relationship can be written as the equation $a + 4 = b$.

Geometric Comparison

Lines, Rays, and Line Segments

The basic unit of geometry is a point. A **point** represents an exact location on a plane, or flat surface. The position of a point is indicated with a dot and usually named with a single uppercase letter, such as point *A* or point *T*. A point is a place, not a thing, and therefore has no dimensions or size. A set of points that lies on the same line is called collinear. A set of points that lies on the same plane is called coplanar.

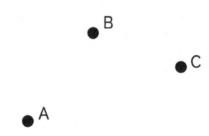

The image above displays point *A*, point *B*, and point *C*.

A **line** is as series of points that extends in both directions without ending. It consists of an infinite number of points and is drawn with arrows on both ends to indicate it extends infinitely. Lines can be named by two points on the line or with a single, cursive, lower case letter. The two lines below could be named line *AB* or line *BA* or $\overleftrightarrow{AB}$ or $\overleftrightarrow{BA}$; and line *m*.

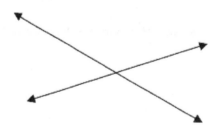

Two lines are considered **parallel** to each other if, while extending infinitely, they will never intersect (or meet). Parallel lines point in the same direction and are always the same distance apart. Two lines are considered

perpendicular if they intersect to form right angles. Right angles are 90°. Typically, a small box is drawn at the intersection point to indicate the right angle.

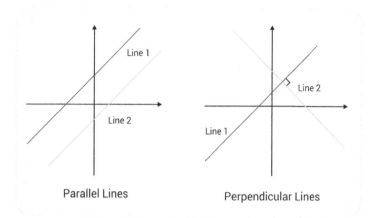

Parallel Lines   Perpendicular Lines

Line 1 is parallel to line 2 in the left image and is written as line 1 || line 2. Line 1 is perpendicular to line 2 in the right image and is written as line 1 ⊥ line 2.

A **ray** has a specific starting point and extends in one direction without ending. The endpoint of a ray is its starting point. Rays are named using the endpoint first, and any other point on the ray. The following ray can be named ray AB and written $\overrightarrow{AB}$.

A **line segment** has specific starting and ending points. A line segment consists of two endpoints and all the points in between. Line segments are named by the two endpoints. The example below is named segment *KL* or segment *LK*, written $\overline{KL}$ or $\overline{LK}$.

Classification of Angles

An **angle** consists of two rays that have a common endpoint. This common endpoint is called the **vertex** of the angle. The two rays can be called sides of the angle. The angle below has a vertex at point *B* and the sides consist of ray *BA* and ray *BC*. An angle can be named in three ways:

- 1. Using the vertex and a point from each side, with the vertex letter in the middle.
- 2. Using only the vertex. This can only be used if it is the only angle with that vertex.
- 3. Using a number that is written inside the angle.

31

The angle below can be written $\angle ABC$ (read angle ABC), $\angle CBA$, $\angle B$, or $\angle 1$.

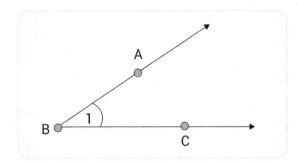

An angle divides a **plane**, or flat surface, into three parts: the angle itself, the interior (inside) of the angle, and the exterior (outside) of the angle. The figure below shows point M on the interior of the angle and point N on the exterior of the angle.

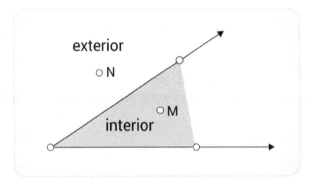

Angles can be measured in units called **degrees**, with the symbol °. The degree measure of an angle is between 0° and 180° and can be obtained by using a **protractor**, which is shown below:

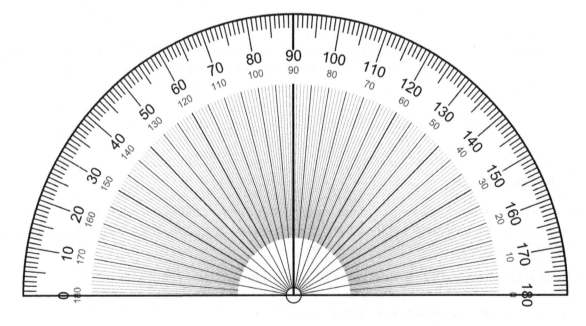

A **straight angle** (or simply a line) measures exactly 180°. A right angle's sides meet at the vertex to create a square corner. A **right angle** measures exactly 90° and is typically indicated by a box drawn in the interior of the angle. An acute angle has an interior that is narrower than a right angle. The measure of an **acute angle** is any value less than 90° and greater than 0°. For example, 89.9°, 47°, 12°, and 1°. An **obtuse angle** has an interior that is wider than a right angle. The measure of an obtuse angle is any value greater than 90° but less than 180°. For example, 90.1°, 110°, 150°, and 179.9°.

- Acute angles: Less than 90°
- Obtuse angles: Greater than 90°
- Right angles: 90°
- Straight angles: 180°

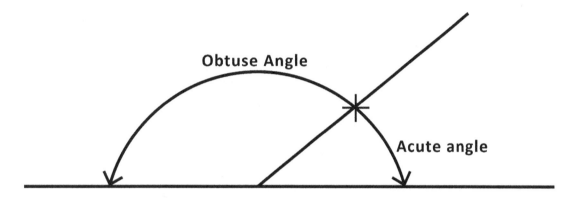

The Parallel Postulate states that if two parallel lines are cut by a transversal, then the corresponding angles are equal. Here is a picture that highlights this postulate:

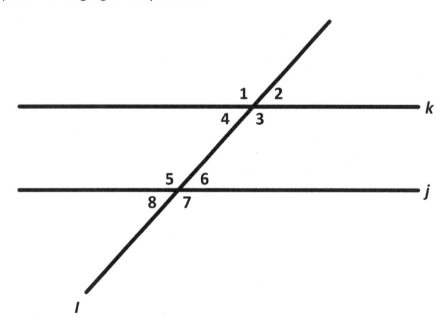

Because lines *k* and *i* are parallel, when cut by transversal *l*, angles 1 and 5 are equal, angles 2 and 6 are equal, angles 4 and 8 are equal, and angles 3 and 7 are equal. Note that angles 1 and 2, 3 and 4, 5 and 6, and 7 and 8 add up to 180 degrees.

This statement is equivalent to the Alternate Interior Angle Theorem, which states that when two parallel lines are cut by a transversal, the resultant interior angles are congruent. In the picture above, angles 3 and 5 are congruent, and angles 4 and 6 are congruent.

The Parallel Postulate or the Alternate Interior Angle Theorem can be used to find the missing angles in the following picture:

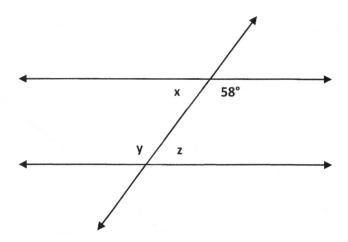

Assuming that the lines are parallel, angle x is found to be 122 degrees. Angle x and the 58-degree angle add up to 180 degrees. The Alternate Interior Angle Theorem states that angle y is equal to 58 degrees. Also, angles y and z add up to 180 degrees, so angle z is 122 degrees. Note that angles x and z are also alternate interior angles, so their equivalence can be used to find angle z as well.

An equivalent statement to the Parallel Postulate is that the sum of all angles in a triangle is 180 degrees. Therefore, given any triangle, if two angles are known, the third can be found accordingly.

Two- and Three-Dimensional Shapes

A **polygon** is a closed geometric figure in a **plane** (flat surface) consisting of at least 3 sides formed by line segments. These are often defined as two-dimensional shapes. Common two-dimensional shapes include circles, triangles, squares, rectangles, pentagons, and hexagons. Note that a circle is a two-dimensional shape without sides.

Two dimensional shapes

Circle	Triangle	Square
Pentagon	Hexagon	Rectangle

34

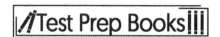

A solid figure, or simply a **solid**, is a figure that encloses a part of space. Some solids consist of flat surfaces only while others include curved surfaces. Solid figures are often defined as three-dimensional shapes. Common three-dimensional shapes include spheres, prisms, cubes, pyramids, cylinders, and cones.

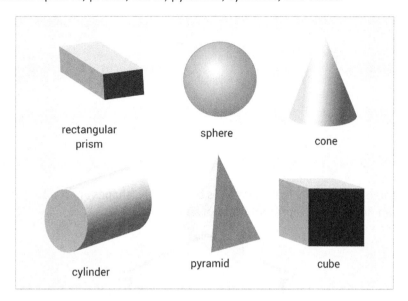

Composing two- or three-dimensional shapes involves putting together two or more shapes to create a new larger figure. For example, a semi-circle (half circle), rectangle, and two triangles can be used to compose the figure of the sailboat shown below.

35

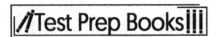

Similarly, solid figures can be placed together to compose an endless number of three-dimensional objects.

Decomposing two- and three-dimensional figures involves breaking the shapes apart into smaller, simpler shapes. Consider the following two-dimensional representations of a house:

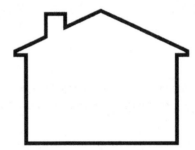

This complex figure can be decomposed into the following basic two-dimensional shapes: large rectangle (body of house); large triangle (roof); small rectangle and small triangle (chimney). Decomposing figures is often done more than one way. To illustrate, the figure of the house could also be decomposed into: two large triangles (body); two medium triangles (roof); two smaller triangles of unequal size (chimney).

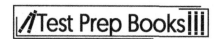

Polygons and Solids

A **polygon** is a closed two-dimensional figure consisting of three or more sides. Polygons can be either convex or concave. A polygon that has interior angles all measuring less than 180° is **convex**. A **concave** polygon has one or more interior angles measuring greater than 180°. Examples are shown below.

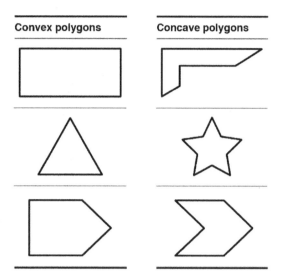

Polygons can be classified by the number of sides (also equal to the number of angles) they have. The following are the names of polygons with a given number of sides or angles:

# of Sides	Name of Polygon
3	Triangle
4	Quadrilateral
5	Pentagon
6	Hexagon
7	Septagon (or heptagon)
8	Octagon
9	Nonagon
10	Decagon

Equiangular polygons are polygons in which the measure of every interior angle is the same. The sides of equilateral polygons are always the same length. If a polygon is both equiangular and equilateral, the polygon is defined as a **regular polygon**. Examples are shown below.

37

Triangles can be further classified by their sides and angles. A triangle with its largest angle measuring 90° is a **right triangle**. A triangle with the largest angle less than 90° is an **acute triangle**. A triangle with the largest angle greater than 90° is an **obtuse triangle**. Below is an example of a right triangle.

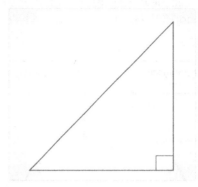

A triangle consisting of two equal sides and two equal angles is an **isosceles triangle**. A triangle with three equal sides and three equal angles is an **equilateral triangle**. A triangle with no equal sides or angles is a **scalene triangle**.

Isosceles triangle:

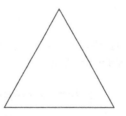

Equilateral triangle:

Scalene triangle:

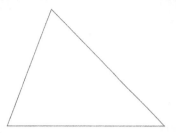

Quadrilaterals can be further classified according to their sides and angles. A quadrilateral with exactly one pair of parallel sides is called a **trapezoid**. A quadrilateral that shows both pairs of opposite sides parallel is a **parallelogram**. Parallelograms include rhombuses, rectangles, and squares. A **rhombus** has four equal sides. A **rectangle** has four equal angles (90° each). A **square** has four 90° angles and four equal sides. Therefore, a square is both a rhombus and a rectangle.

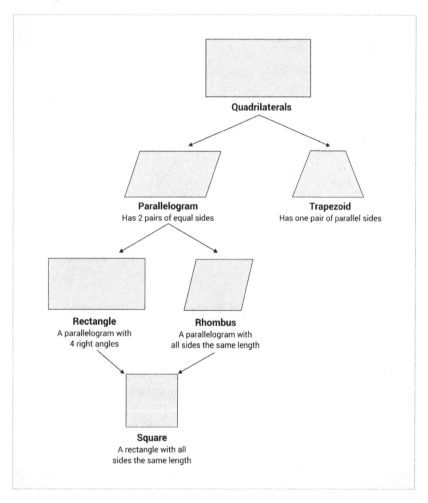

A solid is a three-dimensional figure that encloses a part of space. Solids consisting of all flat surfaces that are polygons are called **polyhedrons**. The two-dimensional surfaces that make up a polyhedron are called **faces**. Types of polyhedrons include prisms and pyramids. A **prism** consists of two parallel faces that are **congruent** (or the same

This material is provided for exam preparation purposes only and does not indicate an endorsement of any specific scientific, political, or religious point of view. © TPB Publishing. You have been licensed one copy of this document for personal use only. Any other reproduction or redistribution is strictly prohibited. All rights reserved.

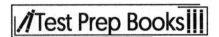
shape and same size), and lateral faces going around (which are parallelograms). A prism is further classified by the shape of its base, as shown below:

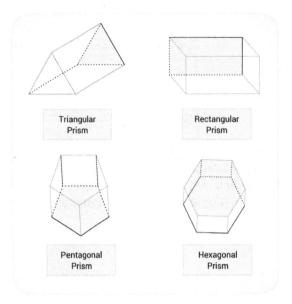

A **pyramid** consists of lateral faces (triangles) that meet at a common point called the **vertex** and one other face that is a polygon, called the **base**. A pyramid can be further classified by the shape of its base, as shown below.

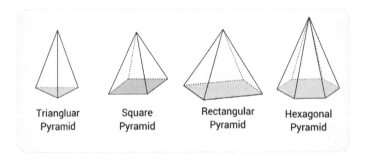

A **tetrahedron** is another name for a triangular pyramid. All the faces of a tetrahedron are triangles.

Solids that are not polyhedrons include spheres, cylinders, and cones. A **sphere** is the set of all points a given distance from a given center point. A sphere is commonly thought of as a three-dimensional circle. A **cylinder** consists of two parallel, congruent (same size) circles and a lateral curved surface. A **cone** consists of a circle as its base and a lateral curved surface that narrows to a point called the vertex.

Similar polygons are the same shape but different sizes. More specifically, their corresponding angle measures are congruent (or equal) and the length of their sides is proportional. For example, all sides of one polygon may be double the length of the sides of another. Likewise, similar solids are the same shape but different sizes. Any corresponding faces or bases of similar solids are the same polygons that are proportional by a consistent value.

Polygons with More than Four Sides
Mathematical problems involving polygons with more than four sides usually involve side length and angle measurements. The sum of all internal angles in a polygon equals $180(n-2)$ degrees, where n is the number of sides. Therefore, the total of all internal angles in a pentagon is 540 degrees because there are five sides so $180(5 -$

40

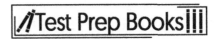

2) = 540 degrees. Unfortunately, area formulas don't exist for polygons with more than four sides. However, their shapes can be split up into triangles, and the formula for area of a triangle can be applied and totaled to obtain the area for the entire figure.

Three-Dimensional Figures with Nets

A **net** is a construction of two-dimensional figures that can be folded to form a given three-dimensional figure. More than one net may exist to fold and produce the same solid, or three-dimensional figure. The bases and faces of the solid figure are analyzed to determine the polygons (two-dimensional figures) needed to form the net.

Consider the following triangular prism:

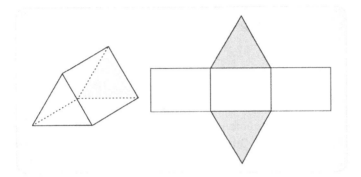

The surface of the prism consists of two triangular bases and three rectangular faces. The net beside it can be used to construct the triangular prism by first folding the triangles up to be parallel to each other, and then folding the two outside rectangles up and to the center with the outer edges touching.

Consider the following cylinder:

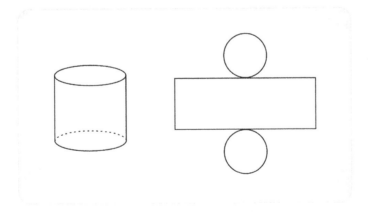

The surface consists of two circular bases and a curved lateral surface that can be opened and flattened into a rectangle. The net beside the cylinder can be used to construct the cylinder by first folding the circles up to be parallel to each other, and then curving the sides of the rectangle up to touch each other. The top and bottom of the folded rectangle should be touching the outside of both circles.

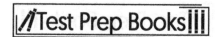

Consider the following square pyramid below on the left. The surface consists of one square base and four triangular faces. The net below on the right can be used to construct the square pyramid by folding each triangle towards the center of the square. The top points of the triangle meet at the vertex.

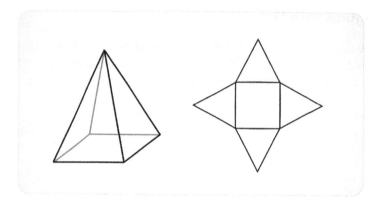

Surface Area and Volume

Surface area and volume are two- and three-dimensional measurements. **Surface area** measures the total surface space of an object, like the six sides of a cube. Questions about surface area will ask how much of something is needed to cover a three-dimensional object, like wrapping a present. **Volume** is the measurement of how much space an object occupies, like how much space is in the cube. Volume questions will ask how much of something is needed to completely fill the object. The most common surface area and volume questions deal with spheres, cubes, and rectangular prisms.

The formula for a cube's surface area is $SA = 6 \times s^2$, where s is the length of a side. A cube has 6 equal sides, so the formula expresses the area of all the sides. Volume is simply measured by taking the cube of the length, so the formula is $V = s^3$.

The surface area formula for a rectangular prism or a general box is $SA = 2(lw + lh + wh)$, where l is the length, h is the height, and w is the width. The volume formula is $V = l \times w \times h$, which is the cube's volume formula adjusted for the unequal lengths of a box's sides.

The formula for a sphere's surface area is $SA = 4\pi r^2$, where r is the sphere's radius. The surface area formula is the area for a circle multiplied by four. To measure volume, the formula is $V = \frac{4}{3}\pi r^3$.

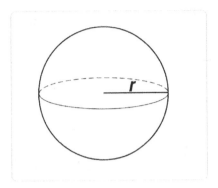

A **rectangular pyramid** is a figure with a rectangular base and four triangular sides that meet at a single vertex. If the rectangle has sides of lengths x and y, then the volume will be given by $V = \frac{1}{3}xyh$.

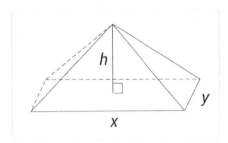

To find the surface area, the dimensions of each triangle must be known. However, these dimensions can differ depending on the problem in question. Therefore, there is no general formula for calculating total surface area.

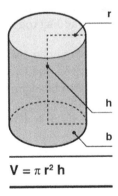

$$V = \pi r^2 h$$

The formula to find the volume of a cylinder is $\pi r^2 h$. This formula contains the formula for the area of a circle (πr^2) because the base of a cylinder is a circle. To calculate the volume of a cylinder, the slices of circles needed to build the entire height of the cylinder are added together. For example, if the radius is 5 feet and the height of the cylinder is 10 feet, the cylinder's volume is calculated by using the following equation: $\pi 5^2 \times 10$. Substituting 3.14 for π, the volume is 785.4 ft³.

43

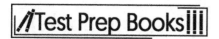
The formula used to calculate the volume of a cone is $\frac{1}{3}\pi r^2 h$.

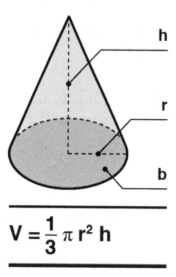

$$V = \frac{1}{3}\pi r^2 h$$

Essentially, the area of the base of the cone is multiplied by the cone's height. In a real-life example where the radius of a cone is 2 meters and the height of a cone is 5 meters, the volume of the cone is calculated by utilizing the formula:

$$\frac{1}{3}\pi 2^2 \times 5 = 21 \, m^3$$

Area and Perimeter of Polygons

The **perimeter** of a polygon is the distance around the outside of the two-dimensional figure. Perimeter is a one-dimensional measurement and is therefore expressed in linear units such as centimeters (*cm*), feet (*ft*), and miles (*mi*). The perimeter (*P*) of a figure can be calculated by adding together each of the sides.

Properties of certain polygons allow that the perimeter may be obtained by using formulas. A rectangle consists of two sides called the length (*l*), which have equal measures, and two sides called the width (*w*), which have equal measures. Therefore, the perimeter (*P*) of a rectangle can be expressed as:

$$P = l + l + w + w$$

This can be simplified to produce the following formula to find the perimeter of a rectangle:

$$P = 2l + 2w \text{ or } P = 2(l + w)$$

As mentioned, a **regular polygon** is one in which all sides have equal length and all interior angles have equal measures, such as a square and an equilateral triangle. To find the perimeter of a regular polygon, the length of one side is multiplied by the number of sides. For example, to find the perimeter of an equilateral triangle with a side of

44

length of 4 feet, 4 feet is multiplied by 3 (number of sides of a triangle). The perimeter of a regular octagon (8 sides) with a side of length of $\frac{1}{2}$ cm is:

$$\frac{1}{2} \, cm \times 8 = 4 \, cm$$

The area of a polygon is the number of square units needed to cover the interior region of the figure. Area is a two-dimensional measurement. Therefore, area is expressed in square units, such as square centimeters (cm^2), square feet (ft^2), or square miles (mi^2). To find the area (A) of a parallelogram, the length of the base (b) is multiplied by the length of the height:

$$(h) \rightarrow A = b \times h$$

Similar to triangles, the height of the parallelogram is measured from one base to the other at a 90° angle (or perpendicular).

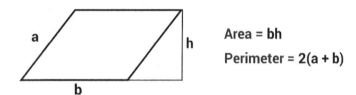

The area of a trapezoid can be calculated using the formula: $A = \frac{1}{2} \times h(b_1 + b_2)$, where h is the height and b_1 and b_2 are the parallel bases of the trapezoid.

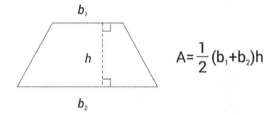

The area of a regular polygon can be determined by using its perimeter and the length of the apothem. The apothem is a line from the center of the regular polygon to any of its sides at a right angle. (Note that the perimeter of a regular polygon can be determined given the length of only one side.) The formula for the area (A) of a regular

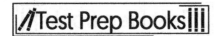
polygon is $A = \frac{1}{2} \times a \times P$, where a is the length of the apothem, and P is the perimeter of the figure. Consider the following regular pentagon:

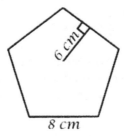

To find the area, the perimeter (P) is calculated first:

$$8cm \times 5 \rightarrow P = 40cm$$

Then the perimeter and the apothem are used to find the area (A):

$$A = \frac{1}{2} \times a \times P$$

$$A = \frac{1}{2} \times (6cm) \times (40cm) \rightarrow A = 120cm^2$$

Note that the unit is:

$$cm^2 \rightarrow cm \times cm = cm^2$$

The area of irregular polygons is found by decomposing, or breaking apart, the figure into smaller shapes. When the area of the smaller shapes is determined, the area of the smaller shapes will produce the area of the original figure when added together.

Consider the example below:

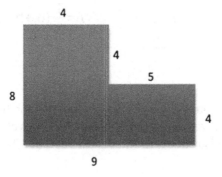

The irregular polygon is decomposed into two rectangles. The area of the large rectangle:

$$(A = l \times w \rightarrow A = 8 \times 4) \text{ is 32 square units}$$

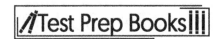

The area of the small rectangle is 20 square units ($A = 4 \times 5$). The sum of the areas of these figures produces the total area of the original polygon:

$$A = 32 + 20 \rightarrow A = 52 \; square \; units$$

Right Rectangular Prisms

A right rectangular prism consists of:

- Two congruent (same size and shape) rectangles as the parallel **bases** (top and bottom).
- Two congruent rectangles as the **side faces.**
- Two congruent rectangles as the **front** and **back faces.**

It is called a **right prism** because the base and sides meet at right angles.

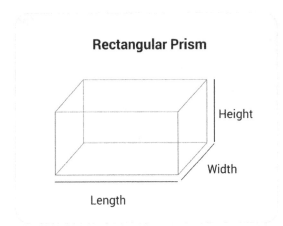

Rectangular Prism

The length and width of the prism is the length and width of the rectangular base. The height of the prism is the measure from one base to the other.

The surface area of three-dimensional figures can be found by adding the areas of each of its bases and faces. The areas of a right rectangular prism are found as follows: two bases → $A = l \times w$; front and back faces → $A = l \times h$; two side faces → $A = w \times h$. The sum of these six areas will equal the surface area of the prism. (Surface area = area of 2 bases + area of front and back + area of 2 sides). This is true for all right rectangular prisms leading to the formula for surface area:

$$SA = 2 \times l \times w + 2 \times l \times h + 2 \times w \times h$$

$$SA = 2(l \times w + l \times h + w \times h)$$

Given the right rectangular prism below, the surface area is calculated as follows:

$$SA = 2\left(3\frac{1}{2}\text{ft}\right)\left(2\frac{1}{2}\text{ft}\right) + 2\left(3\frac{1}{2}\text{ft}\right)\left(1\frac{1}{2}\text{ft}\right) + 2\left(2\frac{1}{2}\text{ft}\right)\left(1\frac{1}{2}\text{ft}\right) \rightarrow SA = 35.5\text{ft}^2$$

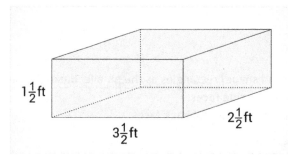

The volume of a solid is the number of cubic units needed to fill the space that the figure occupies. This concept is similar to filling a box with blocks. Volume is a three-dimensional measurement. Therefore, volume is expressed in cubic units such as cubic centimeters (cm^3), cubic feet (ft^3), and cubic yards (yd^3). If a rectangular prism has a volume of 30 cubic meters ($30m^3$), it will take 30 cubes, each with sides one meter in length, to fill the space occupied by the prism. A simple formula can be used to determine the volume of a right rectangular prism. The area of the base of the prism ($l \times w$) will indicate how many "blocks" are needed to cover the base. The height (h) of the prism will indicate how many "levels" of blocks are needed to construct the prism. Therefore, to find the volume (V) of a right rectangular prism, the area of the base ($l \times w$) is multiplied by the height (h):

$$V = l \times w \times h$$

The volume of the prism shown above is calculated:

$$V = \left(3\frac{1}{2}\text{ft}\right) \times \left(2\frac{1}{2}\text{ft}\right) \times \left(1\frac{1}{2}\text{ft}\right) \rightarrow V = 13.125\text{ft}^3$$

Effects of Changes to Dimensions on Area and Volume

Similar polygons are figures that are the same shape but different sizes. Likewise, similar solids are different sizes but are the same shape. In both cases, corresponding angles in the same positions for both figures are congruent, and corresponding sides are proportional in length. For example, the triangles below are similar. The following pairs of corresponding angles are congruent: $\angle A$ and $\angle D$; $\angle B$ and $\angle E$; $\angle C$ and $\angle F$. The corresponding sides are proportional:

$$\frac{AB}{DE} = \frac{6}{3} = 2$$

$$\frac{BC}{EF} = \frac{9}{4.5} = 2$$

$$\frac{CA}{FD} = \frac{10}{5} = 2$$

In other words, triangle *ABC* is the same shape but twice as large as triangle *DEF*.

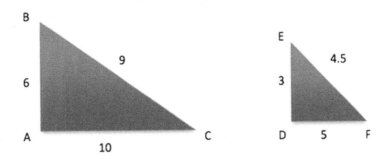

Given the nature of two- and three-dimensional measurements, changing dimensions by a given scale (multiplier) does not change the area of volume by the same scale. Consider a rectangle with a length of 5 centimeters and a width of 4 centimeters. The area of the rectangle is $20cm^2$. Doubling the dimensions of the rectangle (multiplying by a scale factor of 2) to 10 centimeters and 8 centimeters *does not* double the area to $40cm^2$. Area is a two-dimensional measurement (measured in square units). Therefore, the dimensions are multiplied by a scale that is squared (raised to the second power) to determine the scale of the corresponding areas. For the previous example, the length and width are multiplied by 2. Therefore, the area is multiplied by 2^2, or 4. The area of a $5cm \times 4cm$ rectangle is $20cm^2$. The area of a $10cm \times 8cm$ rectangle is $80cm^2$.

Volume is a three-dimensional measurement, which is measured in cubic units. Therefore, the scale between dimensions of similar solids is cubed (raised to the third power) to determine the scale between their volumes. Consider similar right rectangular prisms: one with a length of 8 inches, a width of 24 inches, and a height of 16 inches; the second with a length of 4 inches, a width of 12 inches, and a height of 8 inches. The first prism, multiplied by a scalar of $\frac{1}{2}$, produces the measurement of the second prism. The volume of the first prism, multiplied by $(\frac{1}{2})^3$, which equals $\frac{1}{8}$, produces the volume of the second prism. The volume of the first prism is $8in \times 24in \times 16in$ which equals $3,072in^3$. The volume of the second prism is $4in \times 12in \times 8in$ which equals $384in^3$:

$$3,072 \ in^3 \times \frac{1}{8} = 384in^3$$

The rules for squaring the scalar for area and cubing the scalar for volume only hold true for similar figures. In other words, if only one dimension is changed (changing the width of a rectangle but not the length) or dimensions are changed at different rates (e.g., the length of a prism is doubled and its height is tripled) the figures are not similar (same shape). Therefore, the rules above do not apply.

The Coordinate Plane

The **coordinate plane**, sometimes referred to as the **Cartesian plane**, is a two-dimensional surface consisting of a horizontal and a vertical number line. The horizontal number line is referred to as the **x-axis**, and the vertical number line is referred to as the **y-axis**. The x-axis and y-axis intersect (or cross) at a point called the **origin**. At the origin, the value of the x-axis is zero, and the value of the y-axis is zero. The coordinate plane identifies the exact location of a point that is plotted on the two-dimensional surface. Like a map, the location of all points on the plane are in relation to the origin. Along the x-axis, numbers to the right of the origin are positive and increasing in value (1,2,3, ...) and to the left of the origin numbers are negative and decreasing in value (-1,-2,-3, ...). Along the y-axis, numbers above the origin are positive and increasing in value and numbers below the origin are negative and decreasing in value.

49

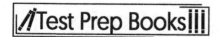

The x- and y-axis divide the coordinate plane into four sections. These sections are referred to as quadrant one, quadrant two, quadrant three, and quadrant four, and are often written with Roman numerals I, II, III, and IV. The upper right section is Quadrant I and consists of points with positive x-values and positive y-values. The upper left section is Quadrant II and consists of points with negative x-values and positive y-values. The bottom left section is Quadrant III and consists of points with negative x-values and negative y-values. The bottom right section is Quadrant IV and consists of points with positive x-values and negative y-values.

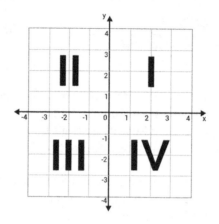

Solving Problems in the Coordinate Plane

The location of a point on a coordinate grid is identified by writing it as an ordered pair. An **ordered pair** is a set of numbers indicating the x-and y-coordinates of the point. Ordered pairs are written in the form (x, y) where x and y are values which indicate their respective coordinates. For example, the point (3, -2) has an x-coordinate of 3 and a y-coordinate of -2.

Plotting a point on the coordinate plane with a given coordinate means starting from the origin (0, 0). To determine the value of the x-coordinate, move right (for positive numbers) or left (for negative numbers) along the x-axis. Next, move up (for positive numbers) or down (for negative numbers) to the value of the y-coordinate. Finally, plot and label the point. For example, plotting the point (1, -2) requires starting from the origin and moving right along

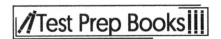

the x-axis to positive one, then moving down until straight across from negative 2 on the y-axis. The point is plotted and labeled. This point, along with three other points, are plotted and labeled on the graph below.

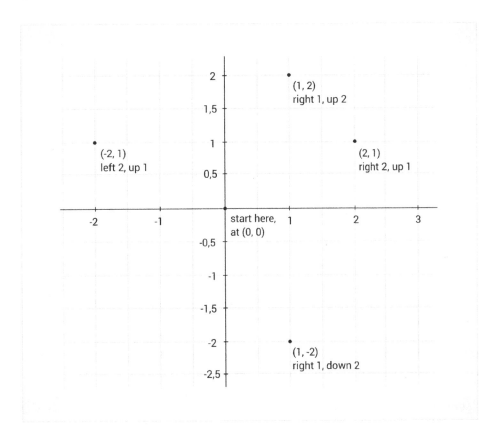

To write the coordinates of a point on the coordinate grid, a line should be traced directly above or below the point until reaching the x-axis (noting the value on the x-axis). Then, returning to the point, a line should be traced directly to the right or left of the point until reaching the y-axis (noting the value on the y-axis). The ordered pair (x, y) should be written with the values determined for the x- and y-coordinates.

Polygons can be drawn in the coordinate plane given the coordinates of their vertices. These coordinates can be used to determine the perimeter and area of the figure. Suppose triangle RQP has vertices located at the points: $R(-2, 0)$, $Q(2, 2)$, and $P(2, 0)$.

By plotting the points for the three vertices, the triangle can be constructed as follows:

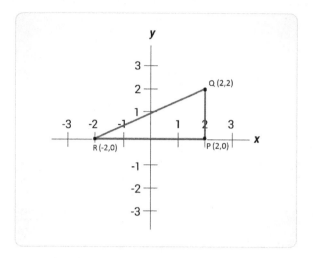

Because points R and P have the same y-coordinates (they are directly across from each other), the distance between them is determined by subtracting their x-coordinates (or simply counting units from one point to the other): $2 - (-2) = 4$. Therefore, the length of side RP is 4 units. Because points Q and P have the same x-coordinate (they are directly above and below each other), the distance between them is determined by subtracting their y-coordinates (or counting units between them): $2 - 0 = 2$. Therefore, the length of side PQ is 2 units. Knowing the length of side RP, which is the base of the triangle, and the length of side PQ, which is the height of the triangle, the area of the figure can be determined by using the formula $A = \frac{1}{2}bh$.

To determine the perimeter of the triangle, the lengths of all three sides are needed. Points R and Q are neither directly across nor directly above and below each other. Therefore, the distance formula must be used to find the length of side RQ. The distance formula is as follows:

$$d = \sqrt{(x_2 - x_1)^2 + (y_2 - y_1)^2}$$

$$d = \sqrt{\left(2 - (-2)\right)^2 + (2 - 0)^2}$$

$$d = \sqrt{(4)^2 + (2)^2}$$

$$d = \sqrt{16 + 4} \rightarrow d = \sqrt{20}$$

The perimeter is determined by adding the lengths of the three sides of the triangle.

The length of side RQ could also be found using the Pythagorean Theorem. The Pythagorean Theorem states that for right triangles $a^2 + b^2 = c^2$, where a and b are side lengths, and c is the hypotenuse.

Elapsed Time, Money, Length, Volume, and Mass

Word problems involving elapsed time, money, length, volume, and mass require determining which operations (addition, subtraction, multiplication, and division) should be performed, and using and/or converting the proper unit for the scenario.

The following table lists key words that can be used to indicate the proper operation:

Addition	Sum, total, in all, combined, increase of, more than, added to
Subtraction	Difference, change, remaining, less than, decreased by
Multiplication	Product, times, twice, triple, each
Division	Quotient, goes into, per, evenly, divided by half, divided by third, split

Identifying and utilizing the proper units for the scenario requires knowing how to apply the conversion rates for money, length, volume, and mass. For example, given a scenario that requires subtracting 8 inches from $2\frac{1}{2}$ feet, both values should first be expressed in the same unit (they could be expressed $\frac{2}{3}$ft & $2\frac{1}{2}$ft, or 8in and 30in). The desired unit for the answer may also require converting back to another unit.

Consider the following scenario: A parking area along the river is only wide enough to fit one row of cars and is $\frac{1}{2}$ kilometers long. The average space needed per car is 5 meters. How many cars can be parked along the river? First, all measurements should be converted to similar units: $\frac{1}{2}km = 500m$. The operation(s) needed should be identified. Because the problem asks for the number of cars, the total space should be divided by the space per car. 500 meters divided by 5 meters per car yields a total of 100 cars. Written as an expression, the meters unit cancels and the cars unit is left: $\frac{500m}{5m/car}$ the same as $500m \times \frac{1\,car}{5m}$ yields 100 cars.

When dealing with problems involving elapsed time, breaking the problem down into workable parts is helpful. For example, suppose the length of time between 1:15pm and 3:45pm must be determined. From 1:15pm to 2:00pm is 45 minutes (knowing there are 60 minutes in an hour). From 2:00pm to 3:00pm is 1 hour. From 3:00pm to 3:45pm is 45 minutes. The total elapsed time is 45 minutes plus 1 hour plus 45 minutes. These blocks of time sum to 1 hour and 90 minutes. 90 minutes is over an hour, so this is converted to 1 hour (60 minutes) and 30 minutes. The total elapsed time can now be expressed as 2 hours and 30 minutes.

Measuring Lengths of Objects

The length of an object can be measured using standard tools such as rulers, yard sticks, meter sticks, and measuring tapes. The following image depicts a yardstick:

Choosing the right tool to perform the measurement requires determining whether United States customary units or metric units are desired, and having a grasp of the approximate length of each unit and the approximate length of each tool. The measurement can still be performed by trial and error without the knowledge of the approximate size of the tool.

For example, to determine the length of a room in feet, a United States customary unit, various tools can be used for this task. These include a ruler (typically 12 inches/1 foot long), a yardstick (3 feet/1 yard long), or a tape measure displaying feet (typically either 25 feet or 50 feet). Because the length of a room is much larger than the length of a ruler or a yardstick, a tape measure should be used to perform the measurement.

When the correct measuring tool is selected, the measurement is performed by first placing the tool directly above or below the object (if making a horizontal measurement) or directly next to the object (if making a vertical

53

measurement). The next step is aligning the tool so that one end of the object is at the mark for zero units, then recording the unit of the mark at the other end of the object. To give the length of a paperclip in metric units, a ruler displaying centimeters is aligned with one end of the paper clip to the mark for zero centimeters.

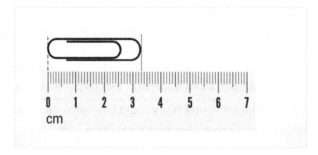

Directly down from the other end of the paperclip is the mark that measures its length. In this case, that mark is three small dashes past the 3 centimeter mark. Each small dash is 1 millimeter (or .1 centimeters). Therefore, the length of the paper clip is 3.3 centimeters.

To compare the lengths of objects, each length must be expressed in the same unit. If possible, the objects should be measured with the same tool or with tools utilizing the same units. For example, a ruler and a yardstick can both measure length in inches. If the lengths of the objects are expressed in different units, these different units must be converted to the same unit before comparing them. If two lengths are expressed in the same unit, the lengths may be compared by subtracting the smaller value from the larger value. For example, suppose the lengths of two gardens are to be compared. Garden A has a length of 4 feet, and garden B has a length of 2 yards. 2 yards is converted to 6 feet so that the measurements have similar units. Then, the smaller length (4 feet) is subtracted from the larger length (6ft): $6ft - 4ft = 2ft$. Therefore, garden B is 2 feet larger than garden A.

Relative Sizes of United States Customary Units and Metric Units

The United States customary system and the metric system each consist of distinct units to measure lengths and volume of liquids. The U.S. customary units for length, from smallest to largest, are: inch (in), foot (ft), yard (yd), and mile (mi). The metric units for length, from smallest to largest, are: millimeter (mm), centimeter (cm), decimeter (dm), meter (m), and kilometer (km). The relative size of each unit of length is shown below.

U.S. Customary	Metric	Conversion
12in = 1ft	10mm = 1cm	1in = 254cm
36in = 3ft = 1yd	10cm = 1dm(decimeter)	1m ≈ 3.28ft ≈ 1.09yd
5,280ft = 1,760yd = 1mi	100cm = 10dm = 1m	1mi ≈ 1.6km
	1,000m = 1km	

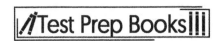

The U.S. customary units for volume of liquids, from smallest to largest, are: fluid ounces (fl oz), cup (c), pint (pt), quart (qt), and gallon (gal). The metric units for volume of liquids, from smallest to largest, are: milliliter (mL), centiliter (cL), deciliter (dL), liter (L), and kiloliter (kL). The relative size of each unit of liquid volume is shown below.

U.S. Customary	Metric	Conversion
8fl oz = 1c	10mL = 1cL	1pt ≈ 0.473L
2c = 1pt	10cL = 1dL	1L ≈ 1.057qt
4c = 2pt = 1qt	1,000mL = 100cL = 10dL = 1L	1gal ≈ 3,785L
4qt = 1gal	1,000L = 1kL	

The U.S. customary system measures weight (how strongly Earth is pulling on an object) in the following units, from least to greatest: ounce (oz), pound (lb), and ton. The metric system measures mass (the quantity of matter within an object) in the following units, from least to greatest: milligram (mg), centigram (cg), gram (g), kilogram (kg), and metric ton (MT). The relative sizes of each unit of weight and mass are shown below.

U.S. Measures of Weight	Metric Measures of Mass
16oz = 1lb	10mg = 1cg
2,000lb = 1 ton	100cg = 1g
	1,000g = 1kg
	1,000kg = 1MT

Note that weight and mass DO NOT measure the same thing.

Time is measured in the following units, from shortest to longest: second (sec), minute (min), hour (h), day (d), week (wk), month (mo), year (yr), decade, century, millennium. The relative sizes of each unit of time is shown below.

- 60 sec = 1min
- 60 min = 1h
- 24 hr = 1d
- 7 d = 1wk
- 52 wk = 1yr
- 12 mo = 1yr
- 10 yr = 1 decade
- 100 yrs = 1 century
- 1,000 yrs = 1 millennium

Conversion of Units

When working with different systems of measurement, conversion from one unit to another may be necessary. The conversion rate must be known to convert units. One method for converting units is to write and solve a proportion. The arrangement of values in a proportion is extremely important. Suppose that a problem requires converting 20 fluid ounces to cups. To do so, a proportion can be written using the conversion rate of $8fl\ oz = 1c$ with x representing the missing value.

The proportion can be written in any of the following ways:

$$\frac{1}{8} = \frac{x}{20} \left(\frac{c \text{ for conversion}}{\text{fl oz for conversion}} = \frac{\text{unknown } c}{\text{fl oz given}} \right)$$

$$\frac{8}{1} = \frac{20}{x} \left(\frac{\text{fl oz for conversion}}{c \text{ for conversion}} = \frac{\text{fl oz given}}{\text{unknown } c} \right)$$

$$\frac{1}{x} = \frac{8}{20} \left(\frac{c \text{ for conversion}}{\text{unknown } c} = \frac{\text{fl oz for conversion}}{\text{fl oz given}} \right)$$

$$\frac{x}{1} = \frac{20}{8} \left(\frac{\text{unknown } c}{c \text{ for conversion}} = \frac{\text{fl oz given}}{\text{fl oz for conversion}} \right)$$

To solve a proportion, the ratios are cross-multiplied and the resulting equation is solved. When cross-multiplying, all four proportions above will produce the same equation: $(8)(x) = (20)(1) \rightarrow 8x = 20$. Divide by 8 to isolate the variable x, which yields $x = 2.5$. The variable x represented the unknown number of cups. Therefore, the conclusion is that 20 fluid ounces converts (is equal to) 2.5 cups.

Sometimes converting units requires writing and solving more than one proportion. Suppose an exam question asks to determine how many hours are in 2 weeks. Without knowing the conversion rate between hours and weeks, this can be determined knowing the conversion rates between weeks and days, and between days and hours. First, weeks are converted to days, then days are converted to hours. To convert from weeks to days, the following proportion can be written:

$$\frac{7}{1} = \frac{x}{2} \left(\frac{\text{days conversion}}{\text{weeks conversion}} = \frac{\text{days unknown}}{\text{weeks given}} \right)$$

Cross-multiplying produces:

$$(7)(2) = (x)(1) \rightarrow 14 = x$$

Therefore, 2 weeks is equal to 14 days. Next, a proportion is written to convert 14 days to hours:

$$\frac{24}{1} = \frac{x}{14} \left(\frac{\text{conversion hours}}{\text{conversion days}} = \frac{\text{unknown hours}}{\text{given days}} \right)$$

Cross-multiplying produces:

$$(24)(14) = (x)(1) \rightarrow 336 = x$$

Therefore, the answer is that there are 336 hours in 2 weeks.

Nongeometric Comparison

Using Ratios, Rates, Proportions, and Scale Drawings to Solve Single- and Multistep Problems

Ratios, rates, proportions, and scale drawings are used when comparing two quantities. Questions on this material will include expressing relationships in simplest terms and solving for missing quantities.

Ratios

A **ratio** is a comparison of two quantities that represent separate groups. For example, if a recipe calls for 2 eggs for every 3 cups of milk, it can be expressed as a ratio. Ratios can be written three ways: (1) with the word "to"; (2) using a colon; or (3) as a fraction. For the previous example, the ratio of eggs to cups of milk can be written as: 2 to 3, 2:3, or $\frac{2}{3}$. When writing ratios, the order is important. The ratio of eggs to cups of milk is not the same as the ratio of cups of milk to eggs, 3:2.

In simplest form, both quantities of a ratio should be written as integers. These should also be reduced just as a fraction would be. For example, 5:10 would reduce to 1:2. Given a ratio where one or both quantities are expressed as a decimal or fraction, both should be multiplied by the same number to produce integers. To write the ratio $\frac{1}{3}$ to 2 in simplest form, both quantities should be multiplied by 3. The resulting ratio is 1 to 6.

When a problem involving ratios gives a comparison between two groups, then: (1) a total should be provided and a part should be requested; or (2) a part should be provided and a total should be requested. Consider the following:

> The ratio of boys to girls in the 11th grade is 5:4. If the total number of 11th grade students is 270, how many are girls?

To solve this, the total number of "ratio pieces" first needs to be determined. The total number of 11th grade students is divided into 9 pieces. The ratio of boys to total students is 5:9; and the ratio of girls to total students is 4:9. Knowing the total number of students, the number of girls can be determined by setting up a proportion:

$$\frac{4}{9} = \frac{x}{270}$$

Solving the proportion via cross-multiplying yields the answer that there are 120 11th grade girls.

Rates

A **rate** is a ratio comparing two quantities expressed in different units. A **unit rate** is one in which the second quantity is one unit of something (e.g., 10 feet/second). Rates often include the word *per*. Examples include miles per hour, beats per minute, and price per pound. The word *per* can be represented with a / symbol or abbreviated with the letter "p" and the units abbreviated. For example, miles per hour would be written mi/h. Given a rate that is not in simplest form (second quantity is not one unit), both quantities should be divided by the value of the second quantity. Suppose a patient had 99 heartbeats in 1½ minutes. To determine the heart rate, both quantities should be divided by 1½. The result is 66 bpm.

Scale Drawings

Scale drawings are used in designs to model the actual measurements of a real-world object. For example, the blueprint of a house might indicate that it is drawn at a scale of 3 inches to 8 feet. Given one value and asked to determine the width of the house, a proportion should be set up to solve the problem. Given the scale of 3in:8ft and a blueprint width of 1 ft (12 in.), to find the actual width of the building, the proportion $\frac{3}{8} = \frac{12}{x}$ should be used. This results in an actual width of 32 ft.

Proportions

A **proportion** is a statement consisting of two equal ratios. Proportions will typically give three of four quantities and require solving for the missing value. The key to solving proportions is to set them up properly. Here's a sample problem:

> If 7 gallons of gas costs $14.70, how many gallons can you get for $20?

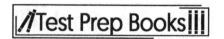

The information should be written as equal ratios with a variable representing the missing quantity:

$$\left(\frac{gallons}{cost} = \frac{gallons}{cost}\right) : \frac{7}{14.70} = \frac{x}{20}$$

To solve, cross-multiply (multiply the numerator of the first ratio by the denominator of the second and vice versa) is used, and the products are set equal to each other. Cross-multiplying results in:

$$(7)(20) = (14.7)(x)$$

After solving the equation for x, it can be determined that 9.5 gallons of gas can be purchased for $20.

For **direct proportions**, as one quantity increases, the other quantity also increases. For **indirect proportions** (also referred to as indirect variations, inverse proportions, or inverse variations), as one quantity increases, the other decreases. Direct proportions can be written:

$$\frac{y_1}{x_1} = \frac{y_2}{x_2}$$

Conversely, indirect proportions are written:

$$y_1 x_1 = y_2 x_2$$

Here's a sample problem:

> It takes 3 carpenters 10 days to build the frame of a house. How long should it take 5 carpenters to build the same frame?

In this scenario, as one quantity increases (number of carpenters), the other decreases (number of days building); therefore, this is an inverse proportion. To solve, the products of the two variables (in this scenario, the total work performed) are set equal to each other ($y_1 x_1 = y_2 x_2$).

Using y to represent carpenters and x to represent days, the resulting equation is:

$$(3)(10) = (5)(x_2)$$

Solving for x_2, it is determined that it should take 5 carpenters 6 days to build the frame of the house.

Solving Single- and Multistep Problems Involving Percentages

The word **percent** means "per hundred." When dealing with percentages, it may be helpful to think of the number as a value in hundredths. For example, 15% can be expressed as "fifteen hundredths" and written as $\frac{15}{100}$ or .15.

Percent Problems

Material on percentages can include questions such as: What is 15% of 25? What percent of 45 is 3? Five is $\frac{1}{2}$% of what number? To solve these problems, the information should be rewritten as an equation where the following helpful steps are completed: (1) "what" is represented by a variable (x); (2) "is" is represented by an = sign; and (3) "of" is represented by multiplication. Any values expressed as a percent should be written as a decimal; and if the

58

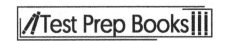

question is asking for a percent, the answer should be converted accordingly. Here are three sample problems based on the information above:

What is 15% of 25?	What percent of 45 is 3?	Five is $\frac{1}{2}$% of what number?
$x = .15 \times 25$	$x \times 45 = 3$	$5 = .005 \times x$
$x = 3.75$	$x = 0.0\overline{6}$	$x = 1,000$
	$x = 6.\overline{6}\%$	

Percent Increase/Decrease

Problems dealing with percentages may involve an original value, a change in that value, and a percentage change. A problem will provide two pieces of information and ask to find the third. To do so, the following formula is used:

$$\frac{change}{original\ value} \times 100 = \text{percent change}$$

Here's a sample problem:

> Attendance at a baseball stadium has dropped 16% from last year. Last year's average attendance was 40,000. What is this year's average attendance?

Using the formula and information, the change is unknown (x), the original value is 40,000, and the percent change is 16%. The formula can be written as:

$$\frac{x}{40,000} \times 100 = 16$$

By solving for x, the change is to determined to be 6,400. The problem asked for this year's average attendance, so to calculate, the change (6,400) is subtracted from last year's attendance (40,000) to determine this year's average attendance is 33,600.

Percent More Than/Less Than

Percentage problems may give a value and what percent that given value is more than or less than an original unknown value. Here's a sample problem:

> A store advertises that all its merchandise has been reduced by 25%. The new price of a pair of shoes is $60. What was the original price?

This problem can be solved by writing a proportion. Two ratios should be written comparing the cost and the percent of the original cost. The new cost is 75% of the original cost ($100\% - 25\%$); and the original cost is 100% of the original cost. The unknown original cost can be represented by x. The proportion would be set up as: $\frac{60}{75} = \frac{x}{100}$. Solving the proportion yields the original cost of $80.

Solving Single- and Multistep Problems Involving Measurement Quantities, Units, and Unit Conversion

Unit conversions apply to many real-world scenarios, including cooking, measurement, construction, and currency. Problems on this material can be solved similarly to those involving unit rates. Given the conversion rate, it can be

written as a fraction (ratio) and multiplied by a quantity in one unit to convert it to the corresponding unit. For example, someone might want to know how many minutes are in $3\frac{1}{2}$ hours. The conversion rate of 60 minutes to 1 hour can be written as:

$$\frac{60 \ min}{1 \ h}$$

Multiplying the quantity by the conversion rate results in:

$$3\frac{1}{2}h \ \times \frac{60 \ min}{1 \ h} = 210 \ min$$

The "h" unit is canceled. To convert a quantity in minutes to hours, the fraction for the conversion rate would be flipped (to cancel the "min" unit). To convert 195 minutes to hours, the equation $195 \ min \ \times \frac{1 \ h}{60 \ min}$ would be used. The result is $\frac{195 \ h}{60}$, which reduces to $3\frac{1}{4}$ hours.

Converting units may require more than one multiplication. The key is to set up the conversion rates so that units cancel out each other and the desired unit is left. Suppose someone wants to convert 3.25 yards to inches, given that $1yd = 3ft$ and $12in = 1ft$. To calculate, the equation use:

$$3.25 \ yd \times \frac{3 \ ft}{1 \ yd} \times \frac{12 \ in}{1 \ ft}$$

The "yd" and "ft" units will cancel, resulting in 117 inches.

Average, Median, and Measures of Central Tendency

Suppose that X is a set of data points $(x_1, x_2, x_3 \ldots x_n)$ and some description of the general properties of this data needs to be found.

The first property that can be defined for this set of data is the **mean**. To find the mean, add up all the data points, then divide by the total number of data points.

This can be expressed using **summation notation** as:

$$\bar{X} = \frac{x_1 + x_2 + x_3 + \ldots + x_n}{n} = \frac{1}{n}\sum_{i=1}^{n} x_i$$

For example, suppose that in a class of 10 students, the scores on a test were 50, 60, 65, 65, 75, 80, 85, 85, 90, 100. Therefore, the average test score will be:

$$\frac{1}{10}(50 + 60 + 65 + 65 + 75 + 80 + 85 + 85 + 90 + 100) = 75.5$$

The mean is a useful number if the distribution of data is normal (more on this later), which roughly means that the frequency of different outcomes has a single peak and is roughly equally distributed on both sides of that peak. However, it is less useful in some cases where the data might be split or where there are some **outliers**. Outliers are data points that are far from the rest of the data. For example, suppose there are 90 employees and 10 executives

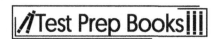

at a company. The executives make $1,000 per hour, and the employees make $10 per hour. Therefore, the average pay rate will be

$$\frac{1,000 \times 10 + 10 \times 90}{100} = 109$$

or $109 per hour. In this case, this average is not very descriptive.

Another useful measurement is the **median**. In a data set X consisting of data points $x_1, x_2, x_3 \ldots x_n$, the median is the point in the middle. The middle refers to the point where half the data comes before it and half comes after, when the data is recorded in numerical order. If n is odd, then the median is:

$$x_{\frac{n+1}{2}}$$

If n is even, it is defined as:

$$\frac{1}{2}\left(x_{\frac{n}{2}} + x_{\frac{n}{2}+1}\right)$$

It is the mean of the two data points closest to the middle of the data points. In the previous example of test scores, the two middle points are 75 and 80. Since there is no single point, the average of these two scores needs to be found. The average is:

$$\frac{75 + 80}{2} = 77.5$$

The median is generally a good value to use if there are a few outliers in the data. It prevents those outliers from affecting the "middle" value as much as when using the mean.

Since an outlier is a data point that is far from most of the other data points in a data set, this means an outlier also is any point that is far from the median of the data set. The outliers can have a substantial effect on the mean of a data set, but they usually do not change the median or mode (the number that appears most frequently in the data set), or do not change them by a large quantity. For example, consider the data set (3, 5, 6, 6, 6, 8). This set has a median of 6 and a mode of 6, with a mean of $\frac{34}{6} \approx 5.67$. Now, suppose a new data point of 1,000 is added so that the data set is now (3, 5, 6, 6, 6, 8, 1,000). The median and mode, which are both still 6, remain unchanged. However, the mean, or average, is now $\frac{1,034}{7}$, which is approximately 147.7. In this case, the median and mode will be better representations for most of the data points.

The reason for outliers in a given data set is a complicated problem. They are sometimes the result of an error by the experimenter, but often they are perfectly valid data points that must be taken into consideration.

One additional measure to define for X is the **mode**. This is the data point that appears more frequently. If two or more data points all tie for the most frequent appearance, then each of them is considered a mode. In the case of the test scores, where the numbers were 50, 60, 65, 65, 75, 80, 85, 85, 90, 100, there are two modes: 65 and 85.

The **first quartile** of a set of data X refers to the largest value from the first ¼ of the data points. In practice, there are sometimes slightly different definitions that can be used, such as the median of the first half of the data points (excluding the median itself if there are an odd number of data points). The term also has a slightly different use: when it is said that a data point lies in the first quartile, it means it is less than or equal to the median of the first half of the data points. Conversely, if it lies *at* the first quartile, then it is equal to the first quartile.

61

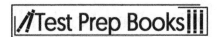

When it is said that a data point lies in the **second quartile**, it means it is between the first quartile and the median.

The **third quartile** refers to data that lies between $\frac{1}{2}$ and $\frac{3}{4}$ of the way through the data set. Again, there are various methods for defining this precisely, but the simplest way is to include all of the data that lie between the median and the median of the top half of the data.

Data that lies in the **fourth quartile** refers to all of the data above the third quartile.

Percentiles may be defined in a similar manner to quartiles. Generally, this is defined in the following manner:

- If a data point lies *in* the n-th percentile, it lies in the range of the first $n\%$ of the data.

- If a data point lies *at* the n-th percentile, $n\%$ of the data lies below this data point.

Given a data set X consisting of data points $(x_1, x_2, x_3 \ldots x_n)$, the **variance of X** is defined to be:

$$\frac{\sum_{i=1}^{n}(x_i - \bar{X})^2}{n}$$

This means that the variance of X is the average of the squares of the differences between each data point and the mean of X. In the formula, $\bar{X}$ is the mean of the values in the data set, and x_i represents each individual value in the data set. The sigma notation indicates that the sum should be found with n being the number of values to add together. $i = 1$ means that the values should begin with the first value.

Given a data set X consisting of data points $(x_1, x_2, x_3 \ldots x_n)$, the **standard deviation of X** is defined to be

$$s_x = \sqrt{\frac{\sum_{i=1}^{n}(x_i - \bar{X})^2}{n}}$$

In other words, the standard deviation is the square root of the variance.

Both the variance and the standard deviation are measures of how much the data tend to be spread out. When the standard deviation is low, the data points are mostly clustered around the mean. When the standard deviation is high, this generally indicates that the data are quite spread out, or else that there are a few substantial outliers.

As a simple example, compute the standard deviation for the data set (1, 3, 3, 5). First, compute the mean, which will be:

$$\frac{1+3+3+5}{4} = \frac{12}{4} = 3$$

Now, find the variance of X with the formula:

$$\sum_{i=1}^{4}(x_i - \bar{X})^2 = (1-3)^2 + (3-3)^2 + (3-3)^2 + (5-3)^2$$

$$-2^2 + 0^2 + 0^2 + 2^2 = 8$$

Therefore, the variance is $\frac{8}{4} = 2$. Taking the square root, the standard deviation will be $\sqrt{2}$.

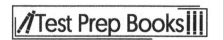

Note that the standard deviation only depends upon the mean, not upon the median or mode(s). Generally, if there are multiple modes that are far apart from one another, the standard deviation will be high. A high standard deviation does not always mean there are multiple modes, however.

Representing Numbers in Various Ways

Concrete Models
Concrete objects are used to develop a tangible understanding of operations of rational numbers. Tools such as tiles, blocks, beads, and hundred charts are used to model problems. For example, a hundred chart (10×10) and beads can be used to model multiplication. If multiplying 5 by 4, beads are placed across 5 rows and down 4 columns producing a product of 20. Similarly, tiles can be used to model division by splitting the total into equal groups. If dividing 12 by 4, 12 tiles are placed one at a time into 4 groups. The result is 4 groups of 3. This is also an effective method for visualizing the concept of remainders.

Representations of objects can be used to expand on the concrete models of operations. Pictures, dots, and tallies can help model these concepts. Utilizing concrete models and representations creates a foundation upon which to build an abstract understanding of the operations.

Rational Numbers on a Number Line
A number line typically consists of integers (...3, 2, 1, 0, -1, -2, -3...), and is used to visually represent the value of a rational number. Each rational number has a distinct position on the line determined by comparing its value with the displayed values on the line. For example, if plotting -1.5 on the number line below, it is necessary to recognize that the value of -1.5 is .5 less than -1 and .5 greater than -2. Therefore, -1.5 is plotted halfway between -1 and -2.

Number lines can also be useful for visualizing sums and differences of rational numbers. Adding a value indicates moving to the right (values increase to the right), and subtracting a value indicates moving to the left (numbers decrease to the left). For example, $-3 - 2$ is displayed by starting at -3 and moving to the left 2 spaces, if the number line is in increments of 1. This will result in an answer of -5.

Rectangular Arrays and Area Models
Rectangular arrays include an arrangement of rows and columns that correspond to the factors and display product totals.

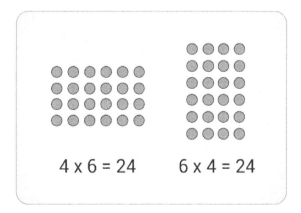

$$4 \times 6 = 24 \qquad 6 \times 4 = 24$$

63

An area model is a rectangle that is divided into rows and columns that match up to the number of place values within each number. Take the example 29 × 65. These two numbers can be split into simpler numbers: $29 = 25 + 4$ and $65 = 60 + 5$. The products of those 4 numbers are found within the rectangle and then summed up to get the answer. The entire process is:

$$(60 \times 25) + (5 \times 25) + (60 \times 4) + (5 \times 4)$$

$$1,500 + 240 + 125 + 20 = 1,885$$

Here is the actual area model:

Area models display multiplication or division problems with one value broken apart to produce simpler calculations. The example below breaks the dividend (3,180) into values that are easily divisible by the divisor (15). The quotients of each piece are then added to obtain the answer.

$$3,180 \div 15 = 212$$

64

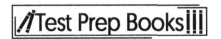

Similarly, area models can be used to break apart multiplication problems as a visual representation of the distributive property. For example:

$$34 \times 28 = 34(20 + 8)$$

$$30(20 + 8) + 4(20 + 8)$$

$$30 \times 20 + 30 \times 8 + 4 \times 20 + 4 \times 8$$

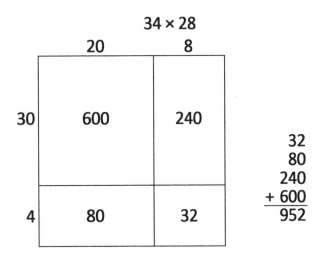

Number Manipulation

Base-10 Numerals, Number Names, and Expanded Form

Numbers used in everyday life are constituted in a **base-10 system**. Each digit in a number, depending on its location, represents some multiple of 10, or quotient of 10 when dealing with decimals. Each digit to the left of the decimal point represents a higher multiple of 10. Each digit to the right of the decimal point represents a quotient of a higher multiple of 10 for the divisor. For example, consider the number 7,631.42. The digit one represents simply the number one. The digit 3 represents 3×10. The digit 6 represents $6 \times 10 \times 10$ (or 6×100). The digit 7 represents $7 \times 10 \times 10 \times 10$ (or $7 \times 1,000$). The digit 4 represents $4 \div 10$. The digit 2 represents:

$$(2 \div 10) \div 10 = 2 \div (10 \times 10) = 2 \div 100$$

A number is written in **expanded form** by expressing it as the sum of the value of each of its digits. The expanded form in the example above, which is written with the highest value first down to the lowest value, is expressed as:

$$7,000 + 600 + 30 + 1 + 0.4 + 0.02$$

When verbally expressing a number, the integer part of the number (the numbers to the left of the decimal point) resembles the expanded form without the addition between values. In the above example, the numbers read "seven thousand six hundred thirty-one." When verbally expressing the decimal portion of a number, the number is read as a whole number, followed by the place value of the furthest digit (non-zero) to the right. In the above example, 0.42 is read "forty-two hundredths." Reading the number 7,631.42 in its entirety is expressed as "seven thousand six hundred thirty-one and forty-two hundredths." The word *and* is used between the integer and decimal parts of the number.

65

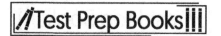
Composing and Decomposing Multi-Digit Numbers

Composing and decomposing numbers aids in conceptualizing what each digit of a multi-digit number represents. The standard, or typical, form in which numbers are written consists of a series of digits representing a given value based on their place value. Consider the number 592.7. This number is composed of 5 hundreds, 9 tens, 2 ones, and 7 tenths.

Composing a number requires adding the given numbers for each place value and writing the numbers in standard form. For example, composing 4 thousands, 5 hundreds, 2 tens, and 8 ones consists of adding as follows: $4,000 + 500 + 20 + 8$, to produce 4,528 (standard form).

Decomposing a number requires taking a number written in standard form and breaking it apart into the sum of each place value. For example, the number 83.17 is decomposed by breaking it into the sum of 4 values (for each of the 4 digits): 8 tens, 3 ones, 1 tenth, and 7 hundredths. The decomposed or "expanded" form of 83.17 is:

$$80 + 3 + 0.1 + 0.07$$

Place Value of a Given Digit

The number system that is used consists of only ten different digits or characters. However, this system is used to represent an infinite number of values. The place value system makes this infinite number of values possible. The position in which a digit is written corresponds to a given value. Starting from the decimal point (which is implied, if not physically present), each subsequent place value to the left represents a value greater than the one before it. Conversely, starting from the decimal point, each subsequent place value to the right represents a value less than the one before it.

The names for the place values to the left of the decimal point are as follows:

...	Billions	Hundred-Millions	Ten-Millions	Millions	Hundred-Thousands	Ten-Thousands	Thousands	Hundreds	Tens	Ones

*Note that this table can be extended infinitely further to the left.

The names for the place values to the right of the decimal point are as follows:

Decimal Point (.)	Tenths	Hundredths	Thousandths	Ten-Thousandths	...

*Note that this table can be extended infinitely further to the right.

When given a multi-digit number, the value of each digit depends on its place value. Consider the number 682,174.953. Referring to the chart above, it can be determined that the digit 8 is in the ten-thousands place. It is in the fifth place to the left of the decimal point. Its value is 8 ten-thousands or 80,000. The digit 5 is two places to the right of the decimal point. Therefore, the digit 5 is in the hundredths place. Its value is 5 hundredths or $\frac{5}{100}$ (equivalent to .05).

Base-10 System

Value of Digits

In accordance with the base-10 system, the value of a digit increases by a factor of ten each place it moves to the left. For example, consider the number 7. Moving the digit one place to the left (70), increases its value by a factor of 10 ($7 \times 10 = 70$). Moving the digit two places to the left (700) increases its value by a factor of 10 twice

66

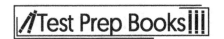

$(7 \times 10 \times 10 = 700)$. Moving the digit three places to the left (7,000) increases its value by a factor of 10 three times $(7 \times 10 \times 10 \times 10 = 7,000)$, and so on.

Conversely, the value of a digit decreases by a factor of ten each place it moves to the right. (Note that multiplying by $\frac{1}{10}$ is equivalent to dividing by 10). For example, consider the number 40. Moving the digit one place to the right (4) decreases its value by a factor of 10 $(40 \div 10 = 4)$. Moving the digit two places to the right (0.4), decreases its value by a factor of 10 twice $(40 \div 10 \div 10 = 0.4)$ or $(40 \times \frac{1}{10} \times \frac{1}{10} = 0.4)$. Moving the digit three places to the right (0.04) decreases its value by a factor of 10 three times $(40 \div 10 \div 10 \div 10 = 0.04)$ or $(40 \times \frac{1}{10} \times \frac{1}{10} \times \frac{1}{10} = 0.04)$, and so on.

Exponents to Denote Powers of 10

The value of a given digit of a number in the base-10 system can be expressed utilizing powers of 10. A power of 10 refers to 10 raised to a given exponent such as 10^0, 10^1, 10^2, 10^3, etc. For the number 10^3, 10 is the **base** and 3 is the **exponent**. A base raised by an exponent represents how many times the base is multiplied by itself. Therefore, $10^1 = 10$, $10^2 = 10 \times 10 = 100$, $10^3 = 10 \times 10 \times 10 = 1,000$, $10^4 = 10 \times 10 \times 10 \times 10 = 10,000$, etc. Any base with a zero exponent equals one.

Powers of 10 are utilized to decompose a multi-digit number without writing all the zeroes. Consider the number 872,349. This number is decomposed to:

$$800,000 + 70,000 + 2,000 + 300 + 40 + 9$$

When utilizing powers of 10, the number 872,349 is decomposed to:

$$(8 \times 10^5) + (7 \times 10^4) + (2 \times 10^3) + (3 \times 10^2) + (4 \times 10^1) + (9 \times 10^0)$$

The power of 10 by which the digit is multiplied corresponds to the number of zeroes following the digit when expressing its value in standard form. For example, 7×10^4 is equivalent to 70,000 or 7 followed by four zeros.

Basic Concepts of Number Theory

Comparing, Classifying, and Ordering Rational Numbers

A **rational number** is any number that can be written as a fraction or ratio. Within the set of rational numbers, several subsets exist that are referenced throughout the mathematics topics. **Counting numbers** are the first numbers learned as a child. Counting numbers consist of 1,2,3,4, and so on. **Whole numbers** include all counting numbers and zero (0,1,2,3,4...). **Integers** include counting numbers, their opposites, and zero (...,-3,-2,-1,0,1,2,3...). **Rational numbers** are inclusive of integers, fractions, and decimals that terminate, or end (1.7, 0.04213) or repeat $(0.136\overline{5})$.

When comparing or ordering numbers, the numbers should be written in the same format (decimal or fraction), if possible. For example, $\sqrt{49}$, 7.3, and $\frac{15}{2}$ are easier to order if each one is converted to a decimal, such as 7, 7.3, and 7.5 (converting fractions and decimals is covered in the following section). A number line is used to order and compare the numbers. Any number that is to the right of another number is greater than that number. Conversely, a number positioned to the left of a given number is less than that number.

Prime and Composite Numbers

Whole numbers are classified as either prime or composite. A **prime number** can only be divided evenly by itself and one. For example, the number 11 can only be divided evenly by 11 and one; therefore, 11 is a prime number. A helpful way to visualize a prime number is to use concrete objects and try to divide them into equal piles. If dividing

11 coins, the only way to divide them into equal piles is to create 1 pile of 11 coins or to create 11 piles of 1 coin each. Other examples of prime numbers include 2, 3, 5, 7, 13, 17, and 19.

A **composite number** is any whole number that is not a prime number. A composite number is a number that can be divided evenly by one or more numbers other than itself and one. For example, the number 6 can be divided evenly by 2 and 3. Therefore, 6 is a composite number. If dividing 6 coins into equal piles, the possibilities are 1 pile of 6 coins, 2 piles of 3 coins, 3 piles of 2 coins, or 6 piles of 1 coin. Other examples of composite numbers include 4, 8, 9, 10, 12, 14, 15, 16, 18, and 20.

To determine if a number is a prime or composite number, the number is divided by every whole number greater than one and less than its own value. If it divides evenly by any of these numbers, then the number is composite. If it does not divide evenly by any of these numbers, then the number is prime. For example, when attempting to divide the number 5 by 2, 3, and 4, none of these numbers divide evenly. Therefore, 5 must be a prime number.

Factors and Multiples of Numbers

The **factors** of a number are all integers that can be multiplied by another integer to produce the given number. For example, 2 is multiplied by 3 to produce 6. Therefore, 2 and 3 are both factors of 6. Similarly, $1 \times 6 = 6$ and $2 \times 3 = 6$, so 1, 2, 3, and 6 are all factors of 6. Another way to explain a factor is to say that a given number divides evenly by each of its factors to produce an integer. For example, 6 does not divide evenly by 5. Therefore, 5 is not a factor of 6.

Multiples of a given number are found by taking that number and multiplying it by any other whole number. For example, 3 is a factor of 6, 9, and 12. Therefore, 6, 9, and 12 are multiples of 3. The multiples of any number are an infinite list. For example, the multiples of 5 are 5, 10, 15, 20, and so on. This list continues without end. A list of multiples is used in finding the least common multiple, or LCM, for fractions when a common denominator is needed. The denominators are written down and their multiples listed until a common number is found in both lists. This common number is the LCM.

Prime factorization breaks down each factor of a whole number until only prime numbers remain. All composite numbers can be factored into prime numbers. For example, the prime factors of 12 are 2, 2, and 3 ($2 \times 2 \times 3 = 12$). To produce the prime factors of a number, the number is factored, and any composite numbers are continuously factored until the result is the product of prime factors only. A factor tree, such as the one below, is helpful when exploring this concept.

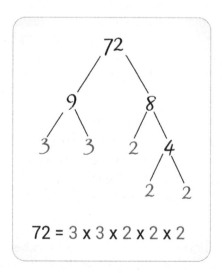

$$72 = 3 \times 3 \times 2 \times 2 \times 2$$

Solving Multistep Mathematical and Real-World Problems

Problem Situations for Operations

Addition and subtraction are **inverse operations**. Adding a number and then subtracting the same number will cancel each other out, resulting in the original number, and vice versa. For example, $8 + 7 - 7 = 8$ and $137 - 100 + 100 = 137$. Similarly, multiplication and division are inverse operations. Therefore, multiplying by a number and then dividing by the same number results in the original number, and vice versa. For example, $8 \times 2 \div 2 = 8$ and $12 \div 4 \times 4 = 12$. Inverse operations are used to work backwards to solve problems. In the case that 7 and a number add to 18, the inverse operation of subtraction is used to find the unknown value ($18 - 7 = 11$). If a school's entire 4th grade was divided evenly into 3 classes each with 22 students, the inverse operation of multiplication is used to determine the total students in the grade:

$$22 \times 3 = 66$$

Additional scenarios involving inverse operations in real-world settings are included in the tables below:

Addition & Subtraction

	Unknown Result	Unknown Change	Unknown Start
Adding to	5 students were in class. 4 more students arrived. How many students are in class? $5 + 4 =?$	8 students were in class. More students arrived late. There are now 18 students in class. How many students arrived late? $8+? = 18$ Solved by inverse operations $18 - 8 =?$	Some students were in class early. 11 more students arrived. There are now 17 students in class. How many students were in class early? $? +11 = 17$ Solved by inverse operations $17 - 11 =?$
Taking from	15 students were in class. 5 students left class. How many students are in class now? $15 - 5 =?$	12 students were in class. Some students left class. There are now 8 students in class. How many students left class? $12-? = 8$ Solved by inverse operations $8+? = 12 \rightarrow 12 - 8 =?$	Some students were in class. 3 students left class. Then there were 13 students in class. How many students were in class before? $?-3 = 13$ Solved by inverse operations $13 + 3 =?$

	Unknown Total	Unknown Addends (Both)	Unknown Addends (One)
Putting together/ taking apart	The homework assignment is 10 addition problems and 8 subtraction problems. How many problems are in the homework assignment? $10 + 8 =?$	Bobby has $9. How much can Bobby spend on candy and how much can Bobby spend on toys? $9 =? +?$	Bobby has 12 pairs of pants. 5 pairs of pants are shorts and the rest are long. How many pairs of long pants does he have? $12 = 5+?$ Solved by inverse operations $12 - 5 =?$

	Unknown Difference	Unknown Larger Value	Unknown Smaller Value
Comparing	Bobby has 5 toys. Tommy has 8 toys. How many more toys does Tommy have than Bobby? $5 + ? = 8$ Solved by inverse operations $8 - 5 = ?$ Bobby has $6. Tommy has $10. How many fewer dollars does Bobby have than Tommy? $10 - 6 = ?$	Tommy has 2 more toys than Bobby. Bobby has 4 toys. How many toys does Tommy have? $2 + 4 = ?$ Bobby has 3 fewer dollars than Tommy. Bobby has $8. How many dollars does Tommy have? $? - 3 = 8$ Solved by inverse operations $8 + 3 = ?$	Tommy has 6 more toys than Bobby. Tommy has 10 toys. How many toys does Bobby have? $? + 6 = 10$ Solved by inverse operations $10 - 6 = ?$ Bobby has $5 less than Tommy. Tommy has $9. How many dollars does Bobby have? $9 - 5 = ?$

Multiplication and Division

	Unknown Product	Unknown Group Size	Unknown Number of Groups
Equal groups	There are 5 students and each student has 4 pieces of candy. How many pieces of candy are there in all? $5 \times 4 = ?$	14 pieces of candy are shared equally by 7 students. How many pieces of candy does each student have? $7 \times ? = 14$ Solved by inverse operations $14 \div 7 = ?$	If 18 pieces of candy are to be given out 3 to each student, how many students will get candy? $? \times 3 = 18$ Solved by inverse operations $18 \div 3 = ?$

	Unknown Product	Unknown Factor	Unknown Factor
Arrays	There are 5 rows of students with 3 students in each row. How many students are there? $5 \times 3 = ?$	If 16 students are arranged into 4 equal rows, how many students will be in each row? $4 \times ? = 16$ Solved by inverse operations $16 \div 4 = ?$	If 24 students are arranged into an array with 6 columns, how many rows are there? $? \times 6 = 24$ Solved by inverse operations $24 \div 6 = ?$

	Larger Unknown	Smaller Unknown	Multiplier Unknown
Comparing	A small popcorn costs $1.50. A large popcorn costs 3 times as much as a small popcorn. How much does a large popcorn cost? $1.50 \times 3 = ?$	A large soda costs $6 and that is 2 times as much as a small soda costs. How much does a small soda cost? $2 \times ? = 6$ Solved by inverse operations $6 \div 2 = ?$	A large pretzel costs $3 and a small pretzel costs $2. How many times as much does the large pretzel cost as the small pretzel? $? \times 2 = 3$ Solved by inverse operations $3 \div 2 = ?$

Remainders in Division Problems

If a given total cannot be divided evenly into a given number of groups, the amount left over is the **remainder**. Consider the following scenario: 32 textbooks must be packed into boxes for storage. Each box holds 6 textbooks.

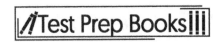

How many boxes are needed? To determine the answer, 32 is divided by 6, resulting in 5 with a remainder of 2. A remainder may be interpreted three ways:

- Add 1 to the quotient
  How many boxes will be needed? Six boxes will be needed because five will not be enough.

- Use only the quotient
  How many boxes will be full? Five boxes will be full.

- Use only the remainder
  If you only have 5 boxes, how many books will not fit? Two books will not fit.

Strategies and Algorithms to Perform Operations on Rational Numbers

A **rational number** is any number that can be written in the form of a ratio or fraction. Integers can be written as fractions with a denominator of 1 ($5 = \frac{5}{1}$; $-342 = \frac{-342}{1}$; etc.). Decimals that terminate and/or repeat can also be written as fractions ($.47 = \frac{47}{100}$; $.\overline{33} = \frac{1}{3}$).

When adding or subtracting fractions, the numbers must have the same denominators. In these cases, numerators are added or subtracted, and denominators are kept the same. For example, $\frac{2}{7} + \frac{3}{7} = \frac{5}{7}$ and $\frac{4}{5} - \frac{3}{5} = \frac{1}{5}$. If the fractions to be added or subtracted do not have the same denominator, a common denominator must be found. This is accomplished by changing one or both fractions to a different but equivalent fraction. Consider the example $\frac{1}{6} + \frac{4}{9}$. First, a **common denominator** must be found. One method is to find the **least common multiple (LCM)** of the denominators 6 and 9. This is the lowest number that both 6 and 9 will divide into evenly. In this case the LCM is 18. Both fractions should be changed to equivalent fractions with a denominator of 18. To obtain the numerator of the new fraction, the old numerator is multiplied by the same number by which the old denominator is multiplied. For the fraction $\frac{1}{6}$, 6 multiplied by 3 will produce a denominator of 18. Therefore, the numerator is multiplied by 3 to produce the new numerator $\left(\frac{1\times3}{6\times3} = \frac{3}{18}\right)$. For the fraction $\frac{4}{9}$, multiplying both the numerator and denominator by 2 produces $\frac{8}{18}$. Since the two new fractions have common denominators, they can be added:

$$\frac{3}{18} + \frac{8}{18} = \frac{11}{18}$$

When multiplying or dividing rational numbers, these numbers may be converted to fractions and multiplied or divided accordingly. When multiplying fractions, all numerators are multiplied by each other and all denominators are multiplied by each other. For example:

$$\frac{1}{3} \times \frac{6}{5} = \frac{1\times6}{3\times5} = \frac{6}{15}$$

$$\frac{-1}{2} \times \frac{3}{1} \times \frac{11}{100} = \frac{-1\times3\times11}{2\times1\times100} = \frac{-33}{200}$$

When dividing fractions, the problem is converted by multiplying by the reciprocal of the divisor. This is done by changing division to multiplication and "flipping" the second fraction, or divisor. For example, $\frac{1}{2} \div \frac{3}{5} \rightarrow \frac{1}{2} \times \frac{5}{3}$ and $\frac{5}{1} \div \frac{1}{3} \rightarrow \frac{5}{1} \times \frac{3}{1}$. To complete the problem, the rules for multiplying fractions should be followed.

Note that when adding, subtracting, multiplying, and dividing mixed numbers (e.g., $4\frac{1}{2}$), it is easiest to convert these to improper fractions (larger numerator than denominator). To do so, the denominator is kept the same. To obtain the numerator, the whole number is multiplied by the denominator and added to the numerator. For example, $4\frac{1}{2} = \frac{9}{2}$ and $7\frac{2}{3} = \frac{23}{3}$. Also, note that answers involving fractions should be converted to the simplest form.

Rational Numbers and Their Operations

Irregular Products and Quotients

The following shows examples where multiplication does not result in a product greater than both factors, and where division does not result in a quotient smaller than the dividend.

If multiplying numbers where one or more has a value less than one, the product will not be greater than both factors. For example, $6 \times \frac{1}{2} = 3$ and $0.75 \times 0.2 = 0.15$. When dividing by a number less than one, the resulting quotient will be greater than the dividend. For example, $8 \div \frac{1}{2} = 16$, because division turns into a multiplication problem, $8 \div \frac{1}{2} \rightarrow 8 \times \frac{2}{1}$. Another example is $0.5 \div 0.2$, which results in 2.5. The problem can be stated by asking how many times 0.2 will go into 0.5. The number being divided is larger than the number that goes into it, so the result will be a number larger than both factors.

Composing and Decomposing Fractions

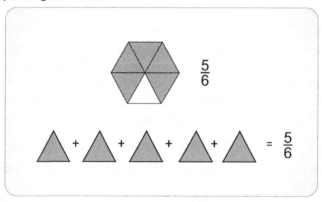

Fractions can be broken apart into sums of fractions with the same denominator. For example, the fraction $\frac{5}{6}$ can be decomposed into sums of fractions with all denominators equal to 6 and the numerators adding to 5. The fraction $\frac{5}{6}$ is decomposed as: $\frac{3}{6} + \frac{2}{6}$; or $\frac{2}{6} + \frac{2}{6} + \frac{1}{6}$; or $\frac{3}{6} + \frac{1}{6} + \frac{1}{6}$; or $\frac{1}{6} + \frac{1}{6} + \frac{1}{6} + \frac{2}{6}$; or:

$$\frac{1}{6} + \frac{1}{6} + \frac{1}{6} + \frac{1}{6} + \frac{1}{6}$$

A **unit fraction** is a fraction in which the numerator is 1. If decomposing a fraction into unit fractions, the sum will consist of a unit fraction added the number of times equal to the numerator. For example:

$$\frac{3}{4} = \frac{1}{4} + \frac{1}{4} + \frac{1}{4} \text{ (unit fractions } \frac{1}{4} \text{ added 3 times)}$$

Composing fractions is simply the opposite of decomposing. It is the process of adding fractions with the same denominators to produce a single fraction. For example:

$$\frac{3}{7} + \frac{2}{7} = \frac{5}{7} \ and \ \frac{1}{5} + \frac{1}{5} + \frac{1}{5} = \frac{3}{5}$$

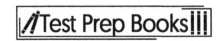

Decrease in Value of a Unit Fraction

A unit fraction is one in which the numerator is 1 ($\frac{1}{2}, \frac{1}{3}, \frac{1}{8}, \frac{1}{20}$, etc.). The denominator indicates the number of equal pieces that the whole is divided into. The greater the number of pieces, the smaller each piece will be. Therefore, the greater the denominator of a unit fraction, the smaller it is in value. Unit fractions can also be compared by converting them to decimals. For example, $\frac{1}{2} = 0.5, \frac{1}{3} = 0.\overline{3}, \frac{1}{8} = 0.125, \frac{1}{20} = 0.05$, etc.

Use of the Same Whole when Comparing Fractions

Fractions all represent parts of the same whole. Fractions may have different denominators, but they represent parts of the same one whole, like a pizza. For example, the fractions $\frac{5}{7}$ and $\frac{2}{3}$ can be difficult to compare because they have different denominators. The first fraction may represent a whole divided into seven parts, where five parts are used. The second fraction represents the same whole divided into three parts, where two are used. It may be helpful to convert one or more of the fractions so that they have common denominators for converting to equivalent fractions by finding the LCM of the denominator. Comparing is much easier if fractions are converted to the equivalent fractions of $\frac{30}{42}$ and $\frac{28}{42}$. These fractions show a whole divided into 42 parts, where the numerators can be compared because the denominators are the same.

Order of Operations

When reviewing calculations consisting of more than one operation, the order in which the operations are performed affects the resulting answer. Consider $5 \times 2 + 7$. Performing multiplication then addition results in an answer of 17 ($5 \times 2 = 10; 10 + 7 = 17$). However, if the problem is written $5 \times (2 + 7)$, the order of operations dictates that the operation inside the parenthesis must be performed first. The resulting answer is 45:

$$2 + 7 = 9$$
$$5 \times 9 = 45$$

The order in which operations should be performed is remembered using the acronym PEMDAS. PEMDAS stands for parenthesis, exponents, multiplication/division, and addition/subtraction. Multiplication and division are performed in the same step, working from left to right with whichever comes first. Addition and subtraction are performed in the same step, working from left to right with whichever comes first.

Consider the following example: $8 \div 4 + 8(7 - 7)$. Performing the operation inside the parenthesis produces $8 \div 4 + 8(0)$ or $8 \div 4 + 8 \times 0$. There are no exponents, so multiplication and division are performed next from left to right resulting in: $2 + 8 \times 0$, then $2 + 0$. Finally, addition and subtraction are performed to obtain an answer of 2. Now consider the following example: $6 \times 3 + 3^2 - 6$. Parentheses are not applicable. Exponents are evaluated first, $6 \times 3 + 9 - 6$. Then multiplication/division forms $18 + 9 - 6$. At last, addition/subtraction leads to the final answer of 21.

Properties of Operations

Properties of operations exist that make calculations easier and solve problems for missing values. The following table summarizes commonly used properties of real numbers.

Property	Addition	Multiplication
Commutative	$a + b = b + a$	$a \times b = b \times a$
Associative	$(a + b) + c = a + (b + c)$	$(a \times b) \times c = a \times (b \times c)$
Identity	$a + 0 = a;\ 0 + a = a$	$a \times 1 = a;\ 1 \times a = a$
Inverse	$a + (-a) = 0$	$a \times \dfrac{1}{a} = 1;\ a \neq 0$
Distributive	$a(b + c) = ab + ac$	

The commutative property of addition states that the order in which numbers are added does not change the sum. Similarly, the commutative property of multiplication states that the order in which numbers are multiplied does not change the product. The associative property of addition and multiplication state that the grouping of numbers being added or multiplied does not change the sum or product, respectively. The commutative and associative properties are useful for performing calculations. For example, $(47 + 25) + 3$ is equivalent to $(47 + 3) + 25$, which is easier to calculate.

The identity property of addition states that adding zero to any number does not change its value. The identity property of multiplication states that multiplying a number by one does not change its value. The inverse property of addition states that the sum of a number and its opposite equals zero. Opposites are numbers that are the same with different signs (e.g., 5 and -5; $-\frac{1}{2}$ and $\frac{1}{2}$). The inverse property of multiplication states that the product of a number (other than zero) and its reciprocal equals one. Reciprocal numbers have numerators and denominators that are inverted (e.g., $\frac{2}{5}$ and $\frac{5}{2}$). Inverse properties are useful for canceling quantities to find missing values (see algebra content). For example, $a + 7 = 12$ is solved by adding the inverse of 7 (which is -7) to both sides in order to isolate a.

The distributive property states that multiplying a sum (or difference) by a number produces the same result as multiplying each value in the sum (or difference) by the number and adding (or subtracting) the products. Consider the following scenario: You are buying three tickets for a baseball game. Each ticket costs $18. You are also charged a fee of $2 per ticket for purchasing the tickets online. The cost is calculated: $3 \times 18 + 3 \times 2$. Using the distributive property, the cost can also be calculated $3(18 + 2)$.

Converting Between Fractions, Decimals, and Percent

To convert a fraction to a decimal, the numerator is divided by the denominator. For example, $\frac{3}{8}$ can be converted to a decimal by dividing 3 by 8 ($\frac{3}{8} = 0.375$). To convert a decimal to a fraction, the decimal point is dropped, and the value is written as the numerator. The denominator is the place value farthest to the right with a digit other than zero. For example, to convert 0.48 to a fraction, the numerator is 48, and the denominator is 100 (the digit 8 is in the hundredths place). Therefore, $0.48 = \frac{48}{100}$. Fractions should be written in the simplest form, or reduced. To reduce a fraction, the numerator and denominator are divided by the largest common factor. In the previous example, 48 and 100 are both divisible by 4. Dividing the numerator and denominator by 4 results in a reduced fraction of $\frac{12}{25}$.

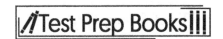

To convert a decimal to a percent, the number is multiplied by 100. To convert .13 to a percent, .13 is multiplied by 100 to get 13 percent. To convert a fraction to a percent, the fraction is converted to a decimal and then multiplied by 100. For example, $\frac{1}{5} = .20$ and .20 multiplied by 100 produces 20 percent.

To convert a percent to a decimal, the value is divided by 100. For example, 125 percent is equal to 1.25 $(\frac{125}{100})$. To convert a percent to a fraction, the percent sign is dropped, and the value is written as the numerator with a denominator of 100. For example, $80\% = \frac{80}{100}$. This fraction can be reduced $(\frac{80}{100} = \frac{4}{5})$.

Rounding Multi-Digit Numbers

Rounding numbers changes the given number to a simpler and less accurate number than the exact given number. Rounding allows for easier calculations which estimate the results of using the exact given number. The accuracy of the estimate and ease of use depends on the place value to which the number is rounded. Rounding numbers consists of:

- Determining what place value the number is being rounded to.

- Examining the digit to the right of the desired place value to decide whether to round up or keep the digit.

- Replacing all digits to the right of the desired place value with zeros.

To round 746,311 to the nearest ten thousands, the digit in the ten thousands place should be located first. In this case, this digit is 4 (7<u>4</u>6,311). Then, the digit to its right is examined. If this digit is 5 or greater, the number will be rounded up by increasing the digit in the desired place by one. If the digit to the right of the place value being rounded is 4 or less, the number will be kept the same. For the given example, the digit being examined is a 6, which means that the number will be rounded up by increasing the digit to the left by one. Therefore, the digit 4 is changed to a 5. Finally, to write the rounded number, any digits to the left of the place value being rounded remain the same and any to its right are replaced with zeros. For the given example, rounding 746,311 to the nearest ten thousand will produce 750,000. To round 746,311 to the nearest hundred, the digit to the right of the three in the hundreds place is examined to determine whether to round up or keep the same number. In this case, that digit is a one, so the number will be kept the same and any digits to its right will be replaced with zeros. The resulting rounded number is 746,300.

Rounding place values to the right of the decimal follows the same procedure, but digits being replaced by zeros can simply be dropped. To round 3.752891 to the nearest thousandth, the desired place value is located (3.75<u>2</u>891) and the digit to the right is examined. In this case, the digit 8 indicates that the number will be rounded up, and the 2 in the thousandths place will increase to a 3. Rounding up and replacing the digits to the right of the thousandths place produces 3.753000 which is equivalent to 3.753. Therefore, the zeros are not necessary, and the rounded number should be written as 3.753.

When rounding up, if the digit to be increased is a 9, the digit to its left is increased by 1 and the digit in the desired place value is changed to a zero. For example, the number 1,598 rounded to the nearest ten is 1,600. Another example shows the number 43.72961 rounded to the nearest thousandth is 43.730 or 43.73.

Determining the Reasonableness of Results

When solving math word problems, the solution obtained should make sense within the given scenario. The step of checking the solution will reduce the possibility of a calculation error or a solution that may be mathematically correct but not applicable in the real world. Consider the following scenarios:

75

A problem states that Lisa got 24 out of 32 questions correct on a test and asks to find the percentage of correct answers. To solve the problem, a student divided 32 by 24 to get 1.33, and then multiplied by 100 to get 133 percent. By examining the solution within the context of the problem, the student should recognize that getting all 32 questions correct will produce a perfect score of 100 percent. Therefore, a score of 133 percent with 8 incorrect answers does not make sense, and the calculations should be checked.

A problem states that the maximum weight on a bridge cannot exceed 22,000 pounds. The problem asks to find the maximum number of cars that can be on the bridge at one time if each car weighs 4,000 pounds. To solve this problem, a student divided 22,000 by 4,000 to get an answer of 5.5. By examining the solution within the context of the problem, the student should recognize that although the calculations are mathematically correct, the solution does not make sense. Half of a car on a bridge is not possible, so the student should determine that a maximum of 5 cars can be on the bridge at the same time.

Mental Math Estimation

Once a result is determined to be logical within the context of a given problem, the result should be evaluated by its nearness to the expected answer. This is performed by approximating given values to perform mental math. Numbers should be rounded to the nearest value possible to check the initial results.

Consider the following example: A problem states that a customer is buying a new sound system for their home. The customer purchases a stereo for $435, 2 speakers for $67 each, and the necessary cables for $12. The customer chooses an option that allows him to spread the costs over equal payments for 4 months. How much will the monthly payments be?

After making calculations for the problem, a student determines that the monthly payment will be $145.25. To check the accuracy of the results, the student rounds each cost to the nearest ten $(440 + 70 + 70 + 10)$ and determines that the total is approximately $590. Dividing by 4 months gives an approximate monthly payment of $147.50. Therefore, the student can conclude that the solution of $145.25 is very close to what should be expected.

When rounding, the place-value that is used in rounding can make a difference. Suppose the student had rounded to the nearest hundred for the estimation. The result $(400 + 100 + 100 + 0 = 600; 600 \div 4 = 150)$ will show that the answer is reasonable but not as close to the actual value as rounding to the nearest ten.

Reading

Comprehension

The Purpose of a Passage

No matter the genre or format, all authors are writing to persuade, inform, entertain, or express feelings. Often, these purposes are blended, with one dominating the rest. It's useful to learn to recognize the author's intent.

Persuasive writing is used to persuade or convince readers of something. It often contains two elements: the argument and the counterargument. The argument takes a stance on an issue, while the counterargument pokes holes in the opposition's stance. Authors rely on logic, emotion, and writer credibility to persuade readers to agree with them. If readers are opposed to the stance before reading, they are unlikely to adopt that stance. However, those who are undecided or committed to the same stance are more likely to agree with the author.

Informative writing tries to teach or inform. Workplace manuals, instructor lessons, statistical reports, and cookbooks are examples of informative texts. Informative writing is usually based on facts and is often void of emotion and persuasion. Informative texts generally contain statistics, charts, and graphs. Although most informative texts lack a persuasive agenda, readers still must examine the text carefully to determine whether one exists within a given passage.

Stories or narratives are designed to entertain. When you go to the movies, you often want to escape for a few hours, not necessarily to think critically. Entertaining writing is designed to delight and engage the reader. However, sometimes this type of writing can be woven into more serious materials, such as persuasive or informative writing to hook the reader before transitioning into a more scholarly discussion.

Emotional writing works to evoke the reader's feelings, such as anger, euphoria, or sadness. The connection between reader and author is an attempt to cause the reader to share the author's intended emotion or tone. Sometimes in order to make a piece more poignant, the author simply wants readers to feel the same emotions that the author has felt. Other times, the author attempts to persuade or manipulate the reader into adopting his stance. While it's okay to sympathize with the author, be aware of the individual's underlying intent.

Types of Passages

Writing can be classified under four passage types: narrative, expository, technical, and persuasive. Though these types are not mutually exclusive, one form tends to dominate the rest. By recognizing the *type* of passage you're reading, you gain insight into *how* you should read. If you're reading a narrative, you can assume the author intends to entertain, which means you may skim the text without losing meaning. A technical document might require a close read because skimming the passage might cause the reader to miss salient details.

1. **Narrative writing**, at its core, is the art of storytelling. For a narrative to exist, certain elements must be present. First, it must have characters. While many characters are human, characters could be defined as anything that thinks, acts, and talks like a human. For example, many recent movies, such as *Lord of the Rings* and *The Chronicles of Narnia*, include animals, fantastical creatures, and even trees that behave like humans. Second, it must have a plot or sequence of events. Typically, those events follow a standard plot diagram, but recent trends start *in medias res* or in the middle (near the climax). In this instance, foreshadowing and flashbacks often fill in plot details. Finally, along with characters and a plot, there must also be conflict. Conflict is usually divided into two types: internal and external. **Internal conflict** indicates the character is in turmoil and is presented through the character's thoughts. **External conflicts** are visible. Types of external conflict include a person versus nature, another person, or society.

77

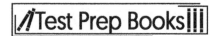

2. **Expository writing** is detached and to the point, while other types of writing—persuasive, narrative, and descriptive—are lively. Since expository writing is designed to instruct or inform, it usually involves directions and steps written in second person ("you" voice) and lacks any persuasive or narrative elements. Sequence words such as *first*, *second*, and *third*, or *in the first place*, *secondly*, and *lastly* are often given to add fluency and cohesion. Common examples of expository writing include instructor's lessons, cookbook recipes, and repair manuals.

3. Due to its empirical nature, **technical writing** is filled with steps, charts, graphs, data, and statistics. The goal of technical writing is to advance understanding in a field through the scientific method. Experts such as teachers, doctors, or mechanics use words unique to the profession in which they operate. These words, which often incorporate acronyms, are called **jargon**. Technical writing is a type of expository writing but is not meant to be understood by the general public. Instead, technical writers assume readers have received a formal education in a particular field of study, and need no explanation as to what the jargon means. Imagine a doctor trying to understand a diagnostic reading for a car or a mechanic trying to interpret lab results. Only professionals with proper training will fully comprehend the text.

4. **Persuasive writing** is designed to change opinions and attitudes. The topic, stance, and arguments are found in the thesis, positioned near the end of the introduction. Later supporting paragraphs offer relevant quotations, paraphrases, and summaries from primary or secondary sources, which are then interpreted, analyzed, and evaluated. The goal of persuasive writers is not to stack quotes but to develop original ideas by using sources as a starting point. Good persuasive writing makes powerful arguments with valid sources and thoughtful analysis. Poor persuasive writing is riddled with bias and logical fallacies. Sometimes logical and illogical arguments are sandwiched together in the same piece. Therefore, readers should display skepticism when reading persuasive arguments.

Text Structure

Depending on what the author is attempting to accomplish, certain formats or text structures work better than others. For example, a sequence structure might work for narration but not for identifying similarities and differences between concepts. Similarly, a comparison-contrast structure is not useful for narration. It's the author's job to put the right information in the correct format.

Readers should be familiar with the five main literary structures:

1. **Sequence structure** (sometimes referred to as the **order structure**) is when the order of events proceed in a predictable order. In many cases, this means the text goes through the plot elements: exposition, rising action, climax, falling action, and resolution. Readers are introduced to characters, setting, and conflict in the **exposition**. In the **rising action**, there's an increase in tension and suspense. The **climax** is the height of tension and the point of no return. Tension decreases during the **falling action**. In the **resolution**, any conflicts presented in the exposition are solved, and the story concludes. An informative text that is structured sequentially will often go in order from one step to the next.

2. In the **problem-solution structure**, authors identify a potential problem and suggest a solution. This form of writing is usually divided into two parts (the problem and the solution) and can be found in informational texts. For example, cell phone, cable, and satellite providers use this structure in manuals to help customers troubleshoot or identify problems with services or products.

3. When authors want to discuss similarities and differences between separate concepts, they arrange thoughts in a **comparison-contrast** paragraph structure. Venn diagrams are an effective graphic organizer for comparison-contrast structures because they feature two overlapping circles that can be used to organize similarities and differences. A comparison-contrast essay organizes one paragraph based on similarities and another based on

78

differences. A comparison-contrast essay can also be arranged with the similarities and differences of individual traits addressed within individual paragraphs. Words such as *however*, *but*, and *nevertheless* help signal a contrast in ideas.

4. **Descriptive writing structure** is designed to appeal to your senses. Much like an artist who constructs a painting, good descriptive writing builds an image in the reader's mind by appealing to the five senses: sight, hearing, taste, touch, and smell. However, overly descriptive writing can become distracting; whereas sparse descriptions can make settings and characters seem flat. Good authors must strike a balance between the two and provide enough detail to enable the reader to really see and experience what is happening in the plot without distracting the reader with excessive details.

5. Passages that use the **cause-and-effect structure** are simply asking *why* by demonstrating some type of connection between ideas. Words such as *if, since, because, then, or consequently* indicate a cause-and-effect relationship. By switching the order of a complex sentence, the writer can rearrange the emphasis on different clauses. Saying, *If Sheryl is late, we'll miss the dance*, is different from saying *We'll miss the dance if Sheryl is late*. One emphasizes Sheryl's tardiness while the other emphasizes missing the dance. Paragraphs can also be arranged in a cause-and-effect format. Cause-and-effect writing discusses the impact of decisions that have been made or could be made. Researchers often apply this paragraph structure to the scientific method.

Point of View

Point of view is an important writing device to consider. In fiction writing, point of view refers to who tells the story or from whose perspective readers are observing the story. In non-fiction writing, the **point of view** refers to whether the author refers to himself/herself, their readers, or chooses not to mention either. Whether fiction or nonfiction, the author will carefully consider the impact the perspective will have on the purpose and main point of the writing.

- **First-person point of view:** The story is told from the writer's perspective. In fiction, this would mean that the main character is also the narrator. First-person point of view is easily recognized by the use of personal pronouns such as *I*, *me*, *we*, *us*, *our*, *my*, and *myself*.

- **Third-person point of view:** In a more formal essay, this would be an appropriate perspective because the focus should be on the subject matter, not the writer or the reader. Third-person point of view is recognized by the use of the pronouns *he*, *she*, *they*, and *it*. In fiction writing, third-person point of view has a few variations.

  o **Third-person limited** point of view refers to a story told by a narrator who has access to the thoughts and feelings of just one character.

  o In **third-person omniscient** point of view, the narrator has access to the thoughts and feelings of all the characters.

  o In **third-person objective** point of view, the narrator is like a fly on the wall and can see and hear what the characters do and say, but does not have access to their thoughts and feelings.

79

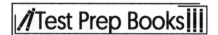

- **Second-person point of view:** This point of view isn't commonly used in fiction or nonfiction writing because it directly addresses the reader using the pronouns *you*, *your*, and *yourself*. Second-person perspective is more appropriate in direct communication, such as business letters or emails.

Point of View	Pronouns Used
First person	I, me, we, us, our, my, myself
Second person	You, your, yourself
Third person	He, she, it, they

Main Ideas and Supporting Details

Topics and main ideas are critical parts of writing. The **topic** is the subject matter of the piece. An example of a topic would be *global warming*.

The **main idea** is what the writer wants to say about that topic. A writer may make the point that global warming is a growing problem that must be addressed in order to save the planet. Therefore, the topic is global warming, and the main idea is that it's *a serious problem needing to be addressed*. The topic can be expressed in a word or two, but the main idea should be a complete thought.

An author will likely identify the topic immediately within the title or the first sentence of a passage. The main idea is usually presented in the introduction. In a single passage, the main idea may be identified in the first or last sentence, but it will most likely be directly stated and easily recognized by the reader. Because it is not always stated immediately in a passage, it's important to carefully read the entire passage to identify the main idea.

The main idea should not be confused with the thesis statement. A **thesis statement** is a clear statement of the writer's specific stance and can often be found in the introduction of a non-fiction piece. The thesis is a specific sentence (or two) that offers the direction and focus of the discussion.

In order to illustrate the main idea, a writer will use **supporting details**, the details that provide evidence or examples to help make a point. Supporting details often appear in the form of quotations, paraphrasing, or analysis. Authors should connect details and analysis to the main point.

In the example of global warming, where the author's main idea is to show the seriousness of this growing problem and the need for change, the use of supporting details in this piece would be critical in effectively making that point. Supporting details used here might include statistics on an increase in global temperatures and studies showing the impact of global warming on the planet. The author could also include projections for future climate change in order to illustrate potential lasting effects of global warming.

It's important to evaluate the author's supporting details to be sure that they are credible, provide evidence of the author's point, and directly support the main idea. Although shocking statistics grab readers' attention, their use could be ineffective information in the piece. Details like this are crucial to understanding the passage and evaluating how well the author presents their argument and evidence.

Also remember that when most authors write, they want to make a point or send a message. This point or message of a text is known as the theme. Authors may state themes explicitly, like in *Aesop's Fables*. More often, especially in modern literature, readers must infer the theme based on text details. Usually after carefully reading and analyzing an entire text, the reader can identify the theme. Typically, the longer the piece, the more themes that readers will encounter, although often one theme dominates the rest, as evidenced by the author's purposeful revisiting of it throughout the passage.

Evaluating a Passage

Determining conclusions requires being an active reader, as a reader must make a prediction and analyze facts presented in the reading to draw a conclusion. There are a few ways to determine a logical conclusion, but careful reading is the most important. It's helpful to read a passage a few times, noting details that seem important to the piece. A reader should also identify key words in a passage to determine the logical conclusion or determination that flows from the information presented.

Textual evidence helps readers draw a conclusion about a passage. **Textual evidence** refers to information—facts and examples—that support the main point; it will likely come from outside sources and can be in the form of quoted or paraphrased material. In order to draw a conclusion from evidence, it's important to examine the credibility and validity of that evidence as well as how (and if) it relates to the main idea.

If an author presents a differing opinion or a **counterargument** in order to refute it, the reader should consider how and why the information is being presented. It is meant to strengthen the original argument and shouldn't be confused with the author's intended conclusion, but it should also be considered in the reader's final evaluation.

Sometimes, authors explicitly state the conclusion they want readers to understand. Alternatively, a conclusion may not be directly stated. In that case, readers must rely on the implications to form a logical conclusion:

> On the way to the bus stop, Michael realized his homework wasn't in his backpack. He ran back to the house to get it and made it back to the bus just in time.

In this example, though it's never explicitly stated, it can be inferred that Michael is a student on his way to school in the morning. When forming a conclusion from implied information, it's important to read the text carefully to find several pieces of evidence to support the conclusion.

Summarizing is an effective way to draw a conclusion from a passage. A **summary** is a shortened version of the original text, written by the reader in their own words. Focusing on the main points of the original text and including only the relevant details can help readers reach a conclusion. It's important to retain the original meaning of the passage.

Like summarizing, **paraphrasing** can also help a reader fully understand different parts of a text. Paraphrasing calls for the reader to take a small part of the passage and list or describe its main points. Paraphrasing is more than rewording the original passage, though. It should be written in the reader's own words, while still retaining the meaning of the original source. This will indicate an understanding of the original source, yet still help the reader expand on their interpretation.

Readers should pay attention to the *sequence*, or the order in which details are laid out in the text, as this can be important to understanding its meaning as a whole. Writers will often use transitional words to help the reader understand the order of events and to stay on track. Words like *next, then, after*, and *finally* show that the order of events is important to the author. In some cases, the author omits these transitional words, and the sequence is implied. Authors may even purposely present the information out of order to make an impact or have an effect on the reader. An example might be when a narrative writer uses flashbacks to reveal information.

Engaging with a Text

There are a few ways for readers to engage actively with the text, such as making inferences and predictions. An **inference** refers to a point that is implied (as opposed to directly stated) by the evidence presented:

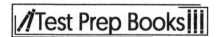

Bradley packed up all of the items from his desk in a box and said goodbye to his coworkers for the last time.

From this sentence, though it is not directly stated, readers can infer that Bradley is leaving his job. It's necessary to use inference in order to draw conclusions about the meaning of a passage. Authors make implications through character dialogue, thoughts, effects on others, actions, and looks. Like in life, readers must assemble all the clues to form a complete picture.

When making an inference about a passage, it's important to rely only on the information that is provided in the text itself. This helps readers ensure that their conclusions are valid.

Readers will also find themselves making predictions when reading a passage or paragraph. **Predictions** are guesses about what's going to happen next. Readers can use prior knowledge to help make accurate predictions. Prior knowledge is best utilized when readers make links between the current text, previously read texts, and life experiences. Some texts use suspense and foreshadowing to captivate readers:

A cat darted across the street just as the car came careening around the curve.

One unfortunate prediction might be that the car will hit the cat. Of course, predictions aren't always accurate, so it's important to read carefully to the end of the text to determine the accuracy of predictions.

Critical Thinking Skills

It's important to read any piece of writing critically. The goal is to discover the point and purpose of what the author is writing about through analysis. It's also crucial to establish the point or stance the author has taken on the topic of the piece. After determining the author's perspective, readers can then more effectively develop their own viewpoints on the subject of the piece.

It is important to distinguish between facts and opinions when reading a piece of writing. A **fact** is information that is true. If information can be disproven, it is not a fact. For example, water freezes at or below thirty-two degrees Fahrenheit. An argument stating that water freezes at seventy degrees Fahrenheit cannot be supported by data and is therefore not a fact. Facts tend to be associated with science, mathematics, and statistics. **Opinions** are information open for debate. Opinions are often tied to subjective concepts like feelings, desires, or manners. They can also be controversial. An affirmative argument for a position—such as gun control—can be just as effective as an opposing argument against it.

Authors often use words like *think, feel, believe,* or *in my opinion* when expressing opinion, but these words won't always appear in an opinion piece, especially if it is formally written. An author's opinion may be backed up by facts, which gives it more credibility, but that opinion should not be taken as fact. A critical reader should be wary of an author's opinion, especially if it is only supported by other opinions.

Fact	Opinion
There are 9 innings in a game of baseball.	Baseball games run too long.
Abraham Lincoln was assassinated on April 14, 1865.	Abraham Lincoln should never have been assassinated.
McDonald's has stores in 118 countries.	McDonald's has the best hamburgers.

Critical readers examine the facts used to support an author's argument. They check the facts against other sources to be sure those facts are correct. They also check the validity of the sources used to be sure those sources are credible, academic, and/or peer reviewed. Consider that when an author uses another person's opinion to support

82

their argument, even if it is an expert's opinion, it is still only an opinion and should not be taken as fact. A strong argument uses valid, measurable facts to support ideas. Even then, the reader may disagree with the argument as it may be rooted in their personal beliefs.

An authoritative argument may use the facts to sway the reader. Because of this, a writer may choose to only use the information and expert opinion that supports their viewpoint.

If the argument is that wind energy is the best solution, the author will use facts that support this idea. That same author may leave out relevant facts on solar energy. The way the author uses facts can influence the reader, so it's important to consider the facts being used, how those facts are being presented, and what information might be left out.

Critical readers should also look for errors in the argument such as bias and logical fallacies. Authors can also reflect **bias** if they ignore an opposing viewpoint or present their side in an unbalanced way. A strong argument considers the opposition and finds a way to refute it. Critical readers should look for an unfair or one-sided presentation of the argument and be skeptical, as a bias may be present. Even if this bias is unintentional, if it exists in the writing, the reader should be wary of the validity of the argument. A **logical fallacy** is a flaw in the logic used to make the argument.

Some of the more common fallacies are shown in the following chart.

Fallacy	Definition
Slippery Slope	A fallacy that is built on the idea that a particular action will lead to a series of events with negative results
Red Herring	The use of an observation or distraction to remove attention from the actual issue
Straw Man	An exaggeration or misrepresentation of an argument so that it is easier to refute
Post Hoc Ergo Propter Hoc	A fallacy that assumes an event to be the consequence of an earlier event merely because it came after it
Bandwagon	A fallacy that assumes because the majority of people feel or believe a certain way then it must be the right way
Ad Hominem	The use of a personal attack on the person or persons associated with a certain argument rather than focusing on the actual argument itself

Readers who are aware of the types of fallacious reasoning are able to weigh the credibility of the author's statements in terms of effective argument. Rhetorical text that contains a myriad of fallacious statements should be considered ineffectual and suspect.

Readers should also look for the use of **stereotypes**. These are the overly simplified beliefs about a person, place, thing, etc. that is indiscriminately applied to a larger group. These can be positive but are usually negative in nature. When a reader comes across the use of stereotypes, they should take that into consideration as they analyze the author's argument. These should generally be avoided. Stereotypes reveal a flaw in the writer's thinking and may suggest a lack of knowledge or understanding about the subject.

Making Inferences

As mentioned previously, making an inference requires the reader to read between the lines and look for what is implied rather than what is explicitly stated. That is, using information that is known from the text, the reader is able to make a logical assumption about information that is not explicitly stated but is probably true. Read the following passage:

"Hey, do you wanna meet my new puppy?" Jonathan asked.

"Oh, I'm sorry but please don't—" Jacinta began to protest, but before she could finish, Jonathan had already opened the passenger side door of his car and a perfect white ball of fur came bouncing towards Jacinta.

"Isn't he the cutest?" beamed Jonathan.

"Yes—achoo!—he's pretty—aaaachooo!!—adora—aaa—aaaachoo!" Jacinta managed to say in between sneezes. "But if you don't mind, I—I—achoo!—need to go inside."

Which of the following can be inferred from Jacinta's reaction to the puppy?
 a. She hates animals.
 b. She is allergic to dogs.
 c. She prefers cats to dogs.
 d. She is angry at Jonathan.

An inference requires the reader to consider the information presented and then form their own idea about what is probably true. Based on the details in the passage, what is the best answer to the question? Important details to pay attention to include the tone of Jacinta's dialogue, which is overall polite and apologetic, as well as her reaction itself, which is a long string of sneezes. Answer choices (a) and (d) both express strong emotions ("hates" and "angry") that are not evident in Jacinta's speech or actions. Answer choice (c) mentions cats, but there is nothing in the passage to indicate Jacinta's feelings about cats. Answer choice (b), "she is allergic to dogs," is the most logical choice. Based on the fact she began sneezing as soon as a fluffy dog approached her, it makes sense to guess that Jacinta might be allergic to dogs. Using the clues in the passage, it is reasonable to guess that this is true even though Jacinta never directly states, "Sorry, I'm allergic to dogs!"

Making inferences is crucial for readers of literature because literary texts often avoid presenting complete and direct information to readers about characters' thoughts or feelings, or they present this information in an unclear way, leaving it up to the reader to interpret clues given in the text. In order to make inferences while reading, readers should ask themselves:

- What details are being presented in the text?
- Is there any important information that seems to be missing?

- Based on the information that the author *does* include, what else is probably true?
- Is this inference reasonable based on what is already known?

Applying Information

A natural extension of being able to make an inference from a given set of information is also being able to apply that information to a new context. This is especially useful in nonfiction or informative writing. Considering the facts and details presented in the text, readers should consider how the same information might be relevant in a different situation. The following is an example of applying an inferential conclusion to a different context:

> Often, individuals behave differently in large groups than they do as individuals. One example of this is the psychological phenomenon known as the bystander effect. According to the bystander effect, the more people who witness an accident or crime occur, the less likely each individual bystander is to respond or offer assistance to the victim. A classic example of this is the murder of Kitty Genovese in New York City in the 1960s. Although there were over thirty witnesses to her killing by a stabber, none of them intervened to help Kitty or contact the police.

Considering the phenomenon of the bystander effect, what would probably happen if somebody tripped on the stairs in a crowded subway station?

    a. Everybody would stop to help the person who tripped
    b. Bystanders would point and laugh at the person who tripped
    c. Someone would call the police after walking away from the station
    d. Few if any bystanders would offer assistance to the person who tripped

This question asks readers to apply the information they learned from the passage, which is an informative paragraph about the bystander effect. According to the passage, this is a concept in psychology that describes the way people in groups respond to an accident—the more people are present, the less likely any one person is to intervene. While the passage illustrates this effect with the example of a woman's murder, the question asks readers to apply it to a different context—in this case, someone falling down the stairs in front of many subway passengers. Although this specific situation is not discussed in the passage, readers should be able to apply the general concepts described in the paragraph. The definition of the bystander effect includes any instance of an accident or crime in front of a large group of people. The question asks about a situation that falls within the same definition, so the general concept should still hold true: in the midst of a large crowd, few individuals are likely to actually respond to an accident. In this case, answer choice (d) is the best response.

Vocabulary

Understanding the Use of Affixes, Context, and Syntax

Affixes

Individual words are constructed from building blocks of meaning. An **affix** is an element that is added to a root or stem word that can change the word's meaning.

For example, the stem word *fix* is a verb meaning *to repair*. When the ending *–able* is added, it becomes the adjective *fixable*, meaning "capable of being repaired." Adding *un–* to the beginning changes the word to *unfixable*, meaning "incapable of being repaired." In this way, affixes attach to the word stem to create a new word and a new meaning. Knowledge of affixes can assist in deciphering the meaning of unfamiliar words.

Affixes are also related to inflection. **Inflection** is the modification of a base word to express a different grammatical or syntactical function. For example, countable nouns such as *car* and *airport* become plural with the addition of *–s* at the end: *cars* and *airports*.

Verb tense is also expressed through inflection. **Regular verbs**—those that follow a standard inflection pattern—can be changed to past tense using the affixes *–ed, –d,* or *–ied,* as in *cooked* and *studied.* Verbs can also be modified for continuous tenses by using *–ing,* as in *working* or *exploring.* Thus, affixes are used not only to express meaning but also to reflect a word's grammatical purpose.

A **prefix** is an affix attached to the beginning of a word. The meanings of English prefixes mainly come from Greek and Latin origins. The chart below contains a few of the most commonly used English prefixes.

Prefix	Meaning	Example
a-	not	amoral, asymptomatic
anti-	against	antidote, antifreeze
auto-	self	automobile, automatic
circum-	around	circumference, circumspect
co-, com-, con-	together	coworker, companion
contra-	against	contradict, contrary
de-	negation or reversal	deflate, deodorant
extra-	outside, beyond	extraterrestrial, extracurricular
in-, im-, il-, ir-	not	impossible, irregular

86

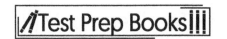

Prefix	Meaning	Example
inter-	between	international, intervene
intra-	within	intramural, intranet
mis-	wrongly	mistake, misunderstand
mono-	one	monolith, monopoly
non-	not	nonpartisan, nonsense
pre-	before	preview, prediction
re-	again	review, renew
semi-	half	semicircle, semicolon
sub-	under	subway, submarine
super-	above	superhuman, superintendent
trans-	across, beyond, through	trans-Siberian, transform
un-	not	unwelcome, unfriendly

While the addition of a prefix alters the meaning of the base word, the addition of a **suffix** may also affect a word's part of speech. For example, adding a suffix can change the noun *material* into the verb *materialize* and back to a noun again in *materialization*.

Suffix	Part of Speech	Meaning	Example
-able, -ible	adjective	having the ability to	honorable, flexible
-acy, -cy	noun	state or quality	intimacy, dependency
-al, -ical	adjective	having the quality of	historical, tribal
-en	verb	to cause to become	strengthen, embolden
-er, -ier	adjective	comparative	happier, longer
-est, -iest	adjective	superlative	sunniest, hottest
-ess	noun	female	waitress, actress
-ful	adjective	full of, characterized by	beautiful, thankful
-fy, -ify	verb	to cause, to come to be	liquefy, intensify
-ism	noun	doctrine, belief, action	Communism, Buddhism
-ive, -ative, -itive	adjective	having the quality of	creative, innovative
-ize	verb	to convert into, to subject to	Americanize, dramatize
-less	adjective	without, missing	emotionless, hopeless
-ly	adverb	in the manner of	quickly, energetically
-ness	noun	quality or state	goodness, darkness
-ous, -ious, -eous	adjective	having the quality of	spontaneous, pious
-ship	noun	status or condition	partnership, ownership
-tion	noun	action or state	renovation, promotion
-y	adjective	characterized by	smoky, dreamy

Through knowledge of prefixes and suffixes, a student's vocabulary can be instantly expanded with an understanding of **etymology**—the origin of words. This, in turn, can be used to add sentence structure variety to academic writing.

Context Clues

Familiarity with common prefixes, suffixes, and root words assists tremendously in unraveling the meaning of an unfamiliar word and making an educated guess as to its meaning. However, some words do not contain many easily-identifiable clues that point to their meaning. In this case, rather than looking at the elements within the

word, it is useful to consider elements around the word—i.e., its context. **Context** refers to the other words and information within the sentence or surrounding sentences that indicate the unknown word's probable meaning. The following sentences provide context for the potentially-unfamiliar word *quixotic*:

> Rebecca had never been one to settle into a predictable, ordinary life. Her quixotic personality led her to leave behind a job with a prestigious law firm in Manhattan and move halfway around the world to pursue her dream of becoming a sushi chef in Tokyo.

A reader unfamiliar with the word *quixotic* doesn't have many clues to use in terms of affixes or root meaning. The suffix *–ic* indicates that the word is an adjective, but that is it. In this case, then, a reader would need to look at surrounding information to obtain some clues about the word. Other adjectives in the passage include *predictable* and *ordinary*, things that Rebecca was definitely not, as indicated by "Rebecca had never been one to settle." Thus, a first clue might be that *quixotic* means the opposite of predictable.

The second sentence doesn't offer any other modifier of *personality* other than *quixotic*, but it does include a story that reveals further information about her personality. She had a stable, respectable job, but she decided to give it up to follow her dream. Combining these two ideas together, then—unpredictable and dream-seeking—gives the reader a general idea of what *quixotic* probably means. In fact, the root of the word is the character Don Quixote, a romantic dreamer who goes on an impulsive adventure.

While context clues are useful for making an approximate definition for newly-encountered words, these types of clues also come in handy when encountering common words that have multiple meanings. The word *reservation* is used differently in each the following sentences:

A. That restaurant is booked solid for the next month; it's impossible to make a reservation unless you know somebody.
B. The hospital plans to open a branch office inside the reservation to better serve Native American patients who cannot easily travel to the main hospital fifty miles away.
C. Janet Clark is a dependable, knowledgeable worker, and I recommend her for the position of team leader without reservation.

All three sentences use the word to express different meanings. In fact, most words in English have more than one meaning—sometimes meanings that are completely different from one another. Thus, context can provide clues as to which meaning is appropriate in a given situation. A quick search in the dictionary reveals several possible meanings for *reservation*:

1. An exception or qualification
2. A tract of public land set aside, such as for the use of American Indian tribes
3. An arrangement for accommodations, such as in a hotel, on a plane, or at a restaurant

Sentence A mentions a restaurant, making the third definition the correct one in this case. In sentence B, some context clues include Native Americans, as well as the implication that a reservation is a place—"inside the reservation," both of which indicate that the second definition should be used here. Finally, sentence C uses *without reservation* to mean "completely" or "without exception," so the first definition can be applied here.

Using context clues in this way can be especially useful for words that have multiple, widely varying meanings. If a word has more than one definition and two of those definitions are the opposite of each other, it is known as an **auto-antonym**—a word that can also be its own antonym. In the case of auto-antonyms, context clues are crucial to determine which definition to employ in a given sentence. For example, the word *sanction* can either mean "to approve or allow" or "a penalty." Approving and penalizing have opposite meanings, so *sanction* is an example of an auto-antonym. The following sentences reflect the distinction in meaning:

88

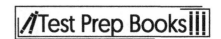

A. In response to North Korea's latest nuclear weapons test, world leaders have called for harsher sanctions to punish the country for its actions.
B. The general has sanctioned a withdrawal of troops from the area.

A context clue can be found in sentence A, which mentions "to punish." A punishment is similar to a penalty, so sentence A is using the word *sanction* according to this definition.

Other examples of auto-antonyms include *oversight*—"to supervise something" or "a missed detail," *resign*—"to quit" or "to sign again, as a contract," and *screen*—"to show" or "to conceal." For these types of words, recognizing context clues is an important way to avoid misinterpreting the sentence's meaning.

Syntax

Syntax refers to the arrangement of words, phrases, and clauses to form a sentence. Knowledge of syntax can also give insight into a word's meaning. The section above considered several examples using the word *reservation* and applied context clues to determine the word's appropriate meaning in each sentence. Here is an example of how the placement of a word can impact its meaning and grammatical function:

A. The development team has reserved the conference room for today.
B. Her quiet and reserved nature is sometimes misinterpreted as unfriendliness when people first meet her.

In addition to using *reserved* to mean different things, each sentence also uses the word to serve a different grammatical function. In sentence A, *reserved* is part of the verb phrase *has reserved*, indicating the meaning "to set aside for a particular use." In sentence B, *reserved* acts as a modifier within the noun phrase "her quiet and reserved nature." Because the word is being used as an adjective to describe a personality characteristic, it calls up a different definition of the word—"restrained or lacking familiarity with others." As this example shows, the function of a word within the overall sentence structure can allude to its meaning. It is also useful to refer to the earlier chart about suffixes and parts of speech as another clue into what grammatical function a word is serving in a sentence.

Analyzing Nuances of Word Meaning and Figures of Speech

By now, it should be apparent that language is not as simple as one word directly correlated to one meaning. Rather, one word can express a vast array of diverse meanings, and similar meanings can be expressed through different words. However, there are very few words that express exactly the same meaning. For this reason, it is important to be able to pick up on the nuances of word meaning.

Many words contain two levels of meaning: connotation and denotation as discussed previously in the informational texts and rhetoric section. A word's **denotation** is its most literal meaning—the definition that can readily be found in the dictionary. A word's **connotation** includes all of its emotional and cultural associations.

In literary writing, authors rely heavily on connotative meaning to create mood and characterization. The following are two descriptions of a rainstorm:

A. The rain slammed against the windowpane, and the wind howled through the fireplace. A pair of hulking oaks next to the house cast eerie shadows as their branches trembled in the wind.
B. The rain pattered against the windowpane, and the wind whistled through the fireplace. A pair of stately oaks next to the house cast curious shadows as their branches swayed in the wind.

Description A paints a creepy picture for readers with strongly emotional words like *slammed*, connoting force and violence. *Howled* connotes pain or wildness, and *eerie* and *trembled* connote fear. Overall, the connotative language in this description serves to inspire fear and anxiety.

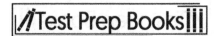

However, as can be seen in description B, swapping out a few key words for those with different connotations completely changes the feeling of the passage. *Slammed* is replaced with the more cheerful *pattered*, and *hulking* has been swapped out for *stately*. Both words imply something large, but *hulking* is more intimidating whereas *stately* is more respectable. *Curious* and *swayed* seem more playful than the language used in the earlier description. Although both descriptions represent roughly the same situation, the nuances of the emotional language used throughout the passages create a very different sense for readers.

Selective choice of connotative language can also be extremely impactful in other forms of writing, such as editorials or persuasive texts. Through connotative language, writers reveal their biases and opinions while trying to inspire feelings and actions in readers:

A. Parents won't stop complaining about standardized tests.
B. Parents continue to raise concerns about standardized tests.

Readers should be able to identify the nuance in meaning between these two sentences. The first one carries a more negative feeling, implying that parents are being bothersome or whiny. Readers of the second sentence, though, might come away with the feeling that parents are concerned and involved in their children's education. Again, the aggregate of even subtle cues can combine to give a specific emotional impression to readers, so from an early age, students should be aware of how language can be used to influence readers' opinions.

Another form of non-literal expression can be found in **figures of speech**. As with connotative language, figures of speech tend to be shared within a cultural group and may be difficult to pick up on for learners outside of that group. In some cases, a figure of speech may be based on the literal denotation of the words it contains, but in other cases, a figure of speech is far removed from its literal meaning. A case in point is **irony,** where what is said is the exact opposite of what is meant:

> The new tax plan is poorly planned, based on faulty economic data, and unable to address the financial struggles of middle-class families. Yet legislators remain committed to passing this brilliant proposal.

When the writer refers to the proposal as brilliant, the opposite is implied—the plan is "faulty" and "poorly planned." By using irony, the writer means that the proposal is anything but brilliant by using the word in a non-literal sense.

Another figure of speech is **hyperbole**—extreme exaggeration or overstatement. Statements like "I love you to the moon and back" or "Let's be friends for a million years" utilize hyperbole to convey a greater depth of emotion, without literally committing oneself to space travel or a life of immortality.

Figures of speech may sometimes use one word in place of another. **Synecdoche**, for example, uses a part of something to refer to its whole. The expression "Don't hurt a hair on her head!" implies protecting more than just an individual hair, but rather her entire body. "The art teacher is training a class of Picassos" uses Picasso, one individual notable artist, to stand in for the entire category of talented artists. Another figure of speech using word replacement is *metonymy*, where a word is replaced with something closely associated to it. For example, news reports may use the word *Washington* to refer to the American government or *the crown* to refer to the British monarch.

Mathematics

Numbers and Numeration

Structure of the Number System

The mathematical number system is made up of two general types of numbers: real and complex. **Real numbers** are both irrational and rational numbers, while **complex numbers** are those composed of both a real number and an imaginary one. Imaginary numbers are the result of taking the square root of -1, and $\sqrt{-1} = i$.

The real number system is often explained using a Venn diagram similar to the one below. After a number has been labeled as a real number, further classification occurs when considering the other groups in this diagram. If a number is a never-ending, non-repeating decimal, it falls in the **irrational** category. Many irrational numbers result from taking roots, such as $\sqrt{2}$ or $\sqrt{3}$. An irrational number may be written as:

$$34.5684952\ldots$$

The ellipsis (...) represents the line of numbers after the decimal that does not repeat and is never-ending.

Rational numbers are any numbers that can be written as a fraction, such as $\frac{1}{3}, \frac{7}{4}$, and -25. More information on these types of numbers is provided in the Quantitative Skills section. Furthermore, if a number does not have a fractional part, it is classified as an **integer**, such as -2, 75, or zero. **Whole numbers** are an even smaller group that only includes positive integers and zero. The last group, **natural numbers**, is made up of only positive integers, such as 2, 56, or 12.

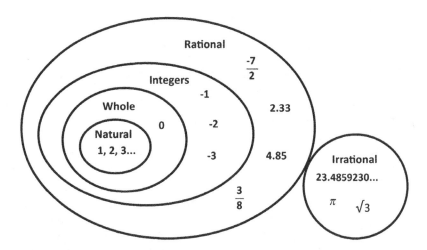

Real numbers can be compared and ordered using the number line. If a number falls to the left on the real number line, it is less than a number on the right. For example, $-2 < 5$ because -2 falls to the left of zero, and 5 falls to the right. Numbers to the left of zero are negative while those to the right are positive.

Complex numbers are made up of the sum of a real number and an imaginary number. Some examples of complex numbers include $6 + 2i$, $5 - 7i$, and $-3 + 12i$. Adding and subtracting complex numbers is similar to collecting like terms. The real numbers are added together, and the imaginary numbers are added together. For example, if the problem asks to simplify the expression $6 + 2i - 3 + 7i$, the 6 and (-3) are combined to make 3, and the $2i$ and $7i$ combine to make $9i$. Multiplying and dividing complex numbers is similar to working with exponents.

One rule to remember when multiplying is that $i \times i = -1$. For example, if a problem asks to simplify the expression $4i(3 + 7i)$, the $4i$ should be distributed throughout the 3 and the $7i$. This leaves the final expression $12i - 28$. The 28 is negative because $i \times i$ results in a negative number. The last type of operation to consider with complex numbers is the conjugate. The **conjugate** of a complex number is a technique used to change the complex number into a real number. For example, the conjugate of $4 - 3i$ is $4 + 3i$. Multiplying $(4 - 3i)(4 + 3i)$ results in $16 + 12i - 12i + 9$, which has a final answer of:

$$16 + 9 = 25$$

The order of operations—PEMDAS—simplifies longer expressions with real or imaginary numbers. Each operation is listed in the order of how they should be completed in a problem containing more than one operation. Parenthesis can also mean grouping symbols, such as brackets and absolute value. Then, exponents are calculated. Multiplication and division should be completed from left to right, and addition and subtraction should be completed from left to right.

Simplification of another type of expression occurs when radicals are involved. **Root** is another word for **radical**. For example, the following expression is a radical that can be simplified: $\sqrt{24x^2}$. First, the number must be factored out to the highest perfect square. Any perfect square can be taken out of a radical. Twenty-four can be factored into 4 and 6, and 4 can be taken out of the radical. $\sqrt{4} = 2$ can be taken out, and 6 stays underneath. If $x > 0$, x can be taken out of the radical because it is a perfect square. The simplified radical is $2x\sqrt{6}$. An approximation can be found using a calculator.

There are also properties of numbers that are true for certain operations. The **commutative property** allows the order of the terms in an expression to change while keeping the same final answer. Both addition and multiplication can be completed in any order and still obtain the same result. However, order does matter in subtraction and division. The **associative property** allows any terms to be "associated" by parenthesis and retain the same final answer. For example:

$$(4 + 3) + 5 = 4 + (3 + 5)$$

Both addition and multiplication are associative; however, subtraction and division do not hold this property. The **distributive property** states that:

$$a(b + c) = ab + ac$$

It is a property that involves both addition and multiplication, and the a is distributed onto each term inside the parentheses.

Interactions Between Rational and Irrational Numbers

When rational and irrational numbers interact, there are different types of number outcomes. For example, when adding or multiplying two rational numbers, the result is a rational number. No matter what two fractions are added or multiplied together, the result can always be written as a fraction. The following expression shows two rational numbers multiplied together:

$$\frac{3}{8} \times \frac{4}{7} = \frac{12}{56}$$

The product of these two fractions is another fraction that can be simplified to $\frac{3}{14}$.

As another interaction, rational numbers added to irrational numbers will always result in irrational numbers. No part of any fraction can be added to a never-ending, non-repeating decimal to make a rational number. The same

92

result is true when multiplying a rational and irrational number. Taking a fractional part of a never-ending, non-repeating decimal will always result in another never-ending, non-repeating decimal. An example of the product of rational and irrational numbers is shown in the following expression: $2 \times \sqrt{7}$.

The last type of interaction concerns two irrational numbers, where the sum or product may be rational or irrational depending on the numbers being used. The following expression shows a rational sum from two irrational numbers:

$$\sqrt{3} + \left(6 - \sqrt{3}\right) = 6$$

The product of two irrational numbers can be rational or irrational. A rational result can be seen in the following expression:

$$\sqrt{2} \times \sqrt{8} = \sqrt{2 \times 8} = \sqrt{16} = 4$$

An irrational result can be seen in the following:

$$\sqrt{3} \times \sqrt{2} = \sqrt{6}$$

Integers
An integer is any number that does not have a fractional part. This includes all positive and negative **whole numbers** and zero. Fractions and decimals—which aren't whole numbers—aren't integers.

Prime Numbers
A **prime** number cannot be divided except by 1 and itself. A prime number has no other factors, which means that no other combination of whole numbers can be multiplied to reach that number. For example, the set of prime numbers between 1 and 27 is {2, 3, 5, 7, 11, 13, 17, 19, 23}.

The number 7 is a prime number because its only factors are 1 and 7. In contrast, 12 isn't a prime number, as it can be divided by other numbers like 2, 3, 4, and 6. Because they are composed of multiple factors, numbers like 12 are called **composite** numbers. All numbers greater than 1 that aren't prime numbers are composite numbers.

Even and Odd Numbers
An integer is **even** if one of its factors is 2, while those integers without a factor of 2 are **odd**. No numbers except for integers can have either of these labels. For example, 2, 40, -16, and 108 are all even numbers, while -1, 13, 59, and 77 are all odd numbers since they are integers that cannot be divided by 2 without a remainder. Numbers like 0.4, $\frac{5}{9}$, π, and $\sqrt{7}$ are neither odd nor even because they are not integers.

Order of Rational Numbers

A common question type on the HSPT asks test takers to order rational numbers from least to greatest or greatest to least. The numbers will come in a variety of formats, including decimals, percentages, roots, fractions, and whole numbers. These questions test for knowledge of different types of numbers and the ability to determine their respective values.

Whether the question asks to order the numbers from greatest to least or least to greatest, the crux of the question is the same—convert the numbers into a common format. Generally, it's easiest to write the numbers as whole numbers and decimals so they can be placed on a number line. The following examples illustrate this strategy:

1. Order the following rational numbers from greatest to least:

$$\sqrt{36}, 0.65, 78\%, 3/4, 7, 90\%, 5/2$$

Of the seven numbers, the whole number (7) and decimal (0.65) are already in an accessible form, so test takers should concentrate on the other five.

First, the square root of 36 equals 6. (If the test asks for the root of a non-perfect root, determine which two whole numbers the root lies between.) Next, the percentages should be converted to decimals. A percentage means "per hundred," so this conversion requires moving the decimal point two places to the left, leaving 0.78 and 0.9. Lastly, the fractions are evaluated:

$$\frac{3}{4} = \frac{75}{100} = 0.75$$

$$\frac{5}{2} = 2\frac{1}{2} = 2.5$$

Now, the only step left is to list the numbers in the requested order:

$$7, \sqrt{36}, \frac{5}{2}, 90\%, 78\%, \frac{3}{4}, 0.65$$

2. Order the following rational numbers from least to greatest:

$2.5, \sqrt{9}, -10.5, 0.853, 175\%, \sqrt{4}, \frac{4}{5}$

$\sqrt{9} = 3$

$175\% = 1.75$

$\sqrt{4} = 2$

$\frac{4}{5} = 0.8$

From least to greatest, the answer is: $-10.5, \frac{4}{5}, 0.853, 175\%, \sqrt{4}, 2.5, \sqrt{9}$

Basic Addition, Subtraction, Multiplication, and Division

Gaining more of something is related to addition, while taking something away relates to subtraction. Vocabulary words such as *total*, *more*, *less*, *left*, and *remain* are common when working with these problems. The + sign means *plus*. This shows that addition is happening. The − sign means *minus*. This shows that subtraction is happening. The symbols will be important when you write out equations.

Addition

Addition can also be defined in equation form. For example, $4 + 5 = 9$ shows that $4 + 5$ is the same as 9. Therefore, $9 = 9$, and "four plus five equals nine." When two quantities are being added together, the result is called the **sum**. Therefore, the sum of 4 and 5 is 9. The numbers being added, such as 4 and 5, are known as the **addends.**

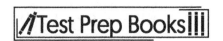

Subtraction

Subtraction can also be in equation form. For example, $9 - 5 = 4$ shows that $9 - 5$ is the same as 4 and that "9 minus 5 is 4." The result of subtraction is known as a **difference**. The difference of $9 - 5$ is 4. 4 represents the amount that is left once the subtraction is done. The order in which subtraction is completed does matter. For example, $9 - 5$ and $5 - 9$ do not result in the same answer. $5 - 9$ results in a negative number. So, subtraction does not adhere to the commutative or associative property. The order in which subtraction is completed is important.

Multiplication

Multiplication is when we add equal amounts. The answer to a multiplication problem is called a **product**. Products stand for the total number of items within different groups. The symbol for multiplication is $\times$ or $\cdot$. We say 2×3 or $2 \cdot 3$ means "2 times 3."

As an example, there are three sets of four apples. The goal is to know how many apples there are in total. Three sets of four apples gives $4 + 4 + 4 = 12$. Also, three times four apples gives $3 \times 4 = 12$. Therefore, for any whole numbers a and b, where a is not equal to zero, $a \times b = b + b + \cdots b$, where b is added a times. Also, $a \times b$ can be thought of as the number of units in a rectangular block consisting of a rows and b columns.

For example, 3×7 is equal to the number of squares in the following rectangle:

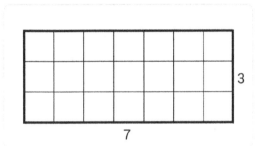

The answer is 21, and there are 21 squares in the rectangle.

When any number is multiplied by one (for example, $8 \times 1 = 8$), the value of original number does not change. Therefore, 1 is the **multiplicative identity**. For any whole number a, $1 \times a = a$. Also, any number multiplied by zero results in zero. Therefore, for any whole number a, $0 \times a = 0$.

Division

Division is based on dividing a given number into parts. The simplest problem involves dividing a number into equal parts. For example, if a pack of 20 pencils is to be divided among 10 children, you would have to divide 20 by 10. In this example, each child would receive 2 pencils.

The symbol for division is $\div$ or $/$. The equation above is written as $20 \div 10 = 2$, or $20/10 = 2$. This means "20 divided by 10 is equal to 2." Division can be explained as the following: for any whole numbers a and b, where b is not equal to zero, $a \div b = c$ if—and only if—$a = b \times c$. This means, division can be thought of as a multiplication problem with a missing part. For instance, calculating $20 \div 10$ is the same as asking the following: "If there are 20 items in total with 10 in each group, how many are in each group?" Therefore, 20 is equal to ten times what value? This question is the same as asking, "If there are 20 items in total with 2 in each group, how many groups are there?"

In a division problem, a is known as the **dividend,** b is the **divisor**, and c is the **quotient.** Zero cannot be divided into parts. Therefore, for any nonzero whole number a, $0 \div a = 0$. Also, division by zero is undefined. Dividing an amount into zero parts is not possible.

More difficult division problems involve dividing a number into equal parts, but having some left over. An example is dividing a pack of 20 pencils among 8 friends so that each friend receives the same number of pencils. In this setting, each friend receives 2 pencils, but there are 4 pencils leftover. 20 is the dividend, 8 is the divisor, 2 is the quotient, and 4 is known as the **remainder**. Within this type of division problem, for whole numbers a, b, c, and d, $a \div b = c$ with a remainder of d. This is true if and only if $a = (b \times c) + d$. When calculating $a \div b$, if there is no remainder, a is said to be *divisible* by b. **Even numbers** are all divisible by the number 2. **Odd numbers** are not divisible by 2. An odd number of items cannot be paired up into groups of 2 without having one item leftover.

Dividing a number by a single digit or two digits can be turned into repeated subtraction problems. An area model can be used throughout the problem that represents multiples of the divisor. For example, the answer to $8580 \div 55$ can be found by subtracting 55 from 8580 one at a time and counting the total number of subtractions necessary. However, a simpler process involves using larger multiples of 55. First, $100 \times 55 = 5,500$ is subtracted from 8,580, and 3,080 is leftover. Next, $50 \times 55 = 2,750$ is subtracted from 3,080 to obtain 380. $5 \times 55 = 275$ is subtracted from 330 to obtain 55, and finally, $1 \times 55 = 55$ is subtracted from 55 to obtain zero. Therefore, there is no remainder, and the answer is:

$$100 + 50 + 5 + 1 = 156$$

Here is a picture of the area model and the repeated subtraction process:

If you want to check the answer of a division problem, multiply the answer by the divisor. This will help you check to see if the dividend is obtained. If there is a remainder, the same process is done, but the remainder is added on at the end to try to match the dividend. In the previous example, $156 \times 55 = 8580$ would be the checking procedure. Dividing decimals involves the same repeated subtraction process. The only difference would be that the subtractions would involve numbers that include values in the decimal places. Lining up decimal places is crucial in this type of problem.

Adding and Subtracting Positive and Negative Numbers

Some problems require adding positive and negative numbers or subtracting positive and negative numbers. Adding a negative number to a positive one can be thought of a reducing or subtracting from the positive number, and the result should be less than the original positive number. For example, adding 8 and -3 is the same is subtracting 3

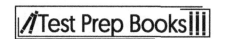

from 8; the result is 5. This can be visualized by imagining that the positive number (8) represents 8 apples that a student has in her basket. The negative number (-3) indicates the number of apples she is in debt or owes to her friend. In order to pay off her debt and "settle the score," she essentially is in possession of three fewer apples than in her basket ($8 - 3 = 5$), so she actually has five apples that are hers to keep. Should the negative addend be of higher magnitude than the positive addend (for example, $-9 + 3$), the result will be negative, but "less negative" or closer to zero than the large negative number. This is because adding a positive value, even if relatively smaller, to a negative value, reduces the magnitude of the negative in the total. Considering the apple example again, if the girl owed 9 apples to her friend (-9) but she picked 3 (+3) off a tree and gave them to her friend, she now would only owe him six apples (-6), which reduced her debt burden (her negative number of apples) by three.

Subtracting positive and negative numbers works the same way with one key distinction: subtracting a negative number from a negative number yields a "less negative" or more positive result because again, this can be considered as removing or alleviating some debt. For example, if the student with the apples owed 5 apples to her friend, she essentially has -5 applies. If her mom gives that friend 10 apples on behalf of the girl, she now has removed the need to pay back the 5 apples and surpassed neutral (no net apples owed) and now her friend owes *her* five apples (+5). Stated mathematically $-5 - -10 = +5$.

When subtracting integers and negative rational numbers, one has to change the problem to adding the opposite and then apply the rules of addition.

- Subtracting two positive numbers is the same as adding one positive and one negative number.

  o For example, $4.9 - 7.1$ is the same as $4.9 + (-7.1)$. The solution is -2.2 since the absolute value of -7.1 is greater than 4.9. Another example is $8.5 - 6.4$ which is the same as $8.5 + (-6.4)$. The solution is 2.1 since the absolute value of 8.5 is greater than 6.4.

- Subtracting a positive number from a negative number results in negative value.

  o For example, $(-12) - 7$ is the same as $(-12) + (-7)$ with a solution of -19.

- Subtracting a negative number from a positive number results in a positive value.

  o For example, $12 - (-7)$ is the same as $12 + 7$ with a solution of 19.

- For multiplication and division of integers and rational numbers, if both numbers are positive or both numbers are negative, the result is a positive value.

  o For example, $(-1.7) \times (-4)$ has a solution of 6.8 since both numbers are negative values.

- If one number is positive and another number is negative, the result is a negative value.

  o For example, $(-15) \div 5$ has a solution of -3 since there is one negative number.

Adding one positive and one negative number requires taking the absolute values and finding the difference between them. Then, the sign of the number that has the higher absolute value for the final solution is used.

Operations with Fractions, Decimals, and Percentages

Fractions
A **fraction** is a part of something that is whole. Items such as apples can be cut into parts to help visualize fractions. If an apple is cut into 2 equal parts, each part represents $\frac{1}{2}$ of the apple. If each half is then cut into two parts, the

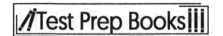

apple now is cut into quarters. Each piece now represents $\frac{1}{4}$ of the apple. In this example, each part is equal because they all have the same size. Geometric shapes, such as circles and squares, can also be utilized to help visualize the idea of fractions. For example, a circle can be drawn on the board and divided into 6 equal parts:

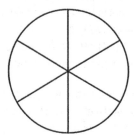

Shading can be used to represent parts of the circle that can be translated into fractions. The top of the fraction, the **numerator,** can represent how many segments are shaded. The bottom of the fraction, the **denominator,** can represent the number of segments that the circle is broken into. A pie is a good analogy to use in this example. If one piece of the circle is shaded, or one piece of pie is cut out, $\frac{1}{6}$ of the object is being referred to. An apple, a pie, or a circle can be utilized in order to compare simple fractions. For example, showing that $\frac{1}{2}$ is larger than $\frac{1}{4}$ and that $\frac{1}{4}$ is smaller than $\frac{1}{3}$ can be accomplished through shading. A **unit fraction** is a fraction in which the numerator is 1, and the denominator is a positive whole number. It represents one part of a whole—one piece of pie.

Imagine that an apple pie has been baked for a holiday party, and the full pie has eight slices. After the party, there are five slices left. How could the amount of the pie that remains be expressed as a fraction? The numerator is 5 since there are 5 pieces left, and the denominator is 8 since there were eight total slices in the whole pie. Thus, expressed as a fraction, the leftover pie totals $\frac{5}{8}$ of the original amount.

Fractions come in three different varieties: proper fractions, improper fractions, and mixed numbers. **Proper fractions** have a numerator less than the denominator, such as $\frac{3}{8}$, but **improper fractions** have a numerator greater than the denominator, such as $\frac{7}{2}$. **Mixed numbers** combine a whole number with a proper fraction, such as $3\frac{1}{2}$. Any mixed number can be written as an improper fraction by multiplying the integer by the denominator, adding the product to the value of the numerator, and dividing the sum by the original denominator. For example:

$$3\frac{1}{2} = \frac{3 \times 2 + 1}{2} = \frac{7}{2}$$

Whole numbers can also be converted into fractions by placing the whole number as the numerator and making the denominator 1. For example, $3 = \frac{3}{1}$.

The bar in a fraction represents division. Therefore $^6/_5$ is the same as $6 \div 5$. In order to rewrite it as a mixed number, division is performed to obtain $6 \div 5 = 1\ R1$. The remainder is then converted into fraction form. The actual remainder becomes the numerator of a fraction, and the divisor becomes the denominator. Therefore $1\ R1$ is written as $1\frac{1}{5}$, a mixed number. A mixed number can also decompose into the addition of a whole number and a fraction. For example,

$$1\frac{1}{5} = 1 + \frac{1}{5} \text{ and } 4\frac{5}{6} = 4 + \frac{1}{6} + \frac{1}{6} + \frac{1}{6} + \frac{1}{6} + \frac{1}{6}$$

98

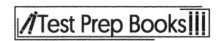

Every fraction can be built from a combination of unit fractions.

One of the most fundamental concepts of fractions is their ability to be manipulated by multiplication or division. This is possible since $\frac{n}{n} = 1$ for any non-zero integer. As a result, multiplying or dividing by $\frac{n}{n}$ will not alter the original fraction since any number multiplied or divided by 1 doesn't change the value of that number. Fractions of the same value are known as equivalent fractions. For example, $\frac{2}{8}$, $\frac{25}{100}$, and $\frac{40}{160}$ are equivalent, as they are all equal to $\frac{1}{4}$.

Like fractions, or **equivalent fractions**, are the terms used to describe these fractions that are made up of different numbers but represent the same quantity. For example, the given fractions are $\frac{4}{8}$ and $\frac{3}{6}$. If a pie was cut into 8 pieces and 4 pieces were removed, half of the pie would remain. Also, if a pie was split into 6 pieces and 3 pieces were eaten, half of the pie would also remain. Therefore, both of the fractions represent half of a pie. These two fractions are referred to as like fractions. **Unlike fractions** are fractions that are different and do not represent equal quantities. When working with fractions in mathematical expressions, like fractions should be simplified. Both $\frac{4}{8}$ and $\frac{3}{6}$ can be simplified into $\frac{1}{2}$.

Comparing fractions can be completed through the use of a number line. For example, if $\frac{3}{5}$ and $\frac{6}{10}$ need to be compared, each fraction should be plotted on a number line. To plot $\frac{3}{5}$, the area from 0 to 1 should be broken into 5 equal segments, and the fraction represents 3 of them. To plot $\frac{6}{10}$, the area from 0 to 1 should be broken into 10 equal segments and the fraction represents 6 of them.

It can be seen that $\frac{3}{5} = \frac{6}{10}$

Like fractions are plotted at the same point on a number line. Unit fractions can also be used to compare fractions. For example, if it is known that,

$$\frac{4}{5} > \frac{1}{2}$$

Also, it known that,

$$\frac{1}{2} > \frac{4}{10}$$

Then, it is also known that,

$$\frac{4}{5} > \frac{4}{10}$$

Also, converting improper fractions to mixed numbers can be helpful in comparing fractions because the whole number portion of the number is more visible.

Adding and subtracting mixed numbers and fractions can be completed by decomposing fractions into a sum of whole numbers and unit fractions. For example, the given problem is

$$5\frac{3}{7} + 2\frac{1}{7}$$

Decomposing into

$$5 + \frac{1}{7} + \frac{1}{7} + \frac{1}{7} + 2 + \frac{1}{7}$$

This shows that the whole numbers can be added separately from the unit fractions. The answer is:

$$5 + 2 + \frac{1}{7} + \frac{1}{7} + \frac{1}{7} + \frac{1}{7} = 7 + \frac{4}{7} = 7\frac{4}{7}$$

Although many equivalent fractions exist, they are easier to compare and interpret when reduced or simplified. The numerator and denominator of a simple fraction will have no factors in common other than 1. When reducing or simplifying fractions, divide the numerator and denominator by the greatest common factor. A simple strategy is to divide the numerator and denominator by low numbers, like 2, 3, or 5 until arriving at a simple fraction, but the same thing could be achieved by determining the greatest common factor for both the numerator and denominator and dividing each by it. Using the first method is preferable when both the numerator and denominator are even, end in 5, or are obviously a multiple of another number. However, if no numbers seem to work, it will be necessary to factor the numerator and denominator to find the GCF. For example:

1) Simplify the fraction $\frac{6}{8}$:

Dividing the numerator and denominator by 2 results in $\frac{3}{4}$, which is a simple fraction.

2) Simplify the fraction $\frac{12}{36}$:

Dividing the numerator and denominator by 2 leaves $\frac{6}{18}$. This isn't a simple fraction, as both the numerator and denominator have factors in common. Dividing each by 3 results in $\frac{2}{6}$, but this can be further simplified by dividing by 2 to get $\frac{1}{3}$. This is the simplest fraction, as the numerator is 1. In cases like this, multiple division operations can be avoided by determining the greatest common factor (12, in this case) between the numerator and denominator.

3) Simplify the fraction $\frac{18}{54}$ by dividing by the greatest common factor:

First, determine the factors for the numerator and denominator. The factors of 18 are 1, 2, 3, 6, 9, and 18. The factors of 54 are 1, 2, 3, 6, 9, 18, 27, and 54. Thus, the greatest common factor is 18. Dividing $\frac{18}{54}$ by 18 leaves $\frac{1}{3}$, which is the simplest fraction. This method takes slightly more work, but it definitively arrives at the simplest fraction.

Adding and Subtracting Fractions

Adding and subtracting fractions that have the same denominators involves adding or subtracting the numerators. The denominator will stay the same. Therefore, the decomposition process can be made simpler, and the fractions do not have to be broken into unit fractions.

For example, the given problem is:

$$4\frac{7}{8} - 2\frac{6}{8}$$

The answer is found by adding the answers to both

$$4 - 2 \text{ and } \frac{7}{8} - \frac{6}{8}$$

$$2 + \frac{1}{8} = 2\frac{1}{8}$$

A common mistake would be to add the denominators so that $\frac{1}{4} + \frac{1}{4} = \frac{1}{8}$ or to add numerators and denominators so that $\frac{1}{4} + \frac{1}{4} = \frac{2}{8}$. However, conceptually, it is known that two quarters make a half, so neither one of these are correct.

If two fractions have different denominators, equivalent fractions must be used to add or subtract them. The fractions must be converted into fractions that have common denominators. A **least common denominator** or the product of the two denominators can be used as the common denominator. For example, in the problem $\frac{5}{6} + \frac{2}{3}$, either 6, which is the least common denominator, or 18, which is the product of the denominators, can be used. In order to use 6, $\frac{2}{3}$ must be converted to sixths. A number line can be used to show the equivalent fraction is $\frac{4}{6}$. What happens is that $\frac{2}{3}$ is multiplied by a fractional form of 1 to obtain a denominator of 6. Hence, $\frac{2}{3} \times \frac{2}{2} = \frac{4}{6}$. Therefore, the problem is now $\frac{5}{6} + \frac{4}{6} = \frac{9}{6}$, which can be simplified into $\frac{3}{2}$. In order to use 18, both fractions must be converted into having 18 as their denominator. $\frac{5}{6}$ would have to be multiplied by $\frac{3}{3}$, and $\frac{2}{3}$ would need to be multiplied by $\frac{6}{6}$. The addition problem would be $\frac{15}{18} + \frac{12}{18} = \frac{27}{18}$, which reduces into $\frac{3}{2}$.

It is always possible to find a common denominator by multiplying the denominators. However, when the denominators are large numbers, this method is unwieldy, especially if the answer must be provided in its simplest form. Thus, it's beneficial to find the **least common denominator** of the fractions—the least common denominator is incidentally also the **least common multiple**.

Once equivalent fractions have been found with common denominators, simply add or subtract the numerators to arrive at the answer:

1) $\frac{1}{2} + \frac{3}{4} = \frac{2}{4} + \frac{3}{4} = \frac{5}{4}$

2) $\frac{3}{12} + \frac{11}{20} = \frac{15}{60} + \frac{33}{60} = \frac{48}{60} = \frac{4}{5}$

3) $\frac{7}{9} - \frac{4}{15} = \frac{35}{45} - \frac{12}{45} = \frac{23}{45}$

4) $\frac{5}{6} - \frac{7}{18} = \frac{15}{18} - \frac{7}{18} = \frac{8}{18} = \frac{4}{9}$

101

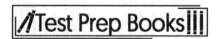

Multiplying and Dividing Fractions

Of the four basic operations that can be performed on fractions, the one that involves the least amount of work is multiplication. To multiply two fractions, simply multiply the numerators together, multiply the denominators together, and place the products of each as a fraction. Whole numbers and mixed numbers can also be expressed as a fraction, as described above, to multiply with a fraction.

Because multiplication is commutative, multiplying a fraction by a whole number is the same as multiplying a whole number by a fraction. The problem involves adding a fraction a specific number of times. The problem $3 \times \frac{1}{4}$ can be translated into adding the unit fraction three times: $\frac{1}{4} + \frac{1}{4} + \frac{1}{4} = \frac{3}{4}$. In the problem $4 \times \frac{2}{5}$, the fraction can be decomposed into $\frac{1}{5} + \frac{1}{5}$ and then added four times to obtain $\frac{8}{5}$. Also, both of these answers can be found by just multiplying the whole number by the numerator of the fraction being multiplied.

The whole numbers can be written in fraction form as:

$$\frac{3}{1} \times \frac{1}{4} = \frac{3}{4}$$

$$\frac{4}{1} \times \frac{2}{5} = \frac{8}{5}$$

Multiplying a fraction times a fraction involves multiplying the numerators together separately and the denominators together separately. For example,

$$\frac{3}{8} \times \frac{2}{3} = \frac{3 \times 2}{8 \times 3} = \frac{6}{24}$$

This can then be reduced to $\frac{1}{4}$.

Dividing a fraction by a fraction is actually a multiplication problem. It involves flipping the divisor and then multiplying normally. For example,

$$\frac{22}{5} \div \frac{1}{2} = \frac{22}{5} \times \frac{2}{1} = \frac{44}{5}$$

The same procedure can be implemented for division problems involving fractions and whole numbers. The whole number can be rewritten as a fraction over a denominator of 1, and then division can be completed.

A common denominator approach can also be used in dividing fractions. Considering the same problem, $\frac{22}{5} \div \frac{1}{2}$, a common denominator between the two fractions is 10. $\frac{22}{5}$ would be rewritten as $\frac{22}{5} \times \frac{2}{2} = \frac{44}{10}$, and $\frac{1}{2}$ would be rewritten as $\frac{1}{2} \times \frac{5}{5} = \frac{5}{10}$. Dividing both numbers straight across results in:

$$\frac{44}{10} \div \frac{5}{10} = \frac{\left(\frac{44}{5}\right)}{\left(\frac{10}{10}\right)} = \frac{\left(\frac{44}{5}\right)}{1} = \frac{44}{5}$$

Many real-world problems will involve the use of fractions. Key words include actual fraction values, such as *half, quarter, third, fourth*, etc. The best approach to solving word problems involving fractions is to draw a picture or diagram that represents the scenario being discussed, while deciding which type of operation is necessary in order

102

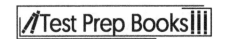

to solve the problem. A phrase such as "one fourth of 60 pounds of coal" creates a scenario in which multiplication should be used, and the mathematical form of the phrase is $\frac{1}{4} \times 60$.

Decimals

The **decimal system** is a way of writing out numbers that uses ten different numerals: 0, 1, 2, 3, 4, 5, 6, 7, 8, and 9. This is also called a "base ten" or "base 10" system. Other bases are also used. For example, computers work with a base of 2. This means they only use the numerals 0 and 1.

The **decimal place** denotes how far to the right of the decimal point a numeral is. The first digit to the right of the decimal point is in the **tenths'** place. The next is the **hundredths'** place. The third is the **thousandths'** place.

So, 3.142 has a 1 in the tenths place, a 4 in the hundredths place, and a 2 in the thousandths place.

The **decimal point** is a period used to separate the **ones'** place from the **tenths'** place when writing out a number as a decimal.

A **decimal number** is a number written out with a decimal point instead of as a fraction, for example, 1.25 instead of $\frac{5}{4}$. Depending on the situation, it may be easier to work with fractions, while other times, it may be easier to work with decimal numbers.

A decimal number is **terminating** if it stops at some point. It is called **repeating** if it never stops but repeats over and over. It is important to note that every rational number can be written as a terminating decimal or as a repeating decimal.

Addition with Decimals

To add decimal numbers, each number needs to be lined up by the decimal point in vertical columns. For each number being added, the zeros to the right of the last number need to be filled in so that each of the numbers has the same number of places to the right of the decimal. Then, the columns can be added together. Here is an example of $2.45 + 1.3 + 8.891$ written in column form:

$$
\begin{array}{r}
2.450 \\
1.300 \\
+\,8.891 \\
\end{array}
$$

Zeros have been added in the columns so that each number has the same number of places to the right of the decimal.

Added together, the correct answer is 12.641:

$$
\begin{array}{r}
2.450 \\
1.300 \\
+\,8.891 \\
\hline
12.641 \\
\end{array}
$$

Subtraction with Decimals

Subtracting decimal numbers is the same process as adding decimals. Here is $7.89 - 4.235$ written in column form:

$$
\begin{array}{r}
7.890 \\
-\,4.235 \\
\hline
3.655 \\
\end{array}
$$

103

A zero has been added in the column so that each number has the same number of places to the right of the decimal.

Multiplication with Decimals

The simplest way to multiply decimals is to calculate the product as if the decimals are not there, then count the number of decimal places in the original problem. Use that total to place the decimal the same number of places over in your answer, counting from right to left. For example, 0.5×1.25 can be rewritten and multiplied as 5×125, which equals 625. Then the decimal is added three places from the right for .625.

The final answer will have the same number of decimal places as the total number of decimal places in the problem. The first number has one decimal place, and the second number has two decimal places. Therefore, the final answer will contain three decimal places:

$$0.5 \times 1.25 = 0.625$$

Division with Decimals

Dividing a decimal by a whole number entails using long division first by ignoring the decimal point. Then, the decimal point is moved the number of places given in the problem.

For example, $6.8 \div 4$ can be rewritten as $68 \div 4$, which is 17. There is one non-zero integer to the right of the decimal point, so the final solution would have one decimal place to the right of the solution. In this case, the solution is 1.7.

Dividing a decimal by another decimal requires changing the divisor to a whole number by moving its decimal point. The decimal place of the dividend should be moved by the same number of places as the divisor. Then, the problem is the same as dividing a decimal by a whole number.

For example, $5.72 \div 1.1$ has a divisor with one decimal point in the denominator. The expression can be rewritten as $57.2 \div 11$ by moving each number one decimal place to the right to eliminate the decimal. The long division can be completed as $572 \div 11$ with a result of 52. Since there is one non-zero integer to the right of the decimal point in the problem, the final solution is 5.2.

In another example, $8 \div 0.16$ has a divisor with two decimal points in the denominator. The expression can be rewritten as $800 \div 16$ by moving each number two decimal places to the right to eliminate the decimal in the divisor. The long division can be completed with a result of 50.

Percentages

Think of percentages as fractions with a denominator of 100. In fact, **percentage** means "per hundred." Problems often require converting numbers from percentages, fractions, and decimals.

The basic percent equation is the following:

$$\frac{is}{of} = \frac{\%}{100}$$

The placement of numbers in the equation depends on what the question asks.

Example 1
Find 40% of 80.

Basically, the problem is asking, "What is 40% of 80?" The 40% is the percent, and 80 is the number to find the percent "of." The equation is:

$$\frac{x}{80} = \frac{40}{100}$$

Solving the equation by cross-multiplication, the problem becomes $100x = 80(40)$. Solving for x gives the answer: $x = 32$.

Example 2
What percent of 90 is 20?

The 20 fills in the "is" portion, while 90 fills in the "of." The question asks for the percent, so that will be x, the unknown. The following equation is set up:

$$\frac{20}{90} = \frac{x}{100}$$

Cross-multiplying yields the equation $90x = 20(100)$. Solving for x gives the answer of 22.2%.

Example 3
30% of what number is 30?

The following equation uses the clues and numbers in the problem:

$$\frac{30}{x} = \frac{30}{100}$$

Cross-multiplying results in the equation $30(100) = 30x$. Solving for x gives the answer $x = 100$.

Conversions
Decimals and Percentages
Since a percentage is based on "per hundred," decimals and percentages can be converted by multiplying or dividing by 100. Practically speaking, this always involves moving the decimal point two places to the right or left, depending on the conversion. To convert a percentage to a decimal, move the decimal point two places to the left and remove the % sign. To convert a decimal to a percentage, move the decimal point two places to the right and add a % sign.

Here are some examples:

$65\% = 0.65$
$0.33 = 33\%$
$0.215 = 21.5\%$
$99.99\% = 0.9999$
$500\% = 5.00$
$7.55 = 755\%$

Fractions and Percentages

Remember that a percentage is a number per one hundred. So, a percentage can be converted to a fraction by making the number in the percentage the numerator and putting 100 as the denominator:

$$43\% = \frac{43}{100}$$

$$97\% = \frac{97}{100}$$

Note that the percent symbol (%) kind of looks like a 0, a 1, and another 0. So think of a percentage like 54% as 54 over 100.

To convert a fraction to a percent, follow the same logic. If the fraction happens to have 100 in the denominator, you're in luck. Just take the numerator and add a percent symbol:

$$\frac{28}{100} = 28\%$$

Otherwise, divide the numerator by the denominator to get a decimal:

$$\frac{9}{12} = 0.75$$

Then convert the decimal to a percentage:

$$0.75 = 75\%$$

Another option is to make the denominator equal to 100. Be sure to multiply the numerator and the denominator by the same number. For example:

$$\frac{3}{20} \times \frac{5}{5} = \frac{15}{100}$$

$$\frac{15}{100} = 15\%$$

Changing Fractions to Decimals

To change a fraction into a decimal, divide the denominator into the numerator until there are no remainders. There may be repeating decimals, so rounding is often acceptable. A straight line above the repeating portion denotes that the decimal repeats.

Example: Express $\frac{4}{5}$ as a decimal.

Set up the division problem.

$$5\overline{)4}$$

5 does not go into 4, so place the decimal and add a zero.

$$5\overline{)4.0}$$

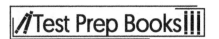

5 goes into 40 eight times. There is no remainder.

$$\begin{array}{r} 0.8 \\ 5\overline{)4.0} \\ -\underline{4.0} \\ 0 \end{array}$$

The solution is 0.8.

Example: Express $33\frac{1}{3}$ as a decimal.

Since the whole portion of the number is known, set it aside to calculate the decimal from the fraction portion.

Set up the division problem.

$$3\overline{)1}$$

3 does not go into 1, so place the decimal and add zeros. 3 goes into 10 three times.

$$\begin{array}{r} 0.3 \\ 3\overline{)1.0} \end{array}$$

This will repeat with a remainder of 1.

$$\begin{array}{r} 0.333 \\ 3\overline{)1.000} \\ -\underline{9} \\ 10 \\ -\underline{9} \\ 10 \end{array}$$

So, we will place a line over the 3 to denote the repetition. The solution is written $0.\overline{3}$.

Changing Decimals to Fractions

To change decimals to fractions, place the decimal portion of the number—the numerator—over the respective place value—the denominator—then reduce, if possible.

Example: Express 0.25 as a fraction.

This is read as twenty-five hundredths, so put 25 over 100. Then reduce to find the solution.

$$\frac{25}{100} = \frac{1}{4}$$

Example: Express 0.455 as a fraction

This is read as four hundred fifty-five thousandths, so put 455 over 1,000. Then reduce to find the solution.

$$\frac{455}{1,000} = \frac{91}{200}$$

There are two types of problems that commonly involve percentages. The first is to calculate some percentage of a given quantity, where you convert the percentage to a decimal, and multiply the quantity by that decimal. Secondly, you are given a quantity and told it is a fixed percent of an unknown quantity. In this case, convert to a decimal, then divide the given quantity by that decimal.

Example: What is 30% of 760?

Convert the percent into a useable number. "Of" means to multiply.

$$30\% = 0.30$$

Set up the problem based on the givens, and solve.

$$0.30 \times 760 = 228$$

Example: 8.4 is 20% of what number?

Convert the percent into a useable number.

$$20\% = 0.20$$

The given number is a percent of the answer needed, so divide the given number by this decimal rather than multiplying it.

$$\frac{8.4}{0.20} = 42$$

Factorization

Factors are the numbers multiplied to achieve a product. Thus, every product in a multiplication equation has, at minimum, two factors. Of course, some products will have more than two factors. For the sake of most discussions, assume that factors are positive integers.

To find a number's factors, start with 1 and the number itself. Then divide the number by 2, 3, 4, and so on, seeing if any divisors can divide the number without a remainder, keeping a list of those that do. Stop upon reaching either the number itself or another factor.

Let's find the factors of 45. Start with 1 and 45. Then try to divide 45 by 2, which fails. Now divide 45 by 3. The answer is 15, so 3 and 15 are now factors. Dividing by 4 doesn't work, and dividing by 5 leaves 9. Lastly, dividing 45 by 6, 7, and 8 all don't work. The next integer to try is 9, but this is already known to be a factor, so the factorization is complete. The factors of 45 are 1, 3, 5, 9, 15 and 45.

Prime Factorization
Prime factorization involves an additional step after breaking a number down to its factors: breaking down the factors until they are all prime numbers. A **prime number** is any number that can only be divided by 1 and itself. The prime numbers between 1 and 20 are 2, 3, 5, 7, 11, 13, 17, and 19. As a simple test, numbers that are even or end in 5 are not prime, though there are other numbers that are not prime, but are odd and do not end in 5. For example, 21 is odd and divisible by 1, 3, 7, and 21, so it is not prime.

Let's break 129 down into its prime factors. First, the factors are 3 and 43. Both 3 and 43 are prime numbers, so we're done. But if 43 was not a prime number, then it would also need to be factorized until all of the factors are expressed as prime numbers.

Common Factor

A **common factor** is a factor shared by two numbers. Let's take 45 and 30 and find the common factors:

The factors of 45 are: 1, 3, 5, 9, 15, and 45.

The factors of 30 are: 1, 2, 3, 5, 6, 10, 15, and 30.

Thus, the common factors are 1, 3, 5, and 15.

Greatest Common Factor

The **greatest common factor** is the largest number among the shared, common factors. From the factors of 45 and 30, the common factors are 3, 5, and 15. Therefore, 15 is the greatest common factor, as it's the largest number.

Least Common Multiple

The **least common multiple** is the smallest number that's a multiple of two numbers. Let's try to find the least common multiple of 4 and 9. The multiples of 4 are 4, 8, 12, 16, 20, 24, 28, 32, 36, and so on. For 9, the multiples are 9, 18, 27, 36, 45, 54, etc. Thus, the least common multiple of 4 and 9 is 36 because this is the lowest number where 4 and 9 share multiples.

If two numbers share no factors besides 1 in common, then their least common multiple will be simply their product. If two numbers have common factors, then their least common multiple will be their product divided by their greatest common factor. This can be visualized by the formula $LCM = \frac{x \times y}{GCF}$, where x and y are some integers, and LCM and GCF are their least common multiple and greatest common factor, respectively.

Exponents

An **exponent** is an operation used as shorthand for a number multiplied or divided by itself for a defined number of times.

$$3^7 = 3 \times 3 \times 3 \times 3 \times 3 \times 3 \times 3$$

In the example above, the 3 is called the **base**, and the 7 is called the **exponent**. The exponent is typically expressed as a superscript number near the upper right side of the base but can also be identified as the number following a caret symbol (^). This operation is verbally expressed as "3 to the 7th power" or "3 raised to the power of 7." Common exponents are 2 and 3. A base raised to the power of 2 is referred to as having been "squared," while a base raised to the power of 3 is referred to as having been "cubed."

Several special rules apply to exponents. First, the **Zero Power Rule** finds that any number raised to the zero power equals 1. For example, 100^0, 2^0, $(-3)^0$ and 0^0 all equal 1 because the bases are raised to the zero power.

Second, exponents can be negative. With negative exponents, the equation is expressed as a fraction, as in the following example:

$$3^{-7} = \frac{1}{3^7} = \frac{1}{3 \times 3 \times 3 \times 3 \times 3 \times 3 \times 3}$$

Third, the **Power Rule** concerns exponents being raised by another exponent. When this occurs, the exponents are multiplied by each other:

$$(x^2)^3 = x^6 = (x^3)^2$$

Fourth, when multiplying two exponents with the same base, the **Product Rule** requires that the base remains the same, and the exponents are added. For example, $a^x \times a^y = a^{x+y}$. Since addition and multiplication are commutative, the two terms being multiplied can be in any order.

$$x^3x^5 = x^{3+5} = x^8 = x^{5+3} = x^5x^3$$

Fifth, when dividing two exponents with the same base, the **Quotient Rule** requires that the base remains the same, but the exponents are subtracted. So, $a^x \div a^y = a^{x-y}$. Since subtraction and division are not commutative, the two terms must remain in order.

$$x^5x^{-3} = x^{5-3} = x^2 = x^5 \div x^3 = \frac{x^5}{x^3}$$

Additionally, 1 raised to any power is still equal to 1, and any number raised to the power of 1 is equal to itself. In other words, $a^1 = a$ and $14^1 = 14$.

Exponents play an important role in scientific notation to present extremely large or small numbers as follows: $a \times 10^b$. To write the number in scientific notation, the decimal is moved until there is only one digit on the left side of the decimal point, indicating that the number a has a value between 1 and 10. The number of times the decimal moves indicates the exponent to which 10 is raised, here represented by b. If the decimal moves to the left, then b is positive, but if the decimal moves to the right, then b is negative.

The following examples demonstrate these concepts:

$$3,050 = 3.05 \times 10^3$$

$$-777 = -7.77 \times 10^2$$

$$0.000123 = 1.23 \times 10^{-4}$$

$$-0.0525 = -5.25 \times 10^{-2}$$

Roots

The **square root** symbol is expressed as $\sqrt{}$ and is commonly known as the **radical**. Taking the root of a number is the inverse operation of multiplying that number by itself some number of times. For example, squaring the number 7 is equal to 7×7, or 49. Finding the square root is the opposite of finding an exponent, as the operation seeks a number that when multiplied by itself, equals the number in the square root symbol.

For example, $\sqrt{36} = 6$ because 6 multiplied by 6 equals 36. Note, the square root of 36 is also -6 since $-6 \times -6 = 36$. This can be indicated using a **plus/minus** symbol like this: ± 6. However, square roots are often just expressed as a positive number for simplicity, with it being understood that the true value can be either positive or negative.

Perfect squares are numbers with whole number square roots. The list of perfect squares begins with 0, 1, 4, 9, 16, 25, 36, 49, 64, 81, and 100.

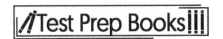

Determining the square root of imperfect squares requires a calculator to reach an exact figure. It's possible, however, to approximate the answer by finding the two perfect squares that the number fits between. For example, the square root of 40 is between 6 and 7 since the squares of those numbers are 36 and 49, respectively.

Square roots are the most common root operation. If the radical doesn't have a number to the upper left of the symbol $\sqrt{}$, then it's a **square root**. Sometimes a radical includes a number in the upper left, like $\sqrt[3]{27}$, as in the other common root type—the **cube root**. Complicated roots, like the cube root, often require a calculator.

Estimation

Estimation is finding a value that is close to a solution but is not the exact answer. For example, if there are values in the thousands to be multiplied, then each value can be estimated to the nearest thousand and the calculation performed. This value provides an approximate solution that can be determined very quickly.

As previously mentioned, **rounding** is the process of either bumping a number up or leaving it the same, based on a specified place value. First, the place value is specified. Then, the digit to its right is looked at. For example, if rounding to the nearest hundreds place, the digit in the tens place is used. If it is a 0, 1, 2, 3, or 4, the digit being rounded to is left alone. If it is a 5, 6, 7, 8 or 9, the digit being rounded to is increased by one. All other digits before the decimal point are then changed to zeros, and the digits in decimal places are dropped. If a decimal place is being rounded to, all subsequent digits are just dropped. For example, if 845,231.45 was to be rounded to the nearest thousands place, the answer would be 845,000. The 5 would remain the same due to the 2 in the hundreds place. Also, if 4.567 was to be rounded to the nearest tenths place, the answer would be 4.6. The 5 increased to 6 due to the 6 in the hundredths place, and the rest of the decimal is dropped.

Sometimes, when performing operations such as multiplying numbers, the result can be estimated by rounding. For example, to estimate the value of 11.2×2.01, each number can be rounded to the nearest integer. This will yield a result of 22.

Vectors

A **vector** can be thought of as an abstract list of numbers or as giving a location in a space. For example, the coordinates (x, y) for points in the Cartesian plane are vectors. Each entry in a vector can be referred to by its location in the list: first, second, third, and so on. The total length of the list is the **dimension** of the vector. A vector is often denoted as such by putting an arrow on top of it. For example:

$$\vec{v} = (v_1, v_2, v_3)$$

Adding Vectors Graphically and Algebraically

There are two basic operations for vectors. First, two vectors can be added together. Let:

$$\vec{v} = (v_1, v_2, v_3)$$

$$\vec{w} = (w_1, w_2, w_3)$$

Then, the sum of the two vectors is defined to be:

$$\vec{v} + \vec{w} = (v_1 + w_1, v_2 + w_2, v_3 + w_3)$$

Subtraction of vectors can be defined similarly.

Vector addition can be visualized in the following manner. First, each vector can be visualized as an arrow. Then, the base of one arrow is placed at the tip of the other arrow. The tip of this first arrow now hits some point in space,

111

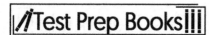

and there will be an arrow from the origin to this point. This new arrow corresponds to the new vector. In subtraction, the direction of the arrow being subtracted is reversed.

For example, if adding together the vectors (-2, 3) and (4, 1), the new vector will be $(-2 + 4, 3 + 1)$, or (2, 4). Graphically, this may be pictured in the following manner:

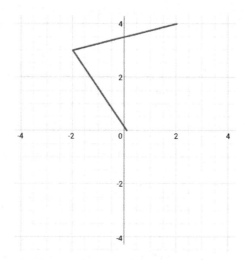

Performing Scalar Multiplications

The second basic operation for vectors is called **scalar multiplication**. Scalar multiplication is multiplying any vector by any real number, which is denoted here as a scalar. Let $\vec{v} = (v_1, v_2, v_3)$, and let a be an arbitrary real number. Then the scalar multiple $a\vec{v} = (av_1, av_2, av_3)$. Graphically, this corresponds to changing the length of the arrow corresponding to the vector by a factor, or scale, of a. That is why the real number is called a **scalar** in this instance.

As an example, let $\vec{v} = (2, -1, 1)$. Then $3\vec{v} = (3 \cdot 2, 3(-1), 3 \cdot 1) = (6, -3, 3)$.

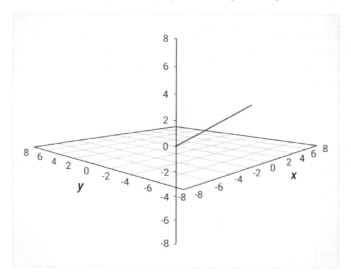

Note that scalar multiplication is **distributive** over vector addition, meaning that:

$$a(\vec{v} + \vec{w}) = a\vec{v} + a\vec{w}$$

112

Matrices

Matrices can be used to represent linear equations, solve systems of equations, and manipulate data to simulate change. Matrices consist of numerical entries in both rows and columns. The following matrix A is a 3 × 4 matrix because it has three rows and four columns:

$$A = \begin{bmatrix} 3 & 2 & -5 & 3 \\ 3 & 6 & 2 & -5 \\ -1 & 3 & 7 & 0 \end{bmatrix}$$

Matrices can be added or subtracted only if they have the same dimensions. For example, the following matrices can be added by adding corresponding matrix entries:

$$\begin{bmatrix} 3 & 4 \\ 2 & -6 \end{bmatrix} + \begin{bmatrix} -1 & 4 \\ 4 & 2 \end{bmatrix} = \begin{bmatrix} 2 & 8 \\ 6 & -4 \end{bmatrix}$$

Multiplication can also be used to manipulate matrices. **Scalar multiplication** involves multiplying a matrix by a constant. Each matrix entry needs to be multiplied by the constant. The following example shows a 3 × 2 matrix being multiplied by the constant 6:

$$6 \times \begin{bmatrix} 3 & 4 \\ 2 & -6 \\ 1 & 0 \end{bmatrix} = \begin{bmatrix} 18 & 24 \\ 12 & -36 \\ 6 & 0 \end{bmatrix}$$

Matrix multiplication of two matrices involves finding multiple dot products. The **dot product** of a row and column is the sum of the products of each corresponding row and column entry. In the following example, a 2 × 2 matrix is multiplied by a 2 × 2 matrix. The dot product of the first row and column is:

$$(2 \times 1) + (1 \times 2) = (2) + (2) = 4$$

$$\begin{bmatrix} 2 & 1 \\ 3 & 5 \end{bmatrix} \times \begin{bmatrix} 1 & 4 \\ 2 & 0 \end{bmatrix} = \begin{bmatrix} 4 & 8 \\ 13 & 12 \end{bmatrix}$$

The same process is followed to find the other three values in the solution matrix. Matrices can only be multiplied if the number of columns in the first matrix equals the number of rows in the second matrix. The previous example is also an example of square matrix multiplication because they are both square matrices. A **square matrix** has the same number of rows and columns. For square matrices, the order in which they are multiplied does matter. Therefore, matrix multiplication does not satisfy the commutative property. It does, however, satisfy the associative and distributive properties.

Another transformation of matrices can be found by using the **identity matrix**—also referred to as the **"I" matrix**. The identity matrix is similar to the number one in normal multiplication. The identity matrix is a square matrix with ones in the diagonal spots and zeros everywhere else. The identity matrix is also the result of multiplying a matrix by its inverse. This process is similar to multiplying a number by its reciprocal.

The **zero matrix** is also a matrix acting as an additive identity. The zero matrix consists of zeros in every entry. It does not change the values of a matrix when using addition.

The **inverse of a matrix** is useful for solving complex systems of equations. Not all matrices have an inverse, but this can be checked by finding the **determinant** of the matrix. If the determinant of the matrix is 0, it is not invertible. Additionally, only square matrices are invertible. To find the determinant of any matrix, each value of the first row is multiplied by the determinant of submatrix consisting of all except the row and column for that value. The results of

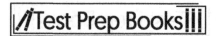

multiplication are alternatingly subtracted and added for 3×3 or larger matrices. The determinant of a matrix can be represented with straight bars (such as $|A|$) or the function det (A), where A is a matrix.

Using the **square 2 x 2 matrix**, the determinant is: $|A| = \begin{vmatrix} a & b \\ c & d \end{vmatrix} = ad - bc$

The absolute value of the determinant of matrix A is equal to the area of a parallelogram with vertices $(0, 0)$, (a, b), (c, d), and $(a + b, c + d)$.

For example, the determinant of the matrix $\begin{bmatrix} -5 & 1 \\ 3 & 4 \end{bmatrix}$ is:

$$-5(4) - 1(3) = -20 - 3 = -23$$

Using a **3 x 3 matrix** $\begin{bmatrix} a & b & c \\ d & e & f \\ g & h & i \end{bmatrix}$, the determinant is $a(ei - fh) - b(di - fg) + c(dh - eg)$.

For example, the determinant of the matrix $A = \begin{bmatrix} 2 & 0 & 1 \\ -1 & 3 & 2 \\ 2 & -2 & -1 \end{bmatrix}$ is:

$$|A| = 2\big(3(-1) - 2(-2)\big) - 0\big(-1(-1) - 2(2)\big) + 1\big(-1(-2) - 3(2)\big)$$

$$|A| = 2(-3 + 4) - 0(1 - 4) + 1(2 - 6)$$

$$|A| = 2(1) - 0(-3) + 1(-4)$$

$$|A| = 2 - 0 - 4 = -2$$

The pattern continues for larger square matrices. For a matrix with real values, this can then be simplified to a real number. If the determinant is non-zero, the square matrix can be inversed.

One way to find an inverse matrix is to use the **matrix of minors**. A **minor** is the determinant of the submatrix found by excluding the row and column of that minor. The matrix formed by all the minors would be M. To use the previous example, the minor of the first row and column is:

$$M_a = ei - fh = 3(-1) - 2(-2) = -3 + 4 = 1$$

When dealing with larger matrices it can be inconvenient to letter the items in a matrix. Another way to refer to them is by the numbers of rows and columns in the matrix. The position of any given value in some matrix A is at row i and column j is thus $A_{i,j}$. Using the previous example, $ie - fh$ was the minor of the first matrix item, which would be:

$$M_{1,1} = A_{2,2}A_{3,3} - A_{2,3}A_{3,2}$$

The following matrix shows all the minors:

$$M = \begin{bmatrix} 1 & -3 & -4 \\ 2 & -4 & -4 \\ -3 & 5 & 6 \end{bmatrix}$$

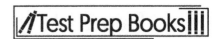

The next step to finding the inverse is to find the **cofactor matrix** from the matrix of minors. This is simply negating every other item in the matrix, in a checkerboard-like pattern. This is done the same for matrices of all sizes. The cofactors of M are:

$$\begin{bmatrix} 1 & 3 & -4 \\ -2 & -4 & 4 \\ -3 & -5 & 6 \end{bmatrix}$$

The last steps to finding the inverse are to transpose the matrix of cofactors and divide it by the determinant of the original matrix, $|A|$. **Transposing** a matrix means turning the rows into columns and vice versa. For example, the third item of the first row would become the third item of the first column. This turns the previous cofactor matrix into an **adjoint matrix**:

$$\begin{bmatrix} 1 & -2 & -3 \\ 3 & -4 & -5 \\ -4 & 4 & 6 \end{bmatrix}$$

Dividing the transposed matrix by the determinant of our original matrix gives the inverse of matrix A:

$$A^{-1} = \frac{1}{|A|} \times \begin{bmatrix} 1 & -2 & -3 \\ 3 & -4 & -5 \\ -4 & 4 & 6 \end{bmatrix}$$

$$\frac{1}{-2} \times \begin{bmatrix} 1 & -2 & -3 \\ 3 & -4 & -5 \\ -4 & 4 & 6 \end{bmatrix} = \begin{bmatrix} -\frac{1}{2} & 1 & \frac{3}{2} \\ -\frac{3}{2} & 2 & \frac{5}{2} \\ 2 & -2 & -3 \end{bmatrix}$$

Given a system of linear equations, a matrix can be used to represent the entire system. Operations can then be performed on the matrix to solve the system. The following system offers an example:

$$x + y + z = 4$$
$$y + 3z = -2$$
$$2x + y - 2z = 12$$

There are three variables and three equations. The coefficients in the equations can be used to form a 3 x 3 matrix:

$$\begin{bmatrix} 1 & 1 & 1 \\ 0 & 1 & 3 \\ 2 & 1 & -2 \end{bmatrix}$$

The number of rows equals the number of equations, and the number of columns equals the number of variables. The numbers on the right side of the equations can be turned into a 3 x 1 matrix. That matrix is shown here:

$$\begin{bmatrix} 4 \\ -2 \\ 12 \end{bmatrix}$$

Such a matrix can also be referred to as a **vector.** The variables are represented in a matrix of their own:

$$\begin{bmatrix} x \\ y \\ z \end{bmatrix}$$

115

The system can be represented by the following matrix equation:

$$\begin{bmatrix} 1 & 1 & 1 \\ 0 & 1 & 3 \\ 2 & 1 & -2 \end{bmatrix} \begin{bmatrix} x \\ y \\ z \end{bmatrix} = \begin{bmatrix} 4 \\ -2 \\ 12 \end{bmatrix}$$

Simply, this is written as $AX = B$. By using the inverse of a matrix, the solution can be found: $X = A^{-1}B$. Once the inverse of A is found, it is then multiplied by B to find the solution to the system: $x = 12, y = -8,$ and $z = 2$.

Measurements

Interpreting Relevant Information from Tables, Charts, and Graphs

Interpretation of Tables, Charts, and Graphs
Data can be represented in many ways. It is important to be able to organize the data into categories that could be represented using one of these methods. Equally important is the ability to read these types of diagrams and interpret their meaning.

Data in Tables
One of the most common ways to express data is in a table. The primary reason for plugging data into a table is to make interpretation more convenient. It's much easier to look at the table than to analyze results in a narrative paragraph. When analyzing a table, pay close attention to the title, variables, and data.

Let's analyze a theoretical antibiotic study. The study has 6 groups, named A through F, and each group receives a different dose of medicine. The results of the study are listed in the table below.

Results of Antibiotic Studies		
Group	Dosage of Antibiotics in milligrams (mg)	Efficacy (% of participants cured)
A	0 mg	20%
B	20 mg	40%
C	40 mg	75%
D	60 mg	95%
E	80 mg	100%
F	100 mg	100%

Tables generally list the title immediately above the data. The title should succinctly explain what is listed below. Here, "Results of Antibiotic Studies" informs the audience that the data pertains to the results of a scientific study on antibiotics.

Identifying the variables at play is one of the most important parts of interpreting data. Remember, the independent variable is intentionally altered, and its change is independent of the other variables. Here, the dosage of antibiotics administered to the different groups is the independent variable. The study is intentionally manipulating the strength of the medicine to study the related results. Efficacy is the dependent variable since its results *depend* on a different variable, the dose of antibiotics. Generally, the independent variable will be listed before the dependent variable in tables.

Also, pay close attention to the variables' labels. Here, the dose is expressed in milligrams (mg) and efficacy in percentages (%). Keep an eye out for questions referencing data in a different unit measurement, or questions asking for a raw number when only the percentage is listed.

116

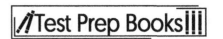

Now that the nature of the study and variables at play have been identified, the data itself needs be interpreted. Group A did not receive any of the medicine. As discussed earlier, Group A is the control, as it reflects the amount of people cured in the same timeframe without medicine. It's important to see that efficacy positively correlates with the dosage of medicine. A question using this study might ask for the lowest dose of antibiotics to achieve 100% efficacy. Although Group E and Group F both achieve 100% efficacy, it's important to note that Group E reaches 100% with a lower dose.

Data in Graphs

Graphs provide a visual representation of data. The variables are placed on the two axes. The bottom of the graph is referred to as the horizontal axis or x-axis. The left-hand side of the graph is known as the vertical axis or y-axis. Typically, the independent variable is placed on the x-axis, and the dependent variable is located on the y-axis. Sometimes the x-axis is a timeline, and the dependent variables for different trials or groups have been measured throughout points in time; time is still an independent variable but is not always immediately thought of as the independent variable being studied.

The most common types of graphs are the bar graph and the line graph.

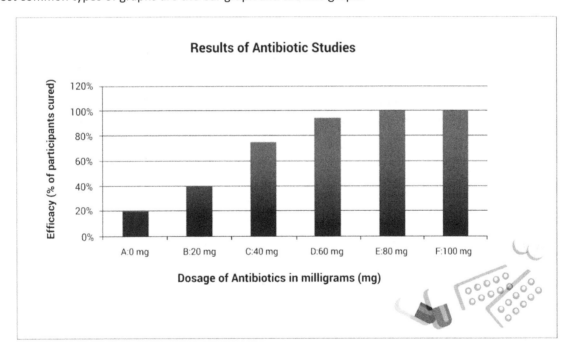

The **bar graph** above expresses the data from the table entitled "Results of Antibiotic Studies." To interpret the data for each group in the study, look at the top of their bars and read the corresponding efficacy on the y-axis.

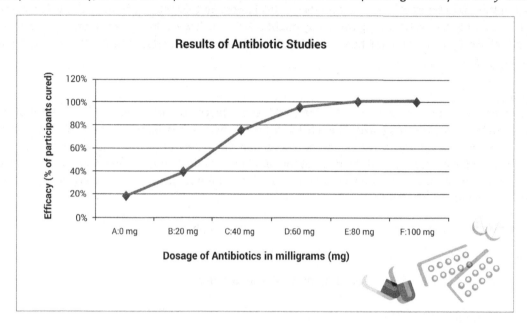

Here, the same data is expressed on a **line graph**. The points on the line correspond with each data entry. Reading the data on the line graph works like the bar graph. The data trend is measured by the slope of the line.

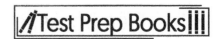

Data in Other Charts

Chart is a broad term that refers to a variety of ways to represent data.

To graph relations, the **Cartesian plane** is used. This means to think of the plane as being given a grid of squares, with one direction being the x-axis and the other direction the y-axis. Generally, the independent variable is placed along the horizontal axis, and the dependent variable is placed along the vertical axis. Any point on the plane can be specified by saying how far to go along the x-axis and how far along the y-axis with a pair of numbers (x, y). Specific values for these pairs can be given names such as $C = (-1, 3)$. Negative values mean to move left or down; positive values mean to move right or up. The point where the axes cross one another is called the **origin**. The origin has coordinates $(0, 0)$ and is usually called O when given a specific label. An illustration of the Cartesian plane, along with the plotted points $(2, 1)$ and $(-1, -1)$, is below.

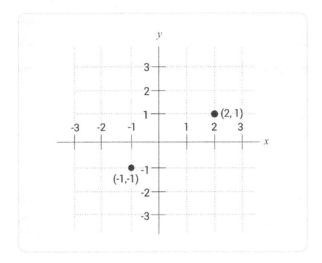

A **line plot** is a diagram that shows quantity of data along a number line. It is a quick way to record data in a structure similar to a bar graph without needing to do the required shading of a bar graph. Here is an example of a line plot:

119

A **tally chart** is a diagram in which tally marks are utilized to represent data. Tally marks are a means of showing a quantity of objects within a specific classification. Here is an example of a tally chart:

Number of days with rain	Number of weeks
0	II
1	⊮⊩ I
2	⊮⊩ IIII
3	⊮⊩ ⊮⊩ ⊮⊩
4	⊮⊩
5	⊮⊩ I
6	⊮⊩
7	I

Data is often recorded using fractions, such as half a mile, and understanding fractions is critical because of their popular use in real-world applications. Also, it is extremely important to label values with their units when using data. For example, regarding length, the number 2 is meaningless unless it is attached to a unit. Writing 2 cm. shows that the number refers to the length of an object.

A **picture graph** is a diagram that shows pictorial representation of data being discussed. The symbols used can represent a certain number of objects. Notice how each fruit symbol in the following graph represents a count of two fruits. One drawback of picture graphs is that they can be less accurate if each symbol represents a large number. For example, if each banana symbol represented ten bananas, and students consumed 22 bananas, it may be challenging to draw and interpret two and one-fifth bananas as a frequency count of 22.

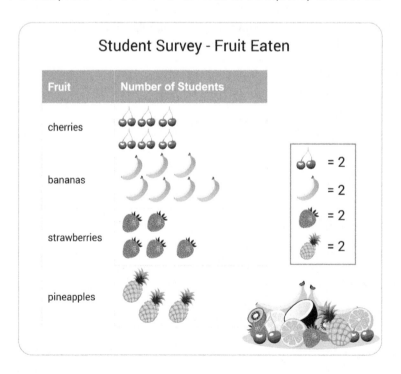

A **circle graph**, also called a **pie chart**, shows categorical data with each category representing a percentage of the whole data set. To make a circle graph, the percent of the data set for each category must be determined. To do so, the frequency of the category is divided by the total number of data points and converted to a percent. For example, if 80 people were asked what their favorite sport is and 20 responded basketball, basketball makes up 25% of the data ($\frac{20}{80} = 0.25 = 25\%$). Each category in a data set is represented by a slice of the circle proportionate to its percentage of the whole.

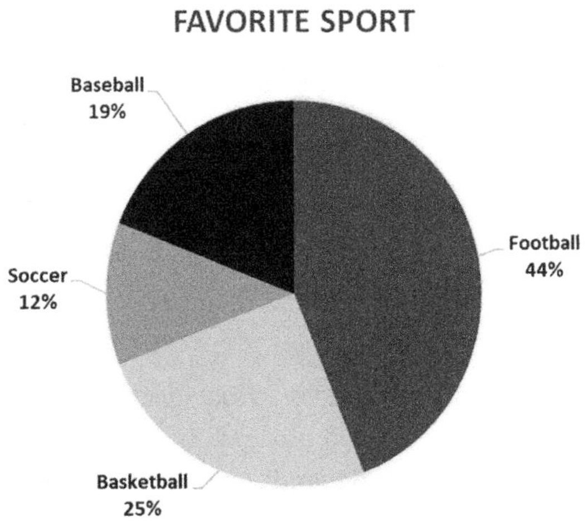

A **scatter plot** displays the relationship between two variables. Values for the independent variable, typically denoted by x, are paired with values for the dependent variable, typically denoted by y. Each set of corresponding values are written as an ordered pair (x, y). To construct the graph, a coordinate grid is labeled with the x-axis representing the independent variable and the y-axis representing the dependent variable. Each ordered pair is graphed.

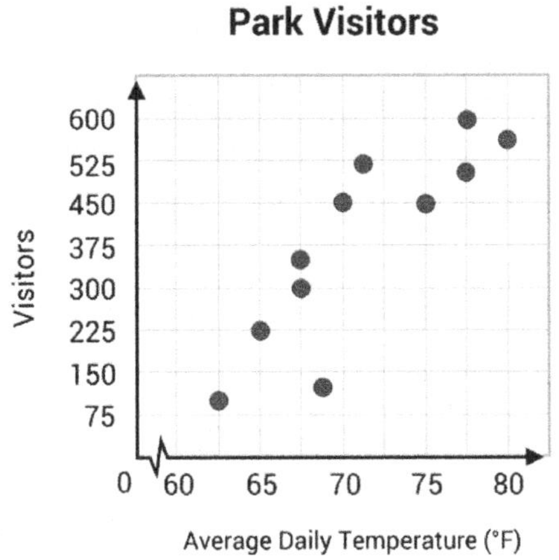

Like a scatter plot, a **line graph** compares two variables that change continuously, typically over time. Paired data values (ordered pair) are plotted on a coordinate grid with the x- and y-axis representing the two variables. A line is drawn from each point to the next, going from left to right. A **double line graph** simply displays two sets of data that contain values for the same two variables. The double line graph below displays the profit for given years (two variables) for Company A and Company B (two data sets).

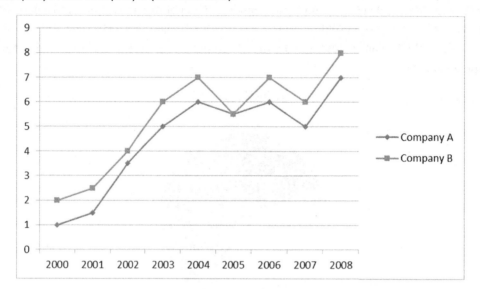

Choosing the appropriate graph to display a data set depends on what type of data is included in the set and what information must be shown.

Scatter plots and line graphs can be used to display data consisting of two variables. Examples include height and weight, or distance and time. A correlation between the variables is determined by examining the points on the graph. Line graphs are used if each value for one variable pairs with a distinct value for the other variable. Line graphs show relationships between variables.

Interpreting Competing Data
Be careful of questions with competing studies. These questions will ask the student to interpret which of two studies shows the greater amount or the higher rate of change between two results.

Here's an example. A research facility runs studies on two different antibiotics: Drug A and Drug B. The Drug A study includes 1,000 participants and cures 600 people. The Drug B study includes 200 participants and cures 150 people. Which drug is more successful?

The first step is to determine the percentage of each drug's rate of success. Drug A was successful in curing 60% of participants, while Drug B achieved a 75% success rate. Thus, Drug B is more successful based on these studies, even though it cured fewer people.

Sample size and experiment consistency should also be considered when answering questions based on competing studies. Is one study significantly larger than the other? In the antibiotics example, the Drug A study is five times larger than Drug B. Thus, Drug B's higher efficacy (desired result) could be a result of the smaller sample size, rather than the quality of drug.

Consistency between studies is directly related to sample size. Let's say the research facility elects to conduct more studies on Drug B. In the next study, there are 400 participants, and 200 are cured. The success rate of the second study is 50%. The results are clearly inconsistent with the first study, which means more testing is needed to determine the drug's efficacy. A hallmark of mathematical or scientific research is repeatability. Studies should be consistent and repeatable, with an appropriately large sample size, before drawing extensive conclusions.

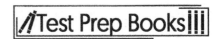

Evaluating the Information in Tables, Charts, and Graphs Using Statistics

Mean, Median, and Mode

As discussed in the Quantitative Skills section, the center of a set of data (statistical values) can be represented by its mean, median, or mode. These are sometimes referred to as **measures of central tendency**. The **mean,** or average, is found by summing the data points then dividing by the total number of data points added together. For example, suppose that in a week (7 days), the daily high temperatures were 68, 72, 77, 80, 80, 81, and 82. Therefore, the average temperature was:

$$\frac{68 + 72 + 77 + 80 + 80 + 81 + 82}{7} = 77.1 \ degrees$$

The **median** is the value in the middle of a data set once the data are arranged in ascending numerical order. The middle refers to the point where half the data comes before it and half comes after, when the data is recorded in numerical order. For instance, in the data set above, the median is 80 degrees.

The **mode** is the data point that appears most frequently. If two or more data points all tie for the most frequent appearance, then each of them is considered a mode. In the case of the temperatures, the mode was 80.

Describing a Set of Data

A set of data can be described in terms of its center, spread, shape and any unusual features. The center of a data set can be measured by its mean, median, or mode. The spread of a data set refers to how far the data points are from the center (mean or median). A data set with all its data points clustered around the center will have a small spread. A data set covering a wide range of values will have a large spread.

When a data set is displayed as a graph like the one below, the shape indicates if a sample is normally distributed, symmetrical, or has measures of skewness. When graphed, a data set with a normal distribution will resemble a bell curve.

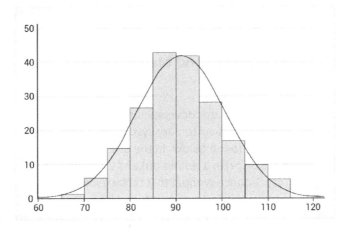

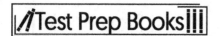
If the data set is symmetrical, each half of the graph when divided at the center is a mirror image of the other. If the graph has fewer data points to the right, the data is skewed right. If it has fewer data points to the left, the data is skewed left.

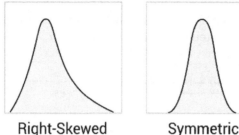

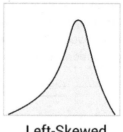

Right-Skewed   Symmetric   Left-Skewed

A description of a data set should include any unusual features such as gaps or outliers. A gap is a span within the range of the data set containing no data points. An outlier is a data point with a value either extremely large or extremely small when compared to the other values in the set.

The graphs above can be referred to as **unimodal** since they all have a single peak. This is in contrast to **bimodal** graphs that have multiple peaks.

Comparing Data

Comparing data sets within statistics can mean many things. The first way to compare data sets is by looking at the center and spread of each set. The center of a data set can mean two things: median or mean. Remember that the median is the value that's halfway into each data set, and it splits the data into two intervals. The mean is the average value of the data within a set. It's calculated by adding up all of the data in the set and dividing the total by the number of data points. Outliers can significantly impact the mean. Additionally, two completely different data sets can have the same mean. For example, a data set with values ranging from 0 to 100 and a data set with values ranging from 44 to 56 can both have means of 50. The first data set has a much wider range, which is known as the **spread** of the data. This measures how varied the data is within each set.

Converting Within and Between Standard and Metric Systems

American Measuring System

The measuring system used today in the United States developed from the British units of measurement during colonial times. The most typically used units in this customary system are those used to measure weight, liquid volume, and length, whose common units are found below. In the customary system, the basic unit for measuring weight is the ounce (oz); there are 16 ounces (oz) in 1 pound (lb) and 2000 pounds in 1 ton. The basic unit for measuring liquid volume is the ounce (oz); 1 ounce is equal to 2 tablespoons (tbsp) or 6 teaspoons (tsp), and there are 8 ounces in 1 cup, 2 cups in 1 pint (pt), 2 pints in 1 quart (qt), and 4 quarts in 1 gallon (gal). For measurements of length, the inch (in) is the base unit; 12 inches make up 1 foot (ft), 3 feet make up 1 yard (yd), and 5280 feet make up 1 mile (mi).

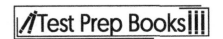

However, as there are only a set number of units in the customary system, with extremely large or extremely small amounts of material, the numbers can become awkward and difficult to compare. Here is a conversion chart for common customary measurements:

Common Customary Measurements		
Length	**Weight**	**Capacity**
1 foot = 12 inches	1 pound = 16 ounces	1 cup = 8 fluid ounces
1 yard = 3 feet	1 ton = 2,000 pounds	1 pint = 2 cups
1 yard = 36 inches		1 quart = 2 pints
1 mile = 1,760 yards		1 quart = 4 cups
1 mile = 5,280 feet		1 gallon = 4 quarts
		1 gallon = 16 cups

Metric System

Aside from the United States, most countries in the world have adopted the metric system embodied in the International System of Units (SI). The three main SI base units used in the metric system are the meter (m), the kilogram (kg), and the liter (L); meters measure length, kilograms measure mass, and liters measure volume.

These three units can use different prefixes, which indicate larger or smaller versions of the unit by powers of ten. This can be thought of as making a new unit which is sized by multiplying the original unit in size by a factor.

These prefixes and associated factors are:

Metric Prefixes			
Prefix	**Symbol**	**Multiplier**	**Exponential**
kilo	k	1,000	10^3
hecto	h	100	10^2
deca	da	10	10^1
no prefix		1	10^0
deci	d	0.1	10^{-1}
centi	c	0.01	10^{-2}
milli	m	0.001	10^{-3}

The correct prefix is then attached to the base. Some examples:

1 milliliter equals .001 liters.
1 kilogram equals 1,000 grams.

Choosing the Appropriate Measuring Unit

Some units of measure are represented as square or cubic units depending on the solution. For example, perimeter is measured in units, area is measured in square units, and volume is measured in cubic units.

Also be sure to use the most appropriate unit for the thing being measured. A building's height might be measured in feet or meters while the length of a nail might be measured in inches or centimeters. Additionally, for SI units, the prefix should be chosen to provide the most succinct available value. For example, the mass of a bag of fruit would likely be measured in kilograms rather than grams or milligrams, and the length of a bacteria cell would likely be measured in micrometers rather than centimeters or kilometers.

125

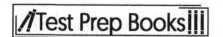

Conversion

Converting measurements in different units between the two systems can be difficult because they follow different rules. The best method is to look up an English to Metric system conversion factor and then use a series of equivalent fractions to set up an equation to convert the units of one of the measurements into those of the other.

The table below lists some common conversion values that are useful for problems involving measurements with units in both systems:

English System	Metric System
1 inch	2.54 cm
1 foot	0.3048 m
1 yard	0.914 m
1 mile	1.609 km
1 ounce	28.35 g
1 pound	0.454 kg
1 fluid ounce	29.574 mL
1 quart	0.946 L
1 gallon	3.785 L

Consider the example where a scientist wants to convert 6.8 inches to centimeters. The table above is used to find that there are 2.54 centimeters in every inch, so the following equation should be set up and solved:

$$\frac{6.8 \text{ in}}{1} \times \frac{2.54 \text{ cm}}{1 \text{ in}} = 17.272 \text{ cm}$$

Notice how the inches in the numerator of the initial figure and the denominator of the conversion factor cancel out. (This equation could have been written simply as 6.8 in × 2.54 cm = 17.272 cm, but it was shown in detail to illustrate the steps). The goal in any conversion equation is to set up the fractions so that the units you are trying to convert from cancel out and the units you desire remain.

For a more complicated example, consider converting 2.15 kilograms into ounces. The first step is to convert kilograms into grams and then grams into ounces. Note that the measurement you begin with does not have to be put in a fraction.

So, in this case, 2.15 kg is by itself although it's technically the numerator of a fraction:

$$2.15 \text{ kg} \times \frac{1{,}000 \text{ g}}{\text{kg}} = 2{,}150 \text{ g}$$

Then, use the conversion factor from the table to convert grams to ounces:

$$2{,}150 \text{ g} \times \frac{1 \text{ oz}}{28.35 \text{ g}} = 75.8 \text{ oz}$$

Geometry

Angles and Diagonals

Diagonals are lines (excluding sides) that connect two vertices within a polygon. **Mutually bisecting diagonals** intersect at their midpoints. Parallelograms, rectangles, squares, and rhombuses have mutually bisecting diagonals. However, trapezoids don't have such lines. **Perpendicular diagonals** occur when they form four right triangles at

126

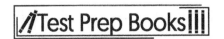

their point of intersection. Squares and rhombuses have perpendicular diagonals, but trapezoids, rectangles, and parallelograms do not. Finally, **perpendicular bisecting diagonals** (also known as **perpendicular bisectors**) form four right triangles at their point of intersection, but this intersection is also the midpoint of the two lines. Both rhombuses and squares have perpendicular bisecting angles, but trapezoids, rectangles, and parallelograms do not. Knowing these definitions can help tremendously in problems that involve both angles and diagonals.

Congruence and Similarity

Sometimes, two figures are **similar**, meaning they have the same basic shape and the same interior angles, but they have different dimensions. If the ratio of two corresponding sides is known, then that ratio, or **scale factor**, holds true for all of the dimensions of the new figure.

Likewise, triangles are similar if they have the same angle measurements, and their sides are proportional to one another. Triangles are **congruent** if the angles of the triangles are equal in measurement and the sides of the triangles are equal in measurement.

There are five ways to show that triangles are congruent:

1. SSS (Side-Side-Side Postulate) – when all three corresponding sides are equal in length, then the two triangles are congruent.

2. SAS (Side-Angle-Side Postulate) – if a pair of corresponding sides and the angle in between those two sides are equal, then the two triangles are congruent.

3. ASA (Angle-Side-Angle Postulate) – if a pair of corresponding angles are equal and the side lengths within those angles are equal, then the two triangles are equal.

4. AAS (Angle-Angle-Side Postulate) – when a pair of corresponding angles for two triangles and a non-included side are equal, then the two triangles are congruent.

5. HL (Hypotenuse-Leg Theorem) – if two right triangles have the same hypotenuse length, and one of the other sides in each triangle are of the same length, then the two triangles are congruent.

If two triangles are discovered to be similar or congruent, this information can assist in determining unknown parts of triangles, such as missing angles and sides.

The example below involves the question of congruent triangles. The first step is to examine whether the triangles are congruent. If the triangles are congruent, then the measure of a missing angle can be found.

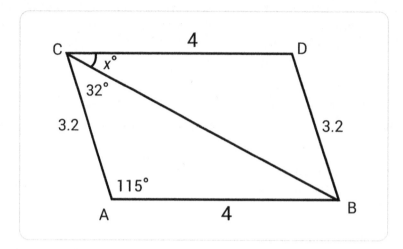

The above diagram provides values for angle measurements and side lengths in triangles *CAB* and *CDB*. Note that side *CA* is 3.2 and side *DB* is 3.2. Side *CD* is 4 and side *AB* is 4. Furthermore, line *CB* is congruent to itself by the reflexive property. Therefore, the two triangles are congruent by SSS (Side-Side-Side). Because the two triangles are congruent, all of the corresponding parts of the triangles are also congruent. Therefore, angle x is congruent to the inside of the angle for which a measurement is not provided in triangle *CAB*. Thus:

$$115° + 32° = 147°$$

A triangle's angles sum 180°, therefore:

$$180° - 147° = 33°$$

Angle $x = 33°$, because the two triangles are reversed.

Transformations of a Plane

Given a figure drawn on a plane, many changes can be made to that figure, including rotation, translation, and reflection. **Rotations** turn the figure about a point, **translations** slide the figure, and **reflections** flip the figure over a specified line. When performing these transformations, the original figure is called the **pre-image**, and the figure after transformation is called the **image**.

More specifically, **translation** means that all points in the figure are moved in the same direction by the same distance. In other words, the figure is slid in some fixed direction. Of course, while the entire figure is slid by the same distance, this does not change any of the measurements of the figures involved. The result will have the same distances and angles as the original figure.

In terms of Cartesian coordinates, a translation means a shift of each of the original points (x, y) by a fixed amount in the x and y directions, to become $(x + a, y + b)$.

Another procedure that can be performed is called **reflection**. To do this, a line in the plane is specified, called the **line of reflection**. Then, take each point and flip it over the line so that it is the same distance from the line but on the opposite side of it. This does not change any of the distances or angles involved, but it does reverse the order in which everything appears.

To reflect something over the x-axis, the points (x, y) are sent to $(x, -y)$. To reflect something over the y-axis, the points (x, y) are sent to the points $(-x, y)$. Flipping over other lines is not something easy to express in Cartesian

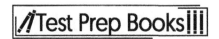

coordinates. However, by drawing the figure and the line of reflection, the distance to the line and the original points can be used to find the reflected figure.

Example: Reflect this triangle with vertices $(-1, 0)$, $(2, 1)$, and $(2, 0)$ over the y-axis. The pre-image is shown below.

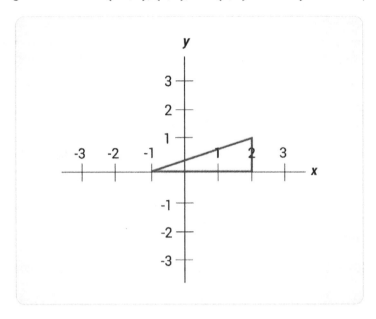

To do this, flip the x values of the points involved to the negatives of themselves, while keeping the y values the same. The image is shown here.

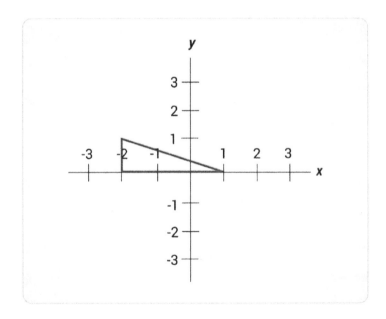

The new vertices will be $(1, 0)$, $(-2, 1)$, and $(-2, 0)$.

Another procedure that does not change the distances and angles in a figure is **rotation**. In this procedure, pick a center point, then rotate every vertex along a circle around that point by the same angle. This procedure is also not easy to express in Cartesian coordinates, and this is not a requirement on this test. However, as with reflections, it's

129

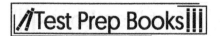

helpful to draw the figures and see what the result of the rotation would look like. This transformation can be performed using a compass and protractor.

Each one of these transformations can be performed on the coordinate plane without changes to the original dimensions or angles.

If two figures in the plane involve the same distances and angles, they are called **congruent figures**. In other words, two figures are congruent when they go from one form to another through reflection, rotation, and translation, or a combination of these.

Remember that rotation and translation will give back a new figure that is identical to the original figure, but reflection will give back a mirror image of it.

To recognize that a figure has undergone a rotation, check to see that the figure has not been changed into a mirror image, but that its orientation has changed (that is, whether the parts of the figure now form different angles with the x- and y-axes).

To recognize that a figure has undergone a translation, check to see that the figure has not been changed into a mirror image, and that the orientation remains the same.

To recognize that a figure has undergone a reflection, check to see that the new figure is a mirror image of the old figure.

Keep in mind that sometimes a combination of translations, reflections, and rotations may be performed on a figure.

Dilation

A **dilation** is a transformation that preserves angles, but not distances. This can be thought of as stretching or shrinking a figure. If a dilation makes figures larger, it is called an **enlargement**. If a dilation makes figures smaller, it is called a **reduction**. The easiest example is to dilate around the origin. In this case, multiply the x and y coordinates by a **scale factor**, k, sending points (x, y) to (kx, ky).

As an example, draw a dilation of the following triangle, whose vertices will be the points $(-1, 0)$, $(1, 0)$, and $(1, 1)$.

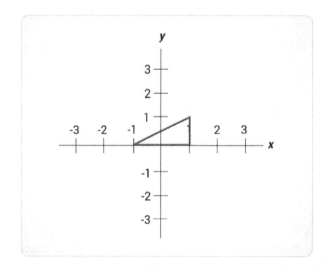

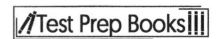

For this problem, dilate by a scale factor of 2, so the new vertices will be $(-2, 0)$, $(2, 0)$, and $(2, 2)$.

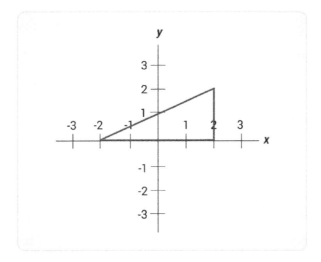

Note that after a dilation, the distances between the vertices of the figure will have changed, but the angles will remain the same. The two figures that are obtained by dilation, along with possibly translation, rotation, and reflection, are all *similar* to one another. Another way to think of this is that similar figures have the same number of vertices and edges, and their angles are all the same. Similar figures have the same basic shape but are different in size.

Surface Area of Three-Dimensional Figures

As mentioned in the Quantitative Skills section, the **area** of a two-dimensional figure refers to the number of square units needed to cover the interior region of the figure. This concept is similar to wallpaper covering the flat surface of a wall. For example, if a rectangle has an area of 10 square centimeters (written $10cm^2$), it will take 10 squares, each with sides one centimeter in length, to cover the interior region of the rectangle. Note that area is measured in square units such as: square centimeters or cm^2; square feet or ft^2; square yards or yd^2; square miles or mi^2.

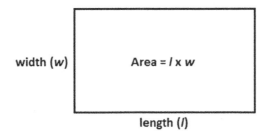

width (*w*)   Area = *l* x *w*

length (*l*)

The **surface area** of a three-dimensional figure refers to the number of square units needed to cover the entire surface of the figure. This concept is similar to using wrapping paper to completely cover the outside of a box. For example, if a triangular pyramid has a surface area of 17 square inches (written $17\ in^2$), it will take 17 squares, each with sides one inch in length, to cover the entire surface of the pyramid. Surface area is also measured in square units.

Many three-dimensional figures (solid figures) can be represented by nets consisting of rectangles and triangles. The surface area of such solids can be determined by adding the areas of each of its faces and bases. Finding the surface

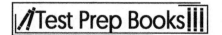

area using this method requires calculating the areas of rectangles and triangles. To find the area (A) of a rectangle, the length (l) is multiplied by the width:

$$(w) \rightarrow A = l \times w$$

The area of the rectangle below is calculated:

$$A = (8cm) \times (4cm) \rightarrow A = 32cm^2$$

To calculate the area (A) of a triangle, the product of $\frac{1}{2}$, the base (b), and the height (h) is found $\rightarrow$

$$A = \frac{1}{2} \times b \times h$$

Note that the height of a triangle is measured from the base to the vertex opposite of it forming a right angle with the base. The area of the triangle below is calculated:

$$A = \frac{1}{2} \times (11 \text{ cm}) \times (6 \text{ cm}) \rightarrow A = 33 \text{ cm}^2$$

Consider the following triangular prism, which is represented by a net consisting of two triangles and three rectangles.

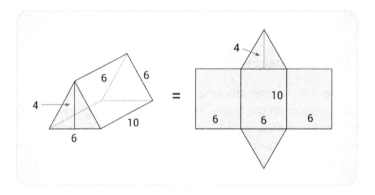

The surface area of the prism can be determined by adding the areas of each of its faces and bases. The surface area (SA) = area of triangle + area of triangle + area of rectangle + area of rectangle + area of rectangle.

$$SA = \left(\frac{1}{2} \times b \times h\right) + \left(\frac{1}{2} \times b \times h\right) + (l \times w) + (l \times w) + (l \times w)$$

$$SA = \left(\frac{1}{2} \times 6 \times 4\right) + \left(\frac{1}{2} \times 6 \times 4\right) + (6 \times 10) + (6 \times 10) + (6 \times 10)$$

$$SA = (12) + (12) + (60) + (60) + (60)$$

$$SA = 204 \text{ square units}$$

Perimeter and Area

As mentioned, **perimeter** is the distance measurement around something. It can be thought of as the length of the boundary, like a fence. In contrast, area is the space occupied by a defined enclosure, like a field enclosed by a fence.

The perimeter of a square is measured by adding together all of the sides. Since a square has four equal sides, its perimeter can be calculated by multiplying the length of one side by 4. Thus, the formula is $P = 4 \times s$, where s equals one side. The area of a square is calculated by squaring the length of one side, which is expressed as the formula $A = s^2$.

Like a square, a rectangle's perimeter is measured by adding together all of the sides. But as the sides are unequal, the formula is different. A rectangle has equal values for its lengths (long sides) and equal values for its widths (short sides), so the perimeter formula for a rectangle is $P = l + l + w + w = 2l + 2w$, where l equals length and w equals width. The area is found by multiplying the length by the width, so the formula is $A = l \times w$.

A triangle's perimeter is measured by adding together the three sides, so the formula is $P = a + b + c$, where a, b, and c are the values of the three sides.

The area is calculated by multiplying the length of the base times the height times $\frac{1}{2}$, so the formula is:

$$A = \frac{1}{2} \times b \times h = \frac{bh}{2}$$

The base is the bottom of the triangle, and the height is the distance from the base to the peak. If a problem asks one to calculate the area of a triangle, it will provide the base and height.

A circle's perimeter—also known as its **circumference**—is measured by multiplying the **diameter** (the straight line measured from one side, through the center, to the direct opposite side of the circle) by π, so the formula is $\pi \times d$. This is sometimes expressed by the formula $C = 2 \times \pi \times r$, where r is the **radius** of the circle. These formulas are equivalent, as the radius equals half of the diameter. The area of a circle is calculated with the formula:

$$A = \pi \times r^2$$

The test will indicate either to leave the answer with π attached or to calculate to the nearest decimal place, which means multiplying by 3.14 for π.

The perimeter of a parallelogram is measured by adding the lengths and widths together. Thus, the formula is the same as for a rectangle:

$$P = l + l + w + w = 2l + 2w$$

However, the area formula differs from the rectangle. For a parallelogram, the area is calculated by multiplying the length by the height:

$$A = h \times l$$

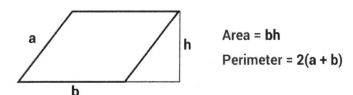

The perimeter of a trapezoid is calculated by adding the two unequal bases and two equal sides, so the formula is:

$$P = a + b_1 + c + b_2$$

133

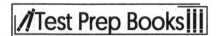

Although unlikely to be a test question, the formula for the area of a trapezoid is $A = \frac{b_1 + b_2}{2} \times h$, where h equals height, and b_1 and b_2 equal the bases.

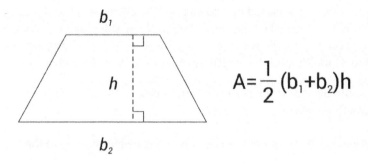

Composite Shapes

The perimeter of an irregular polygon is found by adding the lengths of all of the sides. In cases where all of the sides are given, this will be very straightforward, as it will simply involve finding the sum of the provided lengths. Other times, a side length may be missing and must be determined before the perimeter can be calculated.

Consider the example below:

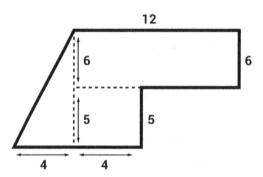

All of the side lengths are provided except for the angled side on the left. Test takers should notice that this is the hypotenuse of a right triangle. The other two sides of the triangle are provided (the base is 4 and the height is $6 + 5 = 11$). The Pythagorean Theorem can be used to find the length of the hypotenuse, remembering that $a^2 + b^2 = c^2$.

Substituting the side values provided yields:

$$(4)^2 = (11)^2 = c^2$$

Therefore, $c = \sqrt{16 + 121} = 11.7$

134

Finally, the perimeter can be found by adding this new side length with the other provided lengths to get the total length around the figure:

$$4 + 4 + 5 + 8 + 6 + 12 + 11.7 = 50.7$$

Although units are not provided in this figure, remember that reporting units with a measurement is important.

The area of irregular polygons is found by decomposing, or breaking apart, the figure into smaller shapes. When the area of the smaller shapes is determined, the area of the smaller shapes will produce the area of the original figure when added together. Consider the earlier example:

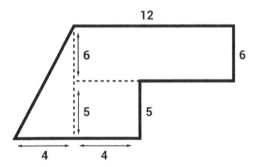

The irregular polygon is decomposed into two rectangles and a triangle. The area of the large rectangle ($A = l \times w \rightarrow A = 12 \times 6$) is 72 square units. The area of the small rectangle is 20 square units:

$$A = 4 \times 5$$

The area of the triangle ($A = \frac{1}{2} \times b \times h \rightarrow A = \frac{1}{2} \times 4 \times 11$) is 22 square units. The sum of the areas of these figures produces the total area of the original polygon:

$$A = 72 + 20 + 22$$
$$A = 114 \; square \; units$$

Here's another example:

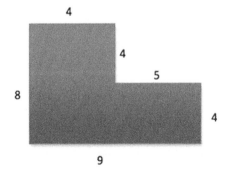

This irregular polygon is decomposed into two rectangles. The area of the large rectangle:

$$(A = l \times w \rightarrow A = 8 \times 4) \text{ is 32 square units}$$

135

The area of the small rectangle is 20 square units ($A = 4 \times 5$). The sum of the areas of these figures produces the total area of the original polygon:

$$A = 32 + 20 \rightarrow A = 52 \; square \; units$$

Solving for Missing Values in Shapes

Using formulas such as perimeter and area for different shapes, it's possible to solve for missing side lengths.

Consider the following problem:

The total perimeter of a rectangular garden is 36 m. If the length of each side is 12 m, what is the width?

The formula for the perimeter of a rectangle is $P = 2L + 2W$, where P is the perimeter, L is the length, and W is the width. The first step is to substitute all of the data into the formula:

$$36 = 2(12) + 2W$$

Simplify by multiplying 2×12:

$$36 = 24 + 2W$$

Simplifying this further by subtracting 24 on each side gives:

$$36 - 24 = 24 - 24 + 2W$$

$$12 = 2W$$

Divide by 2:

$$6 = W$$

The width is 6 cm. Remember to test this answer by substituting this value into the original formula:

$$36 = 2(12) + 2(6)$$

More complicated situations can arise where missing side lengths can be calculated by using concepts of similarity and proportional relationships. Suppose that Lara is 5 feet tall and is standing 30 feet from the base of a light pole, and her shadow is 6 feet long. How high is the light on the pole? To figure this out, it helps to make a sketch of the situation:

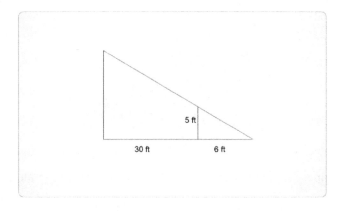

136

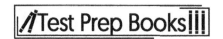

The light pole is the left side of the triangle. Lara is the 5-foot vertical line. Test takers should notice that there are two right triangles here, and that they have all the same angles as one another. Therefore, they form similar triangles. So, the ratio of proportionality between them must be found.

The bases of these triangles are known. The small triangle, formed by Lara and her shadow, has a base of 6 feet. The large triangle formed by the light pole along with the line from the base of the pole out to the end of Lara's shadow is $30 + 6 = 36$ feet long. So, the ratio of the big triangle to the little triangle is $\frac{36}{6} = 6$. The height of the little triangle is 5 feet. Therefore, the height of the big triangle will be $6 \times 5 = 30$ feet, meaning that the light is 30 feet up the pole.

The Pythagorean Theorem and Right Triangles

The Pythagorean Theorem

The Pythagorean theorem is an important concept in geometry. It states that for right triangles, the sum of the squares of the two shorter sides will be equal to the square of the longest side (also called the **hypotenuse**). The longest side will always be the side opposite to the 90° angle. If this side is called c, and the other two sides are a and b, then the Pythagorean theorem states that $c^2 = a^2 + b^2$.

Since lengths are always positive, this also can be written as:

$$c = \sqrt{a^2 + b^2}$$

A diagram to show the parts of a triangle using the Pythagorean theorem is below.

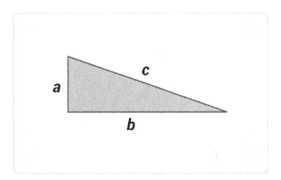

As an example of the theorem, suppose that Shirley has a rectangular field that is 5 feet wide and 12 feet long, and she wants to split it in half using a fence that goes from one corner to the opposite corner. How long will this fence need to be? To figure this out, note that this makes the field into two right triangles, whose hypotenuse will be the fence dividing it in half. Therefore, the fence length will be given by:

$$\sqrt{5^2 + 12^2} = \sqrt{169} = 13 \; feet \; long$$

137

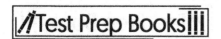
Trigonometric Functions

From the unit circle, the trigonometric ratios were found for the special right triangle with a hypotenuse of 1.

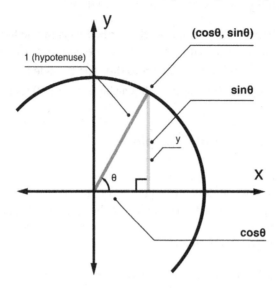

From this triangle, the following Pythagorean identities are formed: $\sin^2 \theta + \cos^2 \theta = 1$, $\tan^2 \theta + 1 = \sec^2 \theta$, and $1 + \cot^2 \theta = \csc^2 \theta$. The second two identities are formed by manipulating the first identity. Since identities are statements that are true for any value of the variable, then they may be used to manipulate equations. For example, a problem may ask for simplification of the expression $\cos^2 x + \cos^2 x \tan^2 x$.

Using the fact that $\tan (x) = \frac{\sin x}{\cos x}$, $\frac{\sin^2 x}{\cos^2 x}$ can then be substituted in for $\tan^2 x$, making the expression:

$$\cos^2 x + \cos^2 x \frac{\sin^2 x}{\cos^2 x}$$

Then the two $\cos^2 x$ terms on top and bottom cancel each other out, simplifying the expression to:

$$\cos^2 x + \sin^2 x$$

By the first Pythagorean identity stated above, the expression can be turned into:

$$\cos^2 x + \sin^2 x = 1$$

Another set of trigonometric identities are the **double-angle formulas**:

$$\sin 2\alpha = 2 \sin \alpha \ \cos \alpha$$

$$\cos 2\alpha = \begin{cases} \cos^2\alpha - \sin^2\alpha \\ 2\cos^2\alpha - 1 \\ 1 - 2\sin^2\alpha \end{cases}$$

138

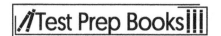

Using these formulas, the following identity can be proved:

$$\sin 2x = \frac{2\tan x}{1 + \tan^2 x}$$

By using one of the Pythagorean identities, the denominator can be rewritten as:

$$1 + \tan^2 x = \sec^2 x$$

By knowing the reciprocals of the trigonometric identities, the secant term can be rewritten to form the equation:

$$\sin 2x = \frac{2\tan x}{1} \times \cos^2 x$$

Replacing $\tan(x)$, the equation becomes $\sin 2x = \frac{2\sin x}{\cos x} \times \cos^2 x$, where the $\cos x$ can cancel out. The new equation is:

$$\sin 2x = 2\sin x \times \cos x$$

This final equation is one of the double-angle formulas.

Other trigonometric identities such as half-angle formulas, sum and difference formulas, and difference of angles formulas can be used to prove and rewrite trigonometric equations. Depending on the given equation or expression, the correct identities need to be chosen to write equivalent statements.

The graph of sine is equal to the graph of cosine, shifted $\frac{\pi}{2}$ units. Therefore, the function $y = \sin x$ is equal to:

$$y = \cos\left(x - \frac{\pi}{2}\right)$$

Within functions, adding a constant to the independent variable shifts the graph either left or right. By shifting the cosine graph, the curve lies on top of the sine function. By transforming the function, the two equations give the same output for any given input.

Complementary Angles
Angles that add up to 90 degrees are **complementary**. Within a right triangle, two complementary angles exist because the third angle is always 90 degrees. In this scenario, the **sine** of one of the complementary angles is equal to the **cosine** of the other angle. The opposite is also true. This relationship exists because sine and cosine will be calculated as the ratios of the same side lengths.

Translating Between a Geometric Description and an Equation for a Conic Section

Equation of a Circle
A **circle** can be defined as the set of all points that are the same distance (known as the **radius**, r) from a single point C (known as the center of the circle). The center has coordinates (h, k), and any point on the circle can be labelled with coordinates (x, y).

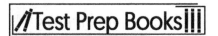

As shown below, a **right triangle** is formed with these two points:

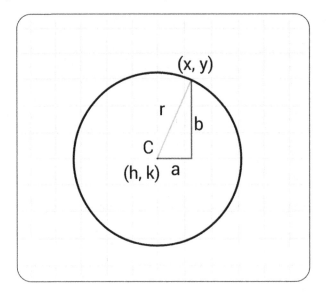

The **Pythagorean theorem** states that:

$$a^2 + b^2 = r^2$$

However, a can be replaced by $|x - h|$ and b can be replaced by $|y - k|$ by using the **distance formula** which is:

$$d = \sqrt{(x_2 - x_1)^2 + (y_2 - y_1)^2}$$

That substitution results in:

$$(x - h)^2 + (y - k)^2 = r^2$$

This is the formula for finding the equation of any circle with a center (h, k) and a radius r. Note that sometimes c is used instead of r.

Finding the Center and Radius

Circles aren't always given in the form of the circle equation where the center and radius can be seen so easily. Oftentimes, they're given in the more general format of:

$$ax^2 + by^2 + cx + dy + e = 0$$

This can be converted to the center-radius form using the algebra technique of completing the square in both variables. First, the constant term is moved over to the other side of the equals sign, and then the x and y variable terms are grouped together. Then the equation is divided through by a and, because this is the equation of a circle, $a = b$. At this point, the x-term coefficient is divided by 2, squared, and then added to both sides of the equation. This value is grouped with the x terms. The same steps then need to be completed with the y-term coefficient. The trinomial in both x and y can now be factored into a square of a binomial, which gives both:

$$(x - h)^2$$
$$\text{and}$$
$$(y - k)^2$$

Parabola Equations

A **parabola** is defined as a specific type of curve such that any point on it is the same distance from a fixed point (called the **focus**) and a fixed straight line (called the **directrix**). A parabola is the shape formed from the intersection of a cone with a plane that's parallel to its side. Every parabola has an **axis of symmetry**, and its **vertex** (h, k) is the

140

Mathematics

point at which the axis of symmetry intersects the curve. If the parabola has an axis of symmetry parallel to the y-axis, the focus is the point $(h, k + f)$ and the directrix is the line $y = k - f$. For example, a parabola may have a vertex at the origin, focus $(0, f)$, and directrix $y = -f$. The equation of this parabola can be derived by using both the focus and the directrix. The distance from any coordinate on the curve to the focus is the same as the distance to the directrix, and the Pythagorean theorem can be used to find the length of d. The triangle has sides with length $|x|$ and $|y - f|$ and therefore:

$$d = \sqrt{x^2 + (y - f)^2}$$

By definition, the **vertex** is halfway between the focus and the directrix and $d = y + f$. Setting these two equations equal to one another, squaring each side, simplifying, and solving for y gives the equation of a parabola with the focus f and the vertex being the origin:

$$y = \frac{1}{4f}x^2$$

If the vertex (h, k) is not the origin, a similar process can be completed to derive the equation $(x - h)^2 = 4f(y - k)$ for a parabola with focus f.

Ellipse and Hyperbola Equations

An **ellipse** is the set of all points for which the sum of the distances from two fixed points (known as the *foci*) is constant. A **hyperbola** is the set of all points for which the difference between the distances from two fixed points (also known as the *foci*) is constant. The **distance formula** can be used to derive the formulas of both an ellipse and a hyperbola, given the coordinates of the foci. Consider an ellipse where its major axis is horizontal (i.e., it's longer along the x-axis) and its foci are the coordinates $(-c, 0)$ and $(c, 0)$. The distance from any point (x, y) to $(-c, 0)$ is

$$d_1 = \sqrt{(x + c)^2 + y^2}$$

and the distance from the same point (x, y) to $(c, 0)$ is:

$$d_1 = \sqrt{(x - c)^2 + y^2}$$

Using the definition of an ellipse, it's true that the sum of the distances from the vertex a to each foci is equal to $d_1 + d_2$. Therefore:

$$d_1 + d_2 = (a + c) + (a - c) = 2a$$

and

$$\sqrt{(x + c)^2 + y^2} + \sqrt{(x - c)^2 + y^2} = 2a$$

After a series of algebraic steps, this equation can be simplified to $\frac{x^2}{a^2} + \frac{y^2}{b^2} = 1$, which is the equation of an ellipse with a horizontal major axis. In this case, $a > b$. When the ellipse has a vertical major axis, similar techniques result in $\frac{x^2}{b^2} + \frac{y^2}{a^2} = 1$, and $a > b$.

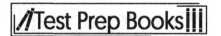

The equation of a hyperbola can be derived in a similar fashion. Consider a hyperbola with a horizontal major axis and its foci are also the coordinates $(-c, 0)$ and $(c, 0)$. Again, the distance from any point (x, y) to $(-c, 0)$ is:

$$d_1 = \sqrt{(x + c)^2 + y^2}$$

and the distance from the same point (x, y) to $(c, 0)$ is:

$$d_1 = \sqrt{(x - c)^2 + y^2}$$

Using the definition of a hyperbola, it's true that the difference of the distances from the vertex a to each foci is equal to $d_1 - d_2$. Therefore:

$$d_1 - d_2 = (c + a) - (c - a) = 2a$$

This means that:

$$\sqrt{(x + c)^2 + y^2} - \sqrt{(x - c)^2 + y^2} = 2a$$

After a series of algebraic steps, this equation can be simplified to:

$$\frac{x^2}{a^2} - \frac{y^2}{b^2} = 1$$

This is the equation of a hyperbola with a horizontal major axis. In this case, $a > b$. Similar techniques result in the equation $\frac{x^2}{b} - \frac{y^2}{a^2} = 1$, where $a > b$ when the hyperbola has a vertical major axis.

Using Coordinate Geometry to Algebraically Prove Simple Geometric Theorems

Proving Theorems with Coordinates

Many important formulas and equations exist in geometry that use coordinates. The distance between two points (x_1, y_1) and (x_2, y_2) is:

$$d = \sqrt{(x_2 - x_1)^2 + (y_2 - y_1)^2}.$$

The slope of the line containing the same two points is:

$$m = \frac{y_2 - y_1}{x_2 - x_1}$$

Also, the midpoint of the line segment with endpoints (x_1, y_1) and (x_2, y_2) is:

$$M = \left(\frac{x_1 + x_2}{2}, \frac{y_1 + y_2}{2} \right)$$

The equations of a circle, parabola, ellipse, and hyperbola can also be used to prove theorems algebraically. Knowing when to use which formula or equation is extremely important, and knowing which formula applies to which property of a given geometric shape is an integral part of the process. In some cases, there are a number of ways to prove a theorem; however, only one way is required.

Solving Problems with Parallel and Perpendicular Lines

Two lines can be parallel, perpendicular, or neither. If two lines are **parallel**, they have the same slope. This is proven using the idea of similar triangles. Consider the following diagram with two parallel lines, L1 and L2:

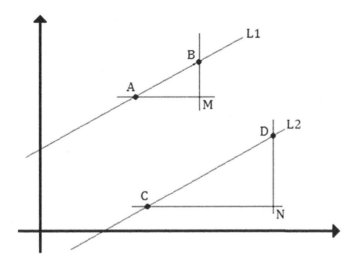

A and B are points on L1, and C and D are points on L2. Right triangles are formed with vertex M and N where lines BM and DN are parallel to the y-axis and AM and CN are parallel to the x-axis. Because all three sets of lines are parallel, the triangles are similar. Therefore:

$$\frac{BM}{DN} = \frac{MA}{NC}$$

This shows that the rise/run is equal for lines L1 and L2. Hence, their slopes are equal.

Secondly, if two lines are **perpendicular**, the product of their slopes equals -1. This means that their slopes are negative reciprocals of each other. Consider two perpendicular lines, l and n:

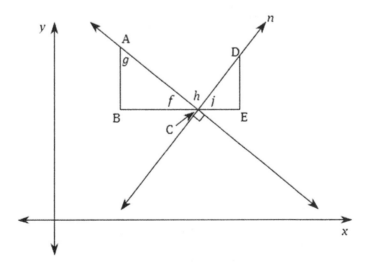

143

Right triangles ABC and CDE are formed so that lines BC and CE are parallel to the x-axis, and AB and DE are parallel to the y-axis. Because line BE is a straight line, angles:

$$f + h + i = 180 \ degrees$$

However, angle h is a right angle, so $f + j = 90 \ degrees$. By construction, $f + g = 90$, which means that $g = j$. Therefore, because angles $B = E$ and $g = j$, the triangles are similar and:

$$\frac{AB}{BC} = \frac{CE}{DE}$$

Because slope is equal to rise/run, the slope of line l is $-\frac{AB}{BC}$ and the slope of line n is $\frac{DE}{CE}$.

Multiplying the slopes together gives:

$$-\frac{AB}{BC} \times \frac{DE}{CE} = -\frac{CE}{DE} \times \frac{DE}{CE} = -1$$

This proves that the product of the slopes of two perpendicular lines equals -1. Both parallel and perpendicular lines can be integral in many geometric proofs, so knowing and understanding their properties is crucial for problem-solving.

Formulas for Ratios

If a line segment with endpoints (x_1, y_1) and (x_2, y_2) is partitioned into two equal parts, the formula for **midpoint** is used. Recall this formula is:

$$M = \left(\frac{x_1 + x_2}{2}, \frac{y_1 + y_2}{2} \right)$$

The ratio of line segments is 1:1. However, if the ratio needs to be anything other than 1:1, a different formula must be used. Consider a ratio that is $a:b$. This means the desired point that partitions the line segment is $\frac{a}{a+b}$ of the way from (x_1, y_1) to (x_2, y_2). The actual formula for the coordinate is:

$$\left(\frac{bx_1 + ax_2}{a + b}, \frac{by_1 + ay_2}{a + b} \right)$$

Computing Side Length, Perimeter, and Area

The side lengths of each shape can be found by plugging the endpoints into the distance formula between two ordered pairs (x_1, y_1) and (x_2, y_2).

As a reminder, this is the **distance formula**:

$$d = \sqrt{(x_2 - x_1)^2 + (y_2 - y_1)^2}$$

The distance formula is derived from the Pythagorean theorem. Once the side lengths are found, they can be added together to obtain the perimeter of the given polygon. Simplifications can be made for specific shapes such as squares and equilateral triangles. For example, one side length can be multiplied by 4 to obtain the perimeter of a square. Also, one side length can be multiplied by 3 to obtain the perimeter of an equilateral triangle. A similar technique can be used to calculate areas. For polygons, both side length and height can be found by using the same distance formula. Areas of triangles and quadrilaterals are straightforward through the use of $A = \frac{1}{2}bh$ or $A = bh$, depending on the shape.

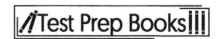

To find the area of other polygons, their shapes can be partitioned into rectangles and triangles. The areas of these simpler shapes can be calculated and then added together to find the total area of the polygon.

Algebra

Algebraic Expressions and Equations

An **algebraic expression** is a statement about an unknown quantity expressed in mathematical symbols. A **variable** is used to represent the unknown quantity, usually denoted by a letter. An equation is a statement in which two expressions (at least one containing a variable) are equal to each other. An algebraic expression can be thought of as a mathematical phrase and an equation can be thought of as a mathematical sentence.

Algebraic expressions and equations both contain numbers, variables, and mathematical operations. The following are examples of algebraic expressions: $5x + 3$, $7xy - 8(x^2 + y)$, and $\sqrt{a^2 + b^2}$. An expression can be simplified or evaluated for given values of variables. The following are examples of equations: $2x + 3 = 7$, $a^2 + b^2 = c^2$, and $2x + 5 = 3x - 2$. An equation contains two sides separated by an equal sign. Equations can be solved to determine the value(s) of the variable for which the statement is true.

Parts of Expressions

Algebraic expressions consist of variables, numbers, and operations. A **term** of an expression is any combination of numbers and/or variables, and terms are separated by addition and subtraction. For example, the expression $5x^2 - 3xy + 4y - 2$ consists of 4 terms: $5x^2$, $-3xy$, $4y$, and -2. Note that each term includes its given sign (+ or −). The **variable** part of a term is a letter that represents an unknown quantity. The **coefficient** of a term is the number by which the variable is multiplied. For the term $4y$, the variable is y, and the coefficient is 4. Terms are identified by the power (or exponent) of its variable.

A number without a variable is referred to as a **constant**. If the variable is to the first power (x^1, or simply x), it is referred to as a linear term. A term with a variable to the second power (x^2) is quadratic, and a term to the third power (x^3) is **cubic**. Consider the expression $x^3 + 3x - 1$. The constant is -1. The linear term is $3x$. There is no quadratic term. The cubic term is x^3.

An algebraic expression can also be classified by how many terms exist in the expression. Any like terms should be combined before classifying. A **monomial** is an expression consisting of only one term. Examples of monomials are: 17, $2x$, and $-5ab^2$. A **binomial** is an expression consisting of two terms separated by addition or subtraction. Examples include $2x - 4$ and $-3y^2 + 2y$. A **trinomial** consists of 3 terms. For example, $5x^2 - 2x + 1$ is a trinomial.

Adding and Subtracting Linear Algebraic Expressions

An algebraic expression is simplified by combining like terms. As mentioned, term is a number, variable, or product of a number and variables separated by addition and subtraction. For the algebraic expression $3x^2 - 4x + 5 - 5x^2 + x - 3$, the terms are $3x^2$, $-4x$, 5, $-5x^2$, x, and -3. Like terms have the same variables raised to the same powers (exponents). The like terms for the previous example are $3x^2$ and $-5x^2$, $-4x$, and x, and 5, and -3. To combine like terms, the coefficients (numerical factor of the term including sign) are added, and the variables and their powers are kept the same. Note that if a coefficient is not written, it is an implied coefficient of 1 ($x = 1x$). The previous example will simplify to:

$$-2x^2 - 3x + 2$$

 Mathematics

When adding or subtracting algebraic expressions, each expression is written in parenthesis. The negative sign is distributed when necessary, and like terms are combined. Consider the following: add $2a + 5b - 2$ to $a - 2b + 8c - 4$. The sum is set as follows:

$$(a - 2b + 8c - 4) + (2a + 5b - 2)$$

In front of each set of parentheses is an implied positive one, which, when distributed, does not change any of the terms. Therefore, the parentheses are dropped and like terms are combined:

$$a - 2b + 8c - 4 + 2a + 5b - 2$$

$$3a + 3b + 8c - 6$$

Consider the following problem: Subtract $2a + 5b - 2$ from $a - 2b + 8c - 4$. The difference is set as follows:
$$(a - 2b + 8c - 4) - (2a + 5b - 2)$$

The implied one in front of the first set of parentheses will not change those four terms. However, distributing the implied -1 in front of the second set of parentheses will change the sign of each of those three terms:
$$a - 2b + 8c - 4 - 2a - 5b + 2$$

Combining like terms yields the simplified expression: $-a - 7b + 8c - 2$.

Distributive Property
The distributive property states that multiplying a sum (or difference) by a number produces the same result as multiplying each value in the sum (or difference) by the number and adding (or subtracting) the products.

Using mathematical symbols, the distributive property states:

$$a(b + c) = ab + ac$$

The expression $4(3 + 2)$ is simplified using the order of operations. Simplifying inside the parenthesis first produces 4×5, which equals 20. The expression $4(3 + 2)$ can also be simplified using the distributive property:
$$4(3 + 2)$$
$$4 \times 3 + 4 \times 2$$
$$12 + 8 = 20$$

Consider the following example: $4(3x - 2)$. The expression cannot be simplified inside the parenthesis because $3x$ and -2 are not like terms and therefore cannot be combined. However, the expression can be simplified by using the distributive property and multiplying each term inside of the parenthesis by the term outside of the parenthesis: $12x - 8$. The resulting equivalent expression contains no like terms, so it cannot be further simplified.

Consider the expression:

$$(3x + 2y + 1) - (5x - 3) + 2(3y + 4)$$

Again, there are no like terms, but the distributive property is used to simplify the expression. Note there is an implied one in front of the first set of parentheses and an implied -1 in front of the second set of parentheses.

Distributing the 1, -1, and 2 produces:

$$1(3x) + 1(2y) + 1(1) - 1(5x) - 1(-3) + 2(3y) + 2(4)$$

$$3x + 2y + 1 - 5x + 3 + 6y + 8$$

146

Mathematics

This expression contains like terms that are combined to produce the simplified expression:

$$-2x + 8y + 12$$

Algebraic expressions are tested to be equivalent by choosing values for the variables and evaluating both expressions. For example, $4(3x - 2)$ and $12x - 8$ are tested by substituting 3 for the variable x and calculating to determine if equivalent values result.

Evaluating Expressions for Given Values

An algebraic expression is a statement written in mathematical symbols, typically including one or more unknown values represented by variables. For example, the expression $2x + 3$ states that an unknown number (x) is multiplied by 2 and added to 3. If given a value for the unknown number, or variable, the value of the expression is determined. For example, if the value of the variable x is 4, the value of the variable 4 is multiplied by 2, and 3 is added. This results in a value of 11 for the expression.

When given an algebraic expression and values for the variable(s), the expression is evaluated to determine its numerical value. To evaluate the expression, the given values for the variables are substituted (or replaced), and the expression is simplified using the order of operations. Parenthesis should be used when substituting. Consider the following: Evaluate $a - 2b + ab$ for $a = 3$ and $b = -1$. To evaluate, any variable a is replaced with 3 and any b with -1, producing:

$$(3) - 2(-1) + (3)(-\text{variable } 1)$$

Next, the order of operations is used to calculate the value of the expression, which is 2.

Verbal Statements and Algebraic Expressions

As mentioned, an algebraic expression is a statement about unknown quantities expressed in mathematical symbols. The statement *five times a number added to forty* is expressed as $5x + 40$. An equation is a statement in which two expressions (with at least one containing a variable) are equal to one another.

The statement *five times a number added to forty is equal to ten* is expressed as:

$$5x + 40 = 10$$

Real world scenarios can also be expressed mathematically. Suppose a job pays its employees \$300 per week and \$40 for each sale made. The weekly pay is represented by the expression $40x + 300$ where x is the number of sales made during the week.

Consider the following scenario: Bob had \$20, and Tom had \$4. After selling 4 ice cream cones to Bob, Tom has as much money as Bob. The cost of an ice cream cone is an unknown quantity and can be represented by a variable (x). The amount of money Bob has after his purchase is four times the cost of an ice cream cone subtracted from his original \$20 → $20 - 4x$. The amount of money Tom has after his sale is four times the cost of an ice cream cone added to his original \$4 → $4x + 4$. After the sale, the amount of money that Bob and Tom have is equal:

$$20 - 4x = 4x + 4$$

Solving for x yields $x = 2$.

147

This material is provided for exam preparation purposes only and does not indicate an endorsement of any specific scientific, political, or religious point of view. © TPB Publishing. You have been licensed one copy of this document for personal use only. Any other reproduction or redistribution is strictly prohibited. All rights reserved.

Use of Formulas

Formulas are mathematical expressions that define the value of one quantity, given the value of one or more different quantities. Formulas look like equations because they contain variables, numbers, operators, and an equal sign. All formulas are equations, but not all equations are formulas. A formula must have more than one variable. For example, $2x + 7 = y$ is an equation and a formula (it relates the unknown quantities x and y). However, $2x + 7 = 3$ is an equation but not a formula (it only expresses the value of the unknown quantity x).

Formulas are typically written with one variable alone (or isolated) on one side of the equal sign. This variable can be thought of as the **subject** in that the formula is stating the value of the subject in terms of the relationship between the other variables. Consider the distance formula: $distance = rate \times time$ or $d = rt$. The value of the subject variable d (distance) is the product of the variable r and t (rate and time). Given the rate and time, the distance traveled can easily be determined by substituting the values into the formula and evaluating.

The formula $P = 2l + 2w$ expresses how to calculate the perimeter of a rectangle (P) given its length (l) and width (w). To find the perimeter of a rectangle with a length of 3ft and a width of 2ft, these values are substituted into the formula for l and w:

$$P = 2(3ft) + 2(2ft)$$

Following the order of operations, the perimeter is determined to be 10ft. When working with formulas such as these, including units is an important step.

Given a formula expressed in terms of one variable, the formula can be manipulated to express the relationship in terms of any other variable. In other words, the formula can be rearranged to change which variable is the subject. To solve for a variable of interest by manipulating a formula, the equation may be solved as if all other variables were numbers. The same steps for solving are followed, leaving operations in terms of the variables instead of calculating numerical values. For the formula $P = 2l + 2w$, the perimeter is the subject expressed in terms of the length and width. To write a formula to calculate the width of a rectangle, given its length and perimeter, the previous formula relating the three variables is solved for the variable w. If P and l were numerical values, this is a two-step linear equation solved by subtraction and division.

To solve the equation $P = 2l + 2w$ for w, $2l$ is first subtracted from both sides:

$$P - 2l = 2w$$

Then both sides are divided by 2:

$$\frac{P - 2l}{2} = w$$

Word Problems

Word problems can appear daunting, but prepared test takers shouldn't let the verbiage psyche them out. No matter the scenario or specifics, the key to answering them is to translate the words into a math problem. It is critical to keep in mind what the question is asking and what operations could lead to that answer. The following word problem resembles one of the question types most frequently encountered on the exam.

148

Working with Money

Walter's Coffee Shop sells a variety of drinks and breakfast treats.

Price List	
Hot Coffee	$2.00
Slow Drip Iced Coffee	$3.00
Latte	$4.00
Muffins	$2.00
Crepe	$4.00
Egg Sandwich	$5.00

Costs	
Hot Coffee	$0.25
Slow Drip Iced Coffee	$0.75
Latte	$1.00
Muffins	$1.00
Crepe	$2.00
Egg Sandwich	$3.00

Walter's utilities, rent, and labor costs him $500 per day. Today, Walter sold 200 hot coffees, 100 slow drip iced coffees, 50 lattes, 75 muffins, 45 crepes, and 60 egg sandwiches. What was Walter's total profit today?

To accurately answer this type of question, the first step is to determine the total cost of making his drinks and treats, then determine how much revenue he earned from selling those products. After arriving at these two totals, the profit is measured by deducting the total cost from the total revenue.

Walter's costs for today:

200 hot coffees	× $0.25	= $50
100 slow drip iced coffees	× $0.75	= $75
50 lattes	× $1.00	= $50
75 muffins	× $1.00	= $75
45 crepes	× $2.00	= $90
60 egg sandwiches	× $3.00	= $180
Utilities, Rent, and Labor		= $500
Total costs		= $1,020

Walter's revenue for today:

200 hot coffees	× $2.00	= $400
100 slow drip iced coffees	× $3.00	= $300
50 lattes	× $4.00	= $200
75 muffins	× $2.00	= $150
45 crepes	× $4.00	= $180
60 egg sandwiches	× $5.00	= $300
Total revenue		= $1,530

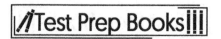

Walter's $Profit = Revenue - Costs = \$1{,}530 - \$1{,}020 = \$510$

This strategy can be applied to other question types. For example, calculating salary after deductions, balancing a checkbook, and calculating a dinner bill are common word problems similar to business planning. In all cases, the most important step is remembering to use the correct operations. When a balance is increased, addition is used. When a balance is decreased, the problem requires subtraction. Common sense and organization are one's greatest assets when answering word problems.

Unit Rate

Unit rate word problems ask test takers to calculate the rate or quantity of something in a different value. For example, a problem might say that a car drove a certain number of miles in a certain number of minutes and then ask how many miles per hour the car was traveling. These questions involve solving proportions. Consider the following examples:

1. Alexandra made $96 during the first 3 hours of her shift as a temporary worker at a law office. She will continue to earn money at this rate until she finishes in 5 more hours. How much does Alexandra make per hour? How much money will Alexandra have made at the end of the day?

This problem can be solved in two ways. The first is to set up a proportion, as the rate of pay is constant. The second is to determine her hourly rate, multiply the 5 hours by that rate, and then adding the $96.

To set up a proportion, the money already earned (numerator) is placed over the hours already worked (denominator) on one side of an equation. The other side has x over 8 hours (the total hours worked in the day). It looks like this: $\frac{96}{3} = \frac{x}{8}$. Now, cross-multiply, which yields $768 = 3x$. To get the value of x, the 768 is divided by 3, which leaves $x = 256$. Alternatively, as x is the numerator of one of the proportions, multiplying by its denominator will reduce the solution by one step. Thus, Alexandra will make $256 at the end of the day. To calculate her hourly rate, the total is divided by 8, giving $32 per hour.

Alternatively, it is possible to figure out the hourly rate by dividing $96 by 3 hours to get $32 per hour. Now her total pay can be figured by multiplying $32 per hour by 8 hours, which comes out to $256.

2. Jonathan is reading a novel. So far, he has read 215 of the 335 total pages. It takes Jonathan 25 minutes to read 10 pages, and the rate is constant. How long does it take Jonathan to read one page? How much longer will it take him to finish the novel? Express the answer in time.

To calculate how long it takes Jonathan to read one page, 25 minutes is divided by 10 pages to determine the page per minute rate. Thus, it takes 2.5 minutes to read one page.

Jonathan must read 120 more pages to complete the novel. (This is calculated by subtracting the number of pages already read from the total.) Now, his rate per page is multiplied by the number of pages remaining. Thus, $120 \times 2.5 = 300$. Expressed in time, 300 minutes is equal to 5 hours.

3. At a hotel, $\frac{4}{5}$ of the 120 rooms are booked for Saturday. On Sunday, $\frac{3}{4}$ of the rooms are booked. On which day are more of the rooms booked, and by how many more?

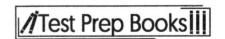

The first step is to calculate the number of rooms booked for each day. This is done by multiplying the fraction of the rooms booked by the total number of rooms.

$$\text{Saturday: } \frac{4}{5} \times 120 = \frac{4}{5} \times \frac{120}{1} = \frac{480}{5} = 96 \text{ rooms}$$

$$\text{Sunday: } \frac{3}{4} \times 120 = \frac{3}{4} \times \frac{120}{1} = \frac{360}{4} = 90 \text{ rooms}$$

Thus, more rooms were booked on Saturday by 6 rooms.

4. In a veterinary hospital, the veterinarian-to-pet ratio is 1:9. The ratio is always constant. If there are 45 pets in the hospital, how many veterinarians are currently in the veterinary hospital?

A proportion is set up to solve for the number of veterinarians: $\frac{1}{9} = \frac{x}{45}$

Cross-multiplying results in $9x = 45$, which works out to 5 veterinarians.

Alternatively, as there are always 9 times as many pets as veterinarians, it is possible to divide the number of pets (45) by 9. This also arrives at the correct answer of 5 veterinarians.

5. At a general practice law firm, 30% of the lawyers work solely on tort cases. If 9 lawyers work solely on tort cases, how many lawyers work at the firm?

The first step is to solve for the total number of lawyers working at the firm, which will be represented here with x. The problem states that 9 lawyers work solely on torts cases, and they make up 30% of the total lawyers at the firm. Thus, 30% multiplied by the total, x, will equal 9. Written as equation, this is:

$$30\% \times x = 9$$

It's easier to deal with the equation after converting the percentage to a decimal, leaving $0.3x = 9$. Thus, $x = \frac{9}{0.3} = 30$ lawyers working at the firm.

6. Xavier was hospitalized with pneumonia. He was originally given 35mg of antibiotics. Later, after his condition continued to worsen, Xavier's dosage was increased to 60mg. What was the percent increase of the antibiotics? Round the percentage to the nearest tenth.

An increase or decrease in percentage can be calculated by dividing the difference in amounts by the original amount and multiplying by 100. Written as an equation, the formula is:

$$\frac{new\ quantity - old\ quantity}{old\ quantity} \times 100$$

Here, the question states that the dosage was increased from 35mg to 60mg, so these values are plugged into the formula to find the percentage increase.

$$\frac{60 - 35}{35} \times 100 = \frac{25}{35} \times 100$$

$$0.7142 \times 100 = 71.4\%$$

Linear Expressions or Equations in One Variable

Linear expressions and equations are concise mathematical statements that can be written to model a variety of scenarios. Questions found pertaining to this topic will contain one variable only. A variable is an unknown quantity, usually denoted by a letter (x, n, p, etc.). In the case of linear expressions and equations, the power of the variable (its exponent) is 1. A variable without a visible exponent is raised to the first power.

Writing Linear Expressions and Equations

When expressing a verbal or written statement mathematically, it is key to understand words or phrases that can be represented with symbols. The following are examples:

Symbol	Phrase
$+$	added to, increased by, sum of, more than
$-$	decreased by, difference between, less than, take away
x	multiplied by, 3 (4, 5 ...) times as large, product of
$\div$	divided by, quotient of, half (third, etc.) of
$=$	is, the same as, results in, as much as
$x, t, n, etc.$	a number, unknown quantity, value of

Solving Linear Equations

When asked to solve a linear equation, one must determine a numerical value for the unknown variable. Given a linear equation involving addition, subtraction, multiplication, and division, isolation of the variable is done by working backward. Addition and subtraction are inverse operations, as are multiplication and division; therefore, they can be used to cancel each other out.

The first steps to solving linear equations are to distribute if necessary and combine any like terms that are on the same side of the equation. Sides of an equation are separated by an $=$ sign. Next, the equation should be manipulated to get the variable on one side. Whatever is done to one side of an equation, must be done to the other side to remain equal. Then, the variable should be isolated by using inverse operations to undo the order of operations backward. Undo addition and subtraction, then undo multiplication and division.

Linear Inequalities in One Variable

Linear inequalities and linear equations are both comparisons of two algebraic expressions. However, unlike equations in which the expressions are equal to each other, linear inequalities compare expressions that are unequal. Linear equations typically have one value for the variable that makes the statement true. Linear inequalities generally have an infinite number of values that make the statement true. Exceptions to these last two statements are covered later on.

152

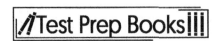

Writing Linear Inequalities

Linear inequalities are a concise mathematical way to express the relationship between unequal values. More specifically, they describe in what way the values are unequal. A value could be greater than ($>$); less than ($<$); greater than or equal to ($\geq$); or less than or equal to ($\leq$) another value. The statement "five times a number added to forty is more than sixty-five" can be expressed as $5x + 40 > 65$. Common words and phrases that express inequalities are:

Symbol	Phrase
$<$	is under, is below, smaller than, beneath
$>$	is above, is over, bigger than, exceeds
$\leq$	no more than, at most, maximum
$\geq$	no less than, at least, minimum

A linear inequality in two variables is a statement expressing an unequal relationship between those two variables. Typically written in slope-intercept form, the variable y can be greater than; less than; greater than or equal to; or less than or equal to a linear expression including the variable x. Examples include $y > 3x$ and $y \leq \frac{1}{2}x - 3$. Questions may instruct students to model real world scenarios such as:

> You work part-time cutting lawns for $15 each and cleaning houses for $25 each. Your goal is to make more than $90 this week. Write an inequality to represent the possible pairs of lawns and houses needed to reach your goal.

This scenario can be expressed as $15x + 25y > 90$ where x is the number of lawns cut and y is the number of houses cleaned.

Solving Linear Inequalities

When solving a linear inequality, the solution is the set of all numbers that makes the statement true. The inequality $x + 2 \geq 6$ has a solution set of 4 and every number greater than 4 (4.0001, 5, 12, 107, etc.). Adding 2 to 4 or any number greater than 4 would result in a value that is greater than or equal to 6. Therefore, $x \geq 4$ would be the solution set.

Solution sets for linear inequalities often will be displayed using a number line. If a value is included in the set ($\geq$ or $\leq$), there is a shaded dot placed on that value and an arrow extending in the direction of the solutions. For a variable $>$ or $\geq$ a number, the arrow would point right on the number line (the direction where the numbers increase); and if a variable is $<$ or $\leq$ a number, the arrow would point left (where the numbers decrease).

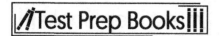

If the value is not included in the set (> or <), an open circle on that value would be used with an arrow in the appropriate direction.

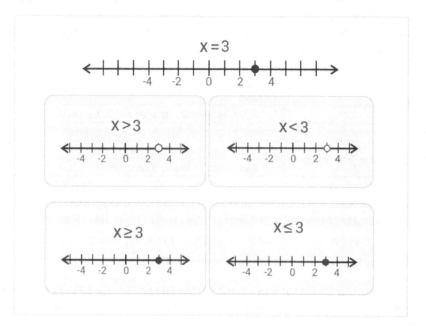

Students may be asked to write a linear inequality given a graph of its solution set. To do so, they should identify whether the value is included (shaded dot or open circle) and the direction in which the arrow is pointing.

In order to algebraically solve a linear inequality, the same steps should be followed as in solving a linear equation (see section on *Solving Linear Equations*). The inequality symbol stays the same for all operations EXCEPT when multiplying or dividing by a negative number. If multiplying or dividing by a negative number while solving an inequality, the relationship reverses (the sign flips). Multiplying or dividing by a positive does not change the relationship, so the sign stays the same. In other words, > switches to < and vice versa. An example is shown below.

Solve $-2(x + 4) \leq 22$ for the value of x.

First, distribute -2 to the binomial by multiplying:

$$-2x - 8 \leq 22$$

Next, add 8 to both sides to isolate the variable:

$$-2x \leq 30$$

Divide both sides by -2 to solve for x:

$$x \geq -15$$

Graphing Solution Sets for Linear Inequalities in Two Variables

A graph of the solution set for a linear inequality shows the ordered pairs that make the statement true. The graph consists of a boundary line dividing the coordinate plane and shading on one side of the boundary. The boundary line should be graphed just as a linear equation would be graphed. If the inequality symbol is > or <, a dashed line can be used to indicate that the line is not part of the solution set. If the inequality symbol is $\geq$ or $\leq$, a solid line can be used to indicate that the boundary line is included in the solution set. An ordered pair (x, y) on either side of the

154

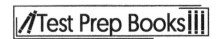

line should be chosen to test in the inequality statement. If substituting the values for x and y results in a true statement $(15(3) + 25(2) > 90)$, that ordered pair and all others on that side of the boundary line are part of the solution set. To indicate this, that region of the graph should be shaded. If substituting the ordered pair results in a false statement, the ordered pair and all others on that side are not part of the solution set.

Therefore, the other region of the graph contains the solutions and should be shaded.

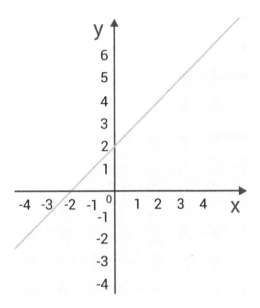

A question may simply ask whether a given ordered pair is a solution to a given inequality. To determine this, the values should be substituted for the ordered pair into the inequality. If the result is a true statement, the ordered pair is a solution; if the result is a false statement, the ordered pair is not a solution.

Quadratic Equations

A **quadratic equation** is an equation in the form:

$$ax^2 + bx + c = 0$$

There are several methods to solve such equations. The easiest method will depend on the quadratic equation in question.

Sometimes, it is possible to solve quadratic equations by manually **factoring** them. This means rewriting them in the form:

$$(x + A)(x + B) = 0$$

If this is done, then they can be solved by remembering that when $ab = 0$, either a or b must be equal to zero. Therefore, to have $(x + A)(x + B) = 0$, $(x + A) = 0$ or $(x + B) = 0$ is needed. These equations have the solutions $x = -A$ and $x = -B$, respectively.

In order to factor a quadratic equation, note that:

$$(x + A)(x + B) = x^2 + (A + B)x + AB$$

So, if an equation is in the form $x^2 + bx + c$, two numbers, *A* and *B,* need to be found that will add up to give us *b*, and multiply together to give us *c*.

As an example, consider solving the equation:

$$-3x^2 + 6x + 9 = 0$$

Start by dividing both sides by -3, leaving:

$$x^2 - 2x - 3 = 0$$

Now, notice that $1 - 3 = -2$, and also that:

$$(1)(-3) = -3$$

This means the equation can be factored into $(x + 1)(x - 3) = 0$. Now, solve $(x + 1) = 0$ and $(x - 3) = 0$ to get $x = -1$ and $x = 3$ as the solutions.

It is useful when trying to factor to remember these three things:

$$x^2 + 2xy + y^2 = (x + y)^2$$

$$x^2 - 2xy + y^2 = (x - y)^2$$

$$\text{and } x^2 - y^2 = (x + y)(x - y).$$

However, factoring by hand is often hard to do. If there are no obvious ways to factor the quadratic equation, solutions can still be found by using the **quadratic formula.**

The quadratic formula is:

$$x = \frac{-b \pm \sqrt{b^2 - 4ac}}{2a}$$

This method will always work, although it sometimes can take longer than factoring by hand, if the factors are easy to guess. Using the standard form $ax^2 + bx + c = 0$, plug the values of *a*, *b*, and *c* from the equation into the formula and solve for x. There will either be two answers, one answer, or no real answer. No real answer comes when the value of the discriminant, the number under the square root, is a negative number. Since there are no real numbers that square to get a negative, the answer will be no real roots.

Here is an example of solving a quadratic equation using the quadratic formula. Suppose the equation to solve is:
$$-2x^2 + 3x + 1 = 0$$

There is no obvious way to factor this, so the quadratic formula is used, with $a = -2, b = 3, c = 1$. After substituting these values into the quadratic formula, it yields this:

$$x = \frac{-3 \pm \sqrt{3^2 - 4(-2)(1)}}{2(-2)}$$

This can be simplified to obtain:

$$\frac{3 \pm \sqrt{9+8}}{4}$$

or

$$\frac{3 \pm \sqrt{17}}{4}$$

Challenges can be encountered when asked to find a quadratic equation with specific roots. Given roots A and B, a quadratic function can be constructed with those roots by taking $(x - A)(x - B)$. So, in constructing a quadratic equation with roots $x = -2, 3$, it would result in:

$$(x + 2)(x - 3) = x^2 - x - 6$$

Multiplying this by a constant also could be done without changing the roots.

Rewriting Expressions

Algebraic expressions are made up of numbers, variables, and combinations of the two, using mathematical operations. Expressions can be rewritten based on their factors. For example, the expression $6x + 4$ can be rewritten as $2(3x + 2)$ because 2 is a factor of both $6x$ and 4. More complex expressions can also be rewritten based on their factors. The expression $x^4 - 16$ can be rewritten as $(x^2 - 4)(x^2 + 4)$. This is a different type of factoring, where a difference of squares is factored into a sum and difference of the same two terms. With some expressions, the factoring process is simple and only leads to a different way to represent the expression. With others, factoring and rewriting the expression leads to more information about the given problem.

In the following quadratic equation, factoring the binomial leads to finding the zeros of the function:

$$x^2 - 5x + 6 = y$$

This equation factors into $(x - 3)(x - 2) = y$, where 2 and 3 are found to be the zeros of the function when y is set equal to zero. The zeros of any function are the x-values where the graph of the function on the coordinate plane crosses the x-axis.

Factoring an equation is a simple way to rewrite the equation and find the zeros, but factoring is not possible for every quadratic. Completing the square is one way to find zeros when factoring is not an option.

The following equation cannot be factored:

$$x^2 + 10x - 9 = 0$$

The first step in this method is to move the constant to the right side of the equation, making it:

$$x^2 + 10x = 9$$

Then, the coefficient of x is divided by 2 and squared. This number is then added to both sides of the equation, to make the equation still true. For this example, $\left(\frac{10}{2}\right)^2 = 25$ is added to both sides of the equation to obtain:

$$x^2 + 10x + 25 = 9 + 25$$

157

This expression simplifies to $x^2 + 10x + 25 = 34$, which can then be factored into:

$$(x + 5)^2 = 34$$

Solving for x then involves taking the square root of both sides and subtracting 5.

This leads to two zeros of the function:

$$x = \pm\sqrt{34} - 5$$

Depending on the type of answer the question seeks, a calculator may be used to find exact numbers.

Given a **quadratic equation in standard form**—$ax^2 + bx + c = 0$—the sign of a tells whether the function has a minimum value or a maximum value. If $a > 0$, the graph opens up and has a minimum value. If $a < 0$, the graph opens down and has a maximum value. Depending on the way the quadratic equation is written, multiplication may need to occur before a max/min value is determined.

Polynomials

An expression of the form ax^n, where n is a non-negative integer, is called a **monomial** because it contains one term. A sum of monomials is called a **polynomial**. For example, $-4x^3 + x$ is a polynomial, while $5x^7$ is a monomial. A function equal to a polynomial is called a **polynomial function**.

The monomials in a polynomial are also called the **terms** of the polynomial.

The constants that precede the variables are called **coefficients.**

The highest value of the exponent of x in a polynomial is called the **degree** of the polynomial. So, $-4x^3 + x$ has a degree of 3, while $-2x^5 + x^3 + 4x + 1$ has a degree of 5. When multiplying polynomials, the degree of the result will be the sum of the degrees of the two polynomials being multiplied.

Addition and subtraction operations can be performed on polynomials with like terms. **Like terms** refers to terms that have the same variable and exponent. The two following polynomials can be added together by collecting like terms:

$$(x^2 + 3x - 4) + (4x^2 - 7x + 8)$$

The x^2 terms can be added as:

$$x^2 + 4x^2 = 5x^2$$

The x terms can be added as $3x + -7x = -4x$, and the constants can be added as:

$$-4 + 8 = 4$$

The following expression is the result of the addition:

$$5x^2 - 4x + 4$$

When subtracting polynomials, the same steps are followed, only subtracting like terms together.

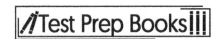

Multiplication of polynomials can also be performed. Given the two polynomials, $(y^3 - 4)$ and $(x^2 + 8x - 7)$, each term in the first polynomial must be multiplied by each term in the second polynomial. The steps to multiply each term in the given example are as follows:

$$(y^3 \times x^2) + (y^3 \times 8x) + (y^3 \times -7) + (-4 \times x^2) + (-4 \times 8x) + (-4 \times -7)$$

Simplifying each multiplied part, yields:

$$x^2y^3 + 8xy^3 - 7y^3 - 4x^2 - 32x + 28$$

None of the terms can be combined because there are no like terms in the final expression. Any polynomials can be multiplied by each other by following the same set of steps, then collecting like terms at the end.

FOIL Method

FOIL is a technique for generating polynomials through the multiplication of binomials. FOIL is an acronym for First, Outer, Inner, and Last. "First" represents the multiplication of the terms appearing first in the binomials. "Outer" means multiplying the outermost terms. "Inner" means multiplying the terms inside. "Last" means multiplying the last terms of each binomial.

After completing FOIL and solving the operations, **like terms** are combined. To identify like terms, test takers should look for terms with the same variable and the same exponent. For example, in $4x^2 - x^2 + 15x + 2x^2 - 8$, the $4x^2, -x^2$, and $2x^2$ are all like terms because they have the same variable (x) and exponent (2). Thus, after combining the like terms, the polynomial has been simplified to:

$$5x^2 + 15x - 8$$

The purpose of FOIL is to simplify an equation involving multiple variables and operations. Although it sounds complicated, working through some examples will provide some clarity:

1. Simplify $(x + 10)(x + 4)$

$$\underset{\text{First}}{(x \times x)} + \underset{\text{Outer}}{(x \times 4)} + \underset{\text{Inner}}{(10 \times x)} + \underset{\text{Last}}{(10 \times 4)}$$

After multiplying these binomials, it's time to solve the operations and combine like terms. Thus, the expression becomes:

$$x^2 + 4x + 10x + 40 = x^2 + 14x + 40$$

2. Simplify $2x(4x^3 - 7y^2 + 3x^2 + 4)$

Here, a monomial ($2x$) is multiplied into a polynomial:

$$(4x^3 - 7y^2 + 3x^2 + 4)$$

Using the distributive property, the monomial gets multiplied by each term in the polynomial. This becomes:

$$2x(4x^3) - 2x(7y^2) + 2x(3x^2) + 2x(4)$$

Now, each monomial is simplified, starting with the coefficients:

$$(2 \times 4)(x \times x^3) - (2 \times 7)(x \times y^2) + (2 \times 3)(x \times x^2) + (2 \times 4)(x)$$

159

When multiplying powers with the same base, their exponents are added. Remember, a variable with no listed exponent has an exponent of 1, and exponents of distinct variables cannot be combined. This produces the answer:

$$8x^{1+3} - 14xy^2 + 6x^{1+2} + 8x = 8x^4 - 14xy^2 + 6x^3 + 8x$$

3. Simplify $(8x^{10}y^2z^4) \div (4x^2y^4z^7)$

The first step is to divide the coefficients of the first two polynomials: $8 \div 4 = 2$. The second step is to divide exponents with the same variable, which requires subtracting the exponents. This results in:

$$2(x^{10-2}y^{2-4}z^{4-7}) = 2x^8y^{-2}z^{-3}$$

However, the most simplified answer should include only positive exponents. Thus, $y^{-2}z^{-3}$ needs to be converted into fractions, respectively $\frac{1}{y^2}$ and $\frac{1}{z^3}$. Since the $2x^8$ has a positive exponent, it is placed in the numerator, and $\frac{1}{y^2}$ and $\frac{1}{z^3}$ are combined into the denominator, leaving $\frac{2x^8}{y^2z^3}$ as the final answer.

Zeros of Polynomials

Finding the **zeros of polynomial functions** is the same process as finding the solutions of polynomial equations. These are the points at which the graph of the function crosses the x-axis. As stated previously, factors can be used to find the zeros of a polynomial function. The degree of the function shows the number of possible zeros. If the highest exponent on the independent variable is 4, then the degree is 4, and the number of possible zeros is 4. If there are complex solutions, the number of roots is less than the degree.

Given the function $y = x^2 + 7x + 6$, y can be set equal to zero, and the polynomial can be factored. The equation turns into $0 = (x + 1)(x + 6)$, where $x = -1$ and $x = -6$ are the zeros. Since this is a quadratic equation, the shape of the graph will be a **parabola** (a U-shaped curve). Knowing that zeros represent the points where the parabola crosses the x-axis, the maximum or minimum point is the only other piece needed to sketch a rough graph of the function. By looking at the function in standard form, the coefficient of x is positive; therefore, the parabola opens up. Using the zeros and the minimum, the following rough sketch of the graph can be constructed:

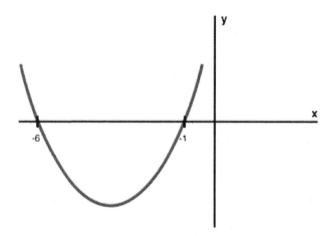

Rational Expressions and Equations

A **rational expression** is a fraction where the numerator and denominator are both polynomials. Some examples of rational expressions include the following: $\frac{4x^3y^5}{3z^4}$, $\frac{4x^3+3x}{x^2}$, and $\frac{x^2+7x+10}{x+2}$. Since these refer to expressions and not equations, they can be simplified but not solved. Using the rules of exponents, some rational expressions with monomials can be simplified. Other rational expressions such as the last example, $\frac{x^2+7x+10}{x+2}$, require more steps to be simplified. First, the polynomial on top can be factored from $x^2 + 7x + 10$ into $(x + 5)(x + 2)$. Then the common factors can be canceled, and the expression can be simplified to $(x + 5)$.

The following problem is an example of using rational expressions:

Reggie wants to lay sod in his rectangular backyard. The length of the yard is given by the expression $4x + 2$ meters, and the width is unknown. The area of the yard is $20x + 10$ square meters. Reggie needs to find the width of the yard. Knowing that the area of a rectangle is length multiplied by width, an expression (area divided by length) can be written to find the width:

$$\frac{20x + 10}{4x + 2}$$

Simplifying this expression by factoring out 10 on the top and 2 on the bottom leads to this expression:

$$\frac{10(2x + 1)}{2(2x + 1)}$$

Canceling out the $2x + 1$ results in $\frac{10}{2} = 5$. The width of the yard is found to be 5 meters by simplifying the rational expression.

A **rational equation** can be as simple as an equation with a ratio of polynomials, $\frac{p(x)}{q(x)}$, set equal to a value, where $p(x)$ and $q(x)$ are both polynomials. A rational equation has an equal sign, which is different from expressions. This leads to solutions, or numbers that make the equation true.

It is possible to solve rational equations by trying to get all of the x terms out of the denominator and then isolating them on one side of the equation. For example, to solve the equation $\frac{3x+2}{2x+3} = 4$, both sides get multiplied by $(2x + 3)$. This will cancel on the left side to yield:

$$3x + 2 = 4(2x + 3)$$

Then:

$$3x + 2 = 8x + 12$$

Now, subtract $8x$ from both sides, which yields $-5x + 2 = 12$. Subtracting 2 from both sides results in $-5x = 10$. Finally, both sides get divided by -5 to obtain $x = -2$.

Sometimes, when solving rational equations, it can be easier to try to simplify the rational expression by factoring the numerator and denominator first, then cancelling out common factors. For example, to solve $\frac{2x^2-8x+6}{x^2-3x+2} = 1$, the first step is to factor:

$$2x^2 - 8x + 6$$
$$2(x^2 - 4x + 3)$$
$$2(x - 1)(x - 3)$$

161

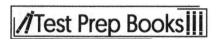

Then, factor $x^2 - 3x + 2$ into $(x-1)(x-2)$. This turns the original equation into:

$$\frac{2(x-1)(x-3)}{(x-1)(x-2)} = 1$$

The common factor of $(x-1)$ can be canceled, leaving:

$$\frac{2(x-3)}{x-2} = 1$$

Now the same method used in the previous example can be followed. Multiplying both sides by $x-2$ and performing the multiplication on the left yields $2x - 6 = x - 2$, which can be simplified to $x = 4$.

Systems of Equations

A **system of equations** is a group of equations that have the same variables or unknowns. These equations can be linear, but they are not always so. Finding a solution to a system of equations means finding the values of the variables that satisfy each equation. For a linear system of two equations and two variables, there could be a single solution, no solution, or infinitely many solutions.

A single solution occurs when there is one value for x and y that satisfies the system. This would be shown on the graph where the lines cross at exactly one point. When there is no solution, the lines are parallel and do not ever cross. With infinitely many solutions, the equations may look different, but they are the same line. One equation will be a multiple of the other, and on the graph, they lie on top of each other.

The **process of elimination** can be used to solve a system of equations. For example, the following equations make up a system: $x + 3y = 10$ and $2x - 5y = 9$. Immediately adding these equations does not eliminate a variable, but it is possible to change the first equation by multiplying the whole equation by -2. This changes the first equation to:

$$-2x - 6y = -20$$

The equations can be then added to obtain:

$$-11y = -11$$

Solving for y yields $y = 1$. To find the rest of the solution, 1 can be substituted in for y in either original equation to find the value of $x = 7$. The solution to the system is (7, 1) because it makes both equations true, and it is the point in which the lines intersect. If the system is **dependent**—having infinitely many solutions—then both variables will cancel out when the elimination method is used, resulting in an equation that is true for many values of x and y. Since the system is dependent, both equations can be simplified to the same equation or line.

A system can also be solved using **substitution.** This involves solving one equation for a variable and then plugging that solved equation into the other equation in the system. For example, $x - y = -2$ and $3x + 2y = 9$ can be solved using substitution. The first equation can be solved for x, where:

$$x = -2 + y$$

Then it can be plugged into the other equation:

$$3(-2 + y) + 2y = 9$$

Solving for y yields $-6 + 3y + 2y = 9$, where $y = 3$. If $y = 3$, then $x = 1$. This solution can be checked by plugging in these values for the variables in each equation to see if it makes a true statement.

Finally, a solution to a system of equations can be found graphically. The solution to a linear system is the point or points where the lines cross. The values of x and y represent the coordinates (x, y) where the lines intersect. Using the same system of equations as above, they can be solved for y to put them in slope-intercept form, $y = mx + b$. These equations become $y = x + 2$ and $y = -\frac{3}{2}x + 4.5$. This system with the solution is shown below:

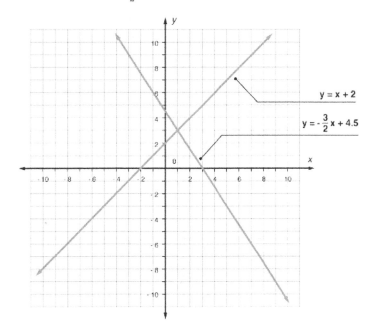

A system of equations may also be made up of a linear and a quadratic equation. These systems may have one solution, two solutions, or no solutions. The graph of these systems involves one straight line and one parabola. Algebraically, these systems can be solved by solving the linear equation for one variable and plugging that answer in to the quadratic equation. If possible, the equation can then be solved to find part of the answer. The graphing method is commonly used for these types of systems. On a graph, these two lines can be found to intersect at one point, at two points across the parabola, or at no points.

Finding solutions to systems of equations is essentially finding what values of the variables make both equations true. It is finding the input value that yields the same output value in both equations. For functions $g(x)$ and $f(x)$, the equation $g(x) = f(x)$ means the output values are being set equal to each other. Solving for the value of x means finding the x-coordinate that gives the same output in both functions. For example, $f(x) = x + 2$ and $g(x) = -3x + 10$ is a system of equations. Setting $f(x) = g(x)$ yields the equation $x + 2 = -3x + 10$. Solving for x, gives the x-coordinate $x = 2$ where the two lines cross. This value can also be found by using a table or a graph. On a table, both equations can be given the same inputs, and the outputs can be recorded to find the point(s) where the lines cross. Any method of solving finds the same solution, but some methods are more appropriate for some systems of equations than others.

A system of linear inequalities consists of two linear inequalities making comparisons between two variables. Students may be given a scenario and asked to express it as a system of inequalities:

> A consumer study calls for at least 60 adult participants. It cannot use more than 25 men. Express these constraints as a system of inequalities.

This can be modeled by the system: $x + y \geq 60; x \leq 25$, where x represents the number of men and y represents the number of women. A solution to the system is an ordered pair that makes both inequalities true when substituting the values for x and y.

163

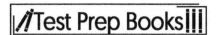

The solution set for a system of inequalities is the region of a graph consisting of ordered pairs that make both inequalities true. To graph the solution set, each linear inequality should first be graphed with appropriate shading. The region of the graph should be identified where the shading for the two inequalities overlaps. This region contains the solution set for the system.

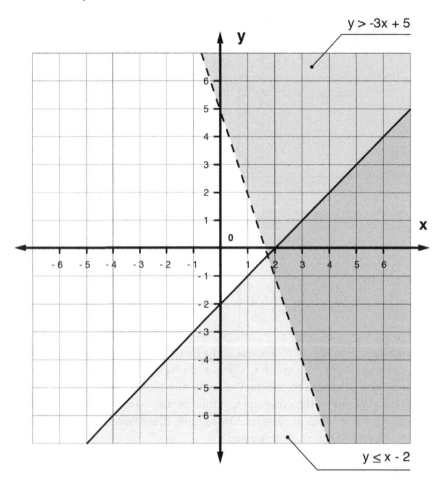

An ordered pair from the region of solutions can be selected to test in the system of inequalities.

Just as with manipulating linear inequalities in one variable, if dividing by a negative number in working with a linear inequality in two variables, the relationship reverses and the inequality sign should be flipped.

Statistics and Probability

Center and Spread of Distributions

Descriptive statistics are utilized to gain an understanding of properties of a data set. This entails examining the center, spread, and shape of the sample data.

Center
The **center** of the sample set can be represented by its mean, median or mode. The **mean** is the average of the data set. It is calculated by adding the data values together and dividing this sum by the sample size (the number of data points). The **median** is the value of the data point in the middle when the sample is arranged in numerical order. If the sample has an even number of data points, the mean of the two middle values is the median. The **mode** is the

164

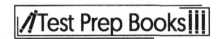

value which appears most often in a data set. It is possible to have multiple modes (if different values repeat equally as often) or no mode (if no value repeats).

Spread

Methods for determining the **spread** of the sample include calculating the range and standard deviation for the data. The *range* is calculated by subtracting the lowest value from the highest value in the set. The **standard deviation** of the sample can be calculated using the formula:

$$\sigma = \sqrt{\frac{\sum(x - \bar{x})^2}{n - 1}}$$

$\bar{x} = sample\ mean$
$n = sample\ size$

Shape

The **shape** of the sample when displayed as a histogram or frequency distribution plot helps to determine if the sample is normally distributed (bell-shaped curve), symmetrical, or displays skewness (lack of symmetry), or kurtosis. **Kurtosis** is a measure of whether the data are heavy-tailed (high number of outliers) or light-tailed (low number of outliers).

Data Collection Methods

Statistical inference, based in probability theory, makes calculated assumptions about an entire population based on data from a sample set from that population.

Population Parameters

A **population** is the entire set of people or things of interest. For example, if researchers wanted to determine the number of hours of sleep per night for college females in the U.S, the population would consist of *every* college female in the country. A **sample** is a subset of the population that may be used for the study. A sample might consist of 100 students per school from 20 different colleges in the country. From the results of the survey, a sample statistic can be calculated. A **sample statistic** is a numerical characteristic of the sample data including mean and variance. A sample statistic can be used to estimate a corresponding **population parameter**, which is a numerical characteristic of the entire population.

Confidence Intervals

A population parameter estimated using a sample statistic may be very accurate or relatively inaccurate based on errors in sampling. A **confidence interval** indicates a range of values likely to include the true population parameter. A given confidence interval such as 95% means that the true population parameter will occur within the interval for 95% of samples.

Measurement Error

The accuracy of a population parameter based on a sample statistic may also be affected by measurement error. **Measurement error** can be divided into random error and systematic error. An example of **random error** for the previous scenario would be a student reporting 8 hours of sleep when she actually sleeps 7 hours per night. **Systematic errors** are those attributed to the measurement system. If the sleep survey gave response options of 2, 4, 6, 8, or 10 hours. This would lead to systematic measurement error because certain values could not be accurately reported.

Evaluating Reports and Determining the Appropriateness of Data Collection Methods

The presentation of statistics can be manipulated to produce a desired outcome. For example, in the statement "four out of five dentists recommend our toothpaste", critical readers should wonder: *who are the five dentists?* While the wording is similar, this statement is very different from "four out of every five dentists recommend our toothpaste." The context of the numerical values allows one to decipher the meaning, intent, and significance of the survey or study.

When analyzing a report, the researchers who conducted the study and their intent must be considered. Was it performed by a neutral party or by a person or group with a vested interest? The sampling method and the data collection method should also be evaluated. Was it a true random sample of the population or was one subgroup over- or underrepresented? Lastly, the measurement system used to obtain the data should be assessed. Was the system accurate and precise or was it a flawed system?

Understanding and Modeling Relationships in Bivariate Data

In an experiment, variables are the key to analyzing data, especially when data is in a graph or table. Variables can represent anything, including objects, conditions, events, and amounts of time.

Covariance is a general term referring to how two variables move in relation to each other. Take for example an employee that gets paid by the hour. For them, hours worked and total pay have a positive covariance. As hours worked increases, so does pay.

Constant variables remain unchanged by the scientist across all trials. Because they are held constant for all groups in an experiment, they aren't being measured in the experiment, and they are usually ignored. Constants can either be controlled by the scientist directly like the nutrition, water, and sunlight given to plants, or they can be selected by the scientist specifically for an experiment like using a certain animal species or choosing to investigate only people of a certain age group.

Independent variables are also controlled by the scientist, but they are the same only for each group or trial in the experiment. Each group might be composed of students that all have the same color of car or each trial may be run on different soda brands. The independent variable of an experiment is what is being indirectly tested because it causes change in the dependent variables.

Dependent variables experience change caused by the independent variable and are what is being measured or observed. For example, college acceptance rates could be a dependent variable of an experiment that sorted a large sample of high school students by an independent variable such as test scores. In this experiment, the scientist groups the high school students by the independent variable (test scores) to see how it affects the dependent variable (their college acceptance rates).

Note that most variables can be held constant in one experiment but independent or dependent in another. For example, when testing how well a fertilizer aids plant growth, its amount of sunlight should be held constant for each group of plants, but if the experiment is being done to determine the proper amount of sunlight a plant should have, the amount of sunlight is an independent variable because it is necessarily changed for each group of plants.

Correlation

An **X-Y diagram**, also known as a **scatter diagram**, visually displays the relationship between two variables. The independent variable is placed on the x-axis, or horizontal axis, and the dependent variable is placed on the y-axis, or vertical axis.

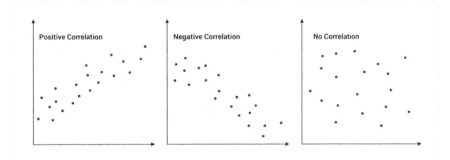

As shown in the figures above, an X-Y diagram may result in positive, negative, or no correlation between the two variables. So, in the first scatter plot, as the y-factor increases the x-factor increases as well. The opposite is true as well: as the x-factor increases the y-factor also increases. Thus, there is a positive correlation because one factor appears to positively affect the other factor.

It's important to note, however, that a positive correlation between two variables doesn't equate to a cause-and-effect relationship. For example, a positive correlation between labor hours and units produced may not equate to a cause-and-effect relationship between the two. Any instance of correlation only indicates how likely the presence of one variable is in the instance of another. The variables should be further analyzed to determine which, if any, other variables (e.g., quality of employee work) may contribute to the positive correlation.

Correlation Coefficient

The **correlation coefficient** (r) measures the association between two variables. Its value is between -1 and 1, where -1 represents a perfect negative linear relationship, 0 represents no relationship, and 1 represents a perfect positive linear relationship. A **negative linear relationship** means that as x-values increase, y-values decrease. A **positive linear relationship** means that as x-values increase, y-values increase. The formula for computing the correlation coefficient is:

$$r = \frac{n(\sum xy) - (\sum x)(\sum y)}{\sqrt{n(\sum x^2) - (\sum x)^2}\sqrt{n(\sum y^2) - (\Sigma y)^2}}$$

n is the number of data points.

Both Microsoft Excel® and a graphing calculator can evaluate this easily once the data points are entered. A correlation greater than 0.8 or less than -0.8 is classified as "strong" while a correlation between -0.5 and 0.5 is classified as "weak."

Calculating Probabilities, Including Related Sample Spaces

Probability, represented by variable p, always has a value from 0 to 1. The total probability for all the possible outcomes (sample space) should equal 1.

Sample Spaces

Probabilities are based on observations of events. The probability of an event occurring is equal to the ratio of the number of favorable outcomes over the total number of possible outcomes. The total number of possible outcomes is found by constructing the sample space. The sum of probabilities of all possible distinct outcomes is equal to 1. A simple example of a sample space involves a deck of cards. They contain 52 distinct cards, and therefore the sample space contains each individual card. To find the probability of selecting a queen on one draw from the deck, the

ratio would be equal to $\frac{4}{52} = \frac{1}{13}$, which equals 4 possible queens over the total number of possibilities in the sample space.

Verifying Independent Events

Two events aren't always independent. For example, having glasses and having brown hair aren't independent characteristics. There definitely can be overlap because people with brown hair can wear glasses. Also, two events that exist at the same time don't have to have a relationship. For example, even if everyone in a given sample is wearing glasses, the characteristics aren't related. In this case, the probability of a brunette wearing glasses is equal to the probability of a person being a brunette multiplied by the probability of a person wearing glasses. This mathematical test of $P(A \cap B) = P(A)P(B)$ verifies that two events are independent.

Simple and Compound Events

A **simple event** consists of only one outcome. The most popular simple event is flipping a coin, which results in either heads or tails. A **compound event** results in more than one outcome and consists of more than one simple event. An example of a compound event is flipping a coin while tossing a die. The result is either heads or tails on the coin and a number from one to six on the die. The probability of a simple event is calculated by dividing the number of possible outcomes by the total number of outcomes. Therefore, the probability of obtaining heads on a coin is $\frac{1}{2}$, and the probability of rolling a 6 on a die is $\frac{1}{6}$. The probability of compound events is calculated using the basic idea of the probability of simple events. If the two events are independent, the probability of one outcome is equal to the product of the probabilities of each simple event. For example, the probability of obtaining heads on a coin and rolling a 6 is equal to:

$$\frac{1}{2} \times \frac{1}{6} = \frac{1}{12}$$

The probability of either A or B occurring is equal to the sum of the probabilities minus the probability that both A and B will occur. Therefore, the probability of obtaining either heads on a coin or rolling a 6 on a die is

$$\frac{1}{2} + \frac{1}{6} - \frac{1}{12} = \frac{7}{12}$$

The two events aren't mutually exclusive because they can happen at the same time. If two events are mutually exclusive, and the probability of both events occurring at the same time is zero, the probability of event A or B occurring equals the sum of both probabilities. An example of calculating the probability of two mutually exclusive events is determining the probability of pulling a king or a queen from a deck of cards. The two events cannot occur at the same time.

Language

Punctuation and Capitalization

Capitalization Rules

Here's a non-exhaustive list of things that should be capitalized:

- The first word of every sentence

- The first word of every line of poetry

- The first letter of proper nouns (World War II)

- Holidays (Valentine's Day)

- Days of the week and months of the year (Tuesday, March)

- The first word, last word, and all major words in the titles of books, movies, songs, and other creative works (*To Kill a Mockingbird,* note that *a* is lowercase since it's not a major word, but *to* is capitalized since it's the first word of the title.

- Titles when preceding a proper noun (President Roberto Gonzales, Aunt Judy)

When simply using a word such as president or secretary, though, the word is not capitalized.

> Officers of the new business must include a *president* and *treasurer*.

Seasons—spring, fall, etc.—are not capitalized.

North, south, east, and *west* are capitalized when referring to regions but are not when being used for directions. In general, if it's preceded by *the* it should be capitalized.

> I'm from the South.
> I drove south.

End Punctuation

Periods (.) are used to end a sentence that is a statement (**declarative**) or a command (**imperative**). They should not be used in a sentence that asks a question or is an exclamation. Periods are also used in abbreviations, which are shortened versions of words.

- Declarative: The boys refused to go to sleep.

- Imperative: Walk down to the bus stop.

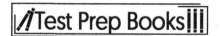

- Abbreviations: Joan Roberts, M.D., Apple Inc., Mrs. Adamson

- If a sentence ends with an abbreviation, it is inappropriate to use two periods. It should end with a single period after the abbreviation.

  The chef gathered the ingredients for the pie, which included apples, flour, sugar, etc.

Question marks (?) are used with direct questions (**interrogative**). An **indirect question** can use a period:

  Interrogative: When does the next bus arrive?

  Indirect Question: I wonder when the next bus arrives.

An **exclamation point (!)** is used to show strong emotion or can be used as an **interjection.** This punctuation should be used sparingly in formal writing situations.

  What an amazing shot!

  Whoa!

Commas

A **comma (,)** is the punctuation mark that signifies a pause—breath—between parts of a sentence. It denotes a break of flow. Proper comma usage helps readers understand the writer's intended emphasis of ideas.

In a **complex sentence**—one that contains a subordinate (dependent) clause or clauses—use a comma if the dependent clause is before the independent clause.

  Because I don't have that much money, I will not pay for the steak.

First, see how the purpose of each comma usage is to designate an interruption in flow. Then, notice how the last clause is dependent because it requires the earlier independent clauses to make sense.

Use a comma on both sides of an interrupting phrase.

  I will pay for the ice cream, *chocolate and vanilla,* and I will eat it all myself.

The words forming the phrase in italics are nonessential (extra) information. To determine if a phrase is nonessential, try reading the sentence without the phrase and see if it's still coherent.

A comma is not necessary in this next sentence to set off *chocolate and vanilla* because no interruption—nonessential or extra information—has occurred. Read sentences aloud when uncertain.

  I will pay for his chocolate and vanilla ice cream, and I will eat it all myself.

If the nonessential phrase comes at the beginning of a sentence, a comma should only go at the end of the phrase. If the phrase comes at the end of a sentence, a comma should only go at the beginning of the phrase.

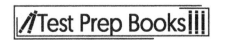

Other types of interruptions include the following:

- Interjections: Oh no, I am not going.
- Abbreviations: Barry Potter, M.D., specializes in heart disorders.
- Direct addresses: Yes, Claudia, I am tired and going to bed.
- Parenthetical phrases: His wife, lovely as she was, was not helpful.
- Transitional phrases: Also, it is not possible.

The second comma in the following sentence is called an **Oxford comma**.

> I will pay for ice cream, syrup, and pop.

It is a comma used after the second-to-last item in a series of three or more items. It comes before the word *or* or *and*. Not everyone uses the Oxford comma; it is optional, but many believe it is needed. The comma functions as a tool to reduce confusion in writing. So, if omitting the Oxford comma would cause confusion, then it's best to include it.

Commas are used in math to mark the place of thousands in numerals, breaking them up so they are easier to read. Other uses for commas are in dates (*March 19, 2016*), letter greetings (*Dear Sally,*), and in between cities and states (*Louisville, KY*).

Semicolons

A **semicolon (;)** is used to connect ideas in a sentence in some way. There are three main ways to use semicolons.

1. To link two independent clauses without the use of a coordinating conjunction:

> I was late for work again; I'm definitely going to get fired.

2. To link two independent clauses with a transitional word:

> The songs were all easy to play; therefore, he didn't need to spend too much time practicing.

3. Between items in a series that are already separated by commas or if necessary to separate lengthy items in a list:

> Starbucks has locations in Media, PA; Swarthmore, PA; and Morton, PA.

> Several classroom management issues presented in the study: the advent of a poor teacher persona in the context of voice, dress, and style; teacher follow-through from the beginning of the school year to the end; and the depth of administrative support, including ISS and OSS protocol.

Colons

A **colon (:)** is used after an independent clause to present an explanation or draw attention to what comes next in the sentence. There are several uses.

Explanations of ideas:

> They soon learned the hardest part about having a new baby: sleep deprivation.

Lists of items:

171

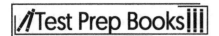
Shari picked up all the supplies she would need for the party: cups, plates, napkins, balloons, streamers, and party favors.

Time, subtitles, general salutations:

The time is 7:15.

I read a book entitled *Pluto: A Planet No More*.

To whom it may concern:

Parentheses and Dashes

Parentheses are half-round brackets that look like this: ( ). They set off a word, phrase, or sentence that is an afterthought, explanation, or side note relevant to the surrounding text but not essential. A pair of commas is often used to set off this sort of information, but parentheses are generally used for information that would not fit well within a sentence or that the writer deems not important enough to be structurally part of the sentence.

The picture of the heart (see above) shows the major parts you should memorize.
Mount Everest is one of three mountains in the world that are over 28,000 feet high (K2 and Kanchenjunga are the other two).

See how the sentences above are complete without the parenthetical statements? In the first example, *see above* would not have fit well within the flow of the sentence. The second parenthetical statement could have been a separate sentence, but the writer deemed the information not pertinent to the topic.

The **em-dash** (—) is a mark longer than a hyphen used as a punctuation mark in sentences and to set apart a relevant thought. Even after plucking out the line separated by the dash marks, the sentence will be intact and make sense.

Looking out the airplane window at the landmarks—Lake Clarke, Thompson Community College, and the bridge—she couldn't help but feel excited to be home.

The dash's use is similar to that of parentheses or a pair of commas. So, what's the difference? Many believe that using dashes makes the clause within them stand out while using parentheses is subtler. It's advised to not use dashes when commas could be used instead.

Ellipses

An **ellipsis (…)** is used to show that there is more to the quoted text than is necessary for the current discussion. Writers use them in place of a word(s), line, phrase, list contents, or paragraph that might just as easily have been omitted from a passage of writing. This can be done to save space or to focus only on the specifically relevant material.

Exercise is good for some unexpected reasons. Watkins writes, "Exercise has many benefits such as …reducing cancer risk."

In the example above, the ellipsis takes the place of the other benefits of exercise that are more expected.

The ellipsis may also be used to show a pause in sentence flow.

"I'm wondering…how this could happen," Dylan said in a soft voice.

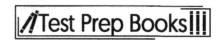

Quotation Marks

Double **quotation marks ("...")** are used at the beginning and end of a direct quote. They are also used with certain titles and to indicate that a term being used is slang or referenced in the sentence. Quotation marks should not be used with an indirect quote. Single quotation marks are used to indicate a quote within a quote.

Direct quote: "The weather is supposed to be beautiful this week," she said.

Indirect quote: One of the customers asked if the sale prices were still in effect.

Quote within a quote: "My little boy just said 'Mama, I want cookie,'" Maria shared.

Titles: Quotation marks should also be used to indicate titles of short works or sections of larger works, such as chapter titles. Other works that use quotation marks include poems, short stories, newspaper articles, magazine articles, web page titles, and songs.

"The Road Not Taken" is my favorite poem by Robert Frost.

"What a Wonderful World" is one of my favorite songs.

Specific or emphasized terms: Quotation marks can also be used to indicate a technical term or to set off a word that is being discussed in a sentence. Quotation marks can also indicate sarcasm.

The new step, called "levigation," is a very difficult technique.

He said he was "hungry" multiple times, but he only ate two bites.

Use with other punctuation: The use of quotation marks with other punctuation varies, depending on the role of the ending or separating punctuation.

In American English, commas and periods go inside quotation marks:

"This is the last time you are allowed to leave early," his boss stated.

The newscaster said, "We have some breaking news to report."

Question marks or exclamation points go inside the quotation marks when they are part of a direct quote:

The doctor shouted, "Get the crash cart!"

When the question mark or exclamation point is part of the sentence, not the quote, it should be placed outside of the quotation marks:

Was it Jackie that said, "Get some potatoes at the store"?

Apostrophes

This punctuation mark, the **apostrophe (')** is a versatile mark. It has several different functions:

- Quotes: Apostrophes are used when a second quote is needed within a quote.

  In my letter to my friend, I wrote, "The girl had to get a new purse, and guess what Mary did? She said, 'I'd like to go with you to the store.' I knew Mary would buy it for her."

173

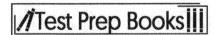

- Contractions: Another use for an apostrophe in the quote above is a contraction. *I'd* is used for *I would.*

- Possession: An apostrophe followed by the letter s shows possession (Mary's purse). If the possessive word is plural, the apostrophe generally just follows the word. Not all possessive pronouns require apostrophes.

    The trees' leaves are all over the ground.

Hyphens

The **hyphen (-)** is a small hash mark that can be used to join words to show that they are linked.

Hyphens can connect two words that work together as a single adjective (a compound adjective).

    honey-covered biscuits

Some words always require hyphens even if not serving as an adjective.

    merry-go-round

Hyphens always go after certain prefixes like *anti-* & *all-.*

Hyphens should also be used when the absence of the hyphen would cause a strange vowel combination (*semi-engineer*) or confusion. For example, *re-collect* should be used to describe something being gathered twice rather than being written as *recollect*, which means to remember.

174

Usage

Understanding the Convention of Standard English

Parts of Speech

The English language has eight parts of speech, each serving a different grammatical function.

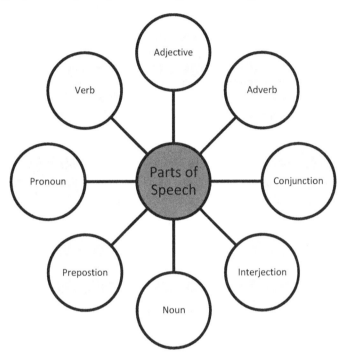

Verb

Verbs describe an action—e.g., *run*, *play*, *eat*—or a state of being—e.g., *is*, *are*, *was*. It is impossible to make a grammatically-complete sentence without a verb.

> He *runs* to the store.

> She *is* eight years old.

Noun

Nouns can be a person, place, or thing. They can refer to concrete objects—e.g., chair, apple, house—or abstract things—love, knowledge, friendliness.

> Look at the *dog*!

> Where are my *keys*?

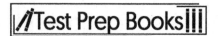

Some nouns are **countable**, meaning they can be counted as separate entities—one chair, two chairs, three chairs. They can be either singular or plural. Others nouns, usually substances or concepts, are **uncountable**—e.g., air, information, wealth—and some nouns can be both countable and uncountable depending on how they are used.

> I bought three *dresses*.

> *Respect* is important to me.

> I ate way too much *food* last night.

> At the international festival, you can sample *foods* from around the world.

Proper nouns are the specific names of people, places, or things and are almost always capitalized.

> *Marie Curie* studied at the *Flying University* in *Warsaw, Poland*.

Pronoun

Pronouns function as substitutes for nouns or noun phrases. Pronouns are often used to avoid constant repetition of a noun or to simplify sentences. **Personal pronouns** are used for people. Some pronouns are **subject pronouns**; they are used to replace the subject in a sentence—I, we, he, she, they.

> Is *he* your friend?

> *We* work together.

Object pronouns can function as the object of a sentence—me, us, him, her, them.

> Give the documents to *her*.

> Did you call *him* back yet?

Some pronouns can function as either the subject or the object—e.g., you, it. The subject of a sentence is the noun of the sentence that is doing or being something.

> *You* should try it.

> *It* tastes great.

Possessive pronouns indicate ownership. They can be used alone—mine, yours, his, hers, theirs, ours—or with a noun—my, your, his, her, their, ours. In the latter case, they function as a determiner, which is described in detail in the below section on adjectives.

> This table is *ours*.

> I can't find *my* phone!

Reflexive pronouns refer back to the person being spoken or written about. These pronouns end in *-self/-selves*.

> I've heard that New York City is gorgeous in the autumn, but I've never seen it for *myself*.

> After moving away from home, young people have to take care of *themselves*.

Indefinite pronouns are used for things that are unknown or unspecified. Some examples are *anybody, something,* and *everything*.

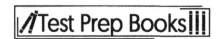

I'm looking for *someone* who knows how to fix computers.

I wanted to buy some shoes today, but I couldn't find *any* that I liked.

Adjective

An **adjective** modifies a noun, making it more precise or giving more information about it. Adjectives answer these questions: What kind? Which one?

I just bought a *red* car.

I don't like *cold* weather.

One special type of word that modifies a noun is a **determiner.** In fact, some grammarians classify determiners as a separate part of speech because whereas adjectives simply describe additional qualities of a noun, a determiner is often a necessary part of a noun phrase, without which the phrase is grammatically incomplete. A determiner indicates whether a noun is definite or indefinite and can identify which noun is being discussed. It also introduces context to the noun in terms of quantity and possession. The most commonly-used determiners are **articles**— a, an, the.

I ordered *a* pizza.

She lives in *the* city.

Possessive pronouns discussed above, such as *my*, *your*, and *our*, are also determiners, along with **demonstratives**— this, that—and **quantifiers**—much, many, some. These determiners can take the place of an article.

Are you using *this* chair?

I need *some* coffee!

Adverb

Adverbs modify verbs, adjectives, and other adverbs. Words that end in *–ly* are usually adverbs. Adverbs answer these questions: When? Where? In what manner? To what degree?

She talks *quickly*.

The mountains are *incredibly* beautiful!

The students arrived *early*.

Please take your phone call *outside*.

Preposition

Prepositions show the relationship between different elements in a phrase or sentence and connect nouns or pronouns to other words in the sentence. Some examples of prepositions are words such as *after*, *at*, *behind*, *by*, *during*, *from*, *in*, *on*, *to*, and *with*.

Let's go *to* class.

Starry Night was painted *by* Vincent van Gogh *in* 1889.

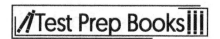

Conjunction

Conjunctions join words, phrases, clauses, or sentences together, indicating the type of connection between these elements.

> I like pizza, *and* I enjoy spaghetti.

> I like to play baseball, *but* I'm allergic to mitts.

Some conjunctions are **coordinating**, meaning they give equal emphasis to two main clauses. Coordinating conjunctions are short, simple words that can be remembered using the mnemonic FANBOYS: for, and, nor, but, or, yet, so. Other conjunctions are **subordinating**. Subordinating conjunctions introduce dependent clauses and include words such as *because*, *since*, *before*, *after*, *if*, and *while*.

Interjection

An **interjection** is a short word that shows greeting or emotion. Examples of interjections include *wow*, *ouch*, *hey*, *oops*, *alas*, and *hey*.

> *Wow*! Look at that sunset!

> Was it your birthday yesterday? *Oops*! I forgot.

Errors in Standard English Grammar, Usage, Syntax, and Mechanics
Sentence Fragments

A complete sentence requires a verb and a subject, and it must express a complete thought. Sometimes, the subject is omitted in the case of the implied *you*, used in sentences that are the command or imperative form—e.g., "Look!" or "Give me that." It is understood that the subject of the command is *you*, the listener or reader, so it is possible to have a structure without an explicit subject. Without these elements, though, the sentence is incomplete—it is a **sentence fragment**. While sentence fragments often occur in conversational English or creative writing, they are generally not appropriate in academic writing. Sentence fragments often occur when dependent clauses are not joined to an independent clause:

> *Sentence fragment*: Because the airline overbooked the flight.

The sentence above is a dependent clause that does not express a complete thought. What happened as a result of this cause? With the addition of an independent clause, this now becomes a complete sentence:

> *Complete sentence*: Because the airline overbooked the flight, several passengers were unable to board.

Sentences fragments may also occur through improper use of conjunctions:

> I'm going to the Bahamas for spring break. And to New York City for New Year's Eve.

While the first sentence above is a complete sentence, the second one is not because it is a prepositional phrase that lacks a subject [I] and a verb [am going]. Joining the two together with the coordinating conjunction forms one grammatically-correct sentence:

> I'm going to the Bahamas for spring break and to New York City for New Year's Eve.

Run-ons

A **run-on** is a sentence with too many independent clauses that are improperly connected to each other:

178

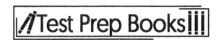

This winter has been very cold some farmers have suffered damage to their crops.

The sentence above has two subject-verb combinations. The first is "this winter has been"; the second is "some farmers have suffered." However, they are simply stuck next to each other without any punctuation or conjunction. Therefore, the sentence is a run-on.

Another type of run-on occurs when writers use inappropriate punctuation:

This winter has been very cold, some farmers have suffered damage to their crops.

Though a comma has been added, this sentence is still not correct. When a comma alone is used to join two independent clauses, it is known as a **comma splice**. Without an appropriate conjunction, a comma cannot join two independent clauses by itself.

Run-on sentences can be corrected by either dividing the independent clauses into two or more separate sentences or inserting appropriate conjunctions and/or punctuation. The run-on sentence can be amended by separating each subject-verb pair into its own sentence:

This winter has been very cold. Some farmers have suffered damage to their crops.

The run-on can also be fixed by adding a comma and conjunction to join the two independent clauses with each other:

This winter has been very cold, so some farmers have suffered damage to their crops.

Parallelism

Parallel structure occurs when phrases or clauses within a sentence contain the same structure. Parallelism increases readability and comprehensibility because it is easy to tell which sentence elements are paired with each other in meaning.

Jennifer enjoys cooking, knitting, and to spend time with her cat.

This sentence is not parallel because the items in the list appear in two different forms. Some are **gerunds,** which is the verb + ing: *cooking, knitting*. The other item uses the **infinitive** form, which is to + verb: *to spend*. To create parallelism, all items in the list may reflect the same form:

Jennifer enjoys cooking, knitting, and spending time with her cat.

All of the items in the list are now in gerund forms, so this sentence exhibits parallel structure. Here's another example:

The company is looking for employees who are responsible and with a lot of experience.

Again, the items that are listed in this sentence are not parallel. "Responsible" is an adjective, yet "with a lot of experience" is a prepositional phrase. The sentence elements do not utilize parallel parts of speech.

The company is looking for employees who are responsible and experienced.

"Responsible" and "experienced" are both adjectives, so this sentence now has parallel structure.

Dangling and Misplaced Modifiers

Modifiers enhance meaning by clarifying or giving greater detail about another part of a sentence. However, incorrectly-placed modifiers have the opposite effect and can cause confusion. A **misplaced modifier** is a modifier that is not located appropriately in relation to the word or phrase that it modifies:

Because he was one of the greatest thinkers of Renaissance Italy, John idolized Leonardo da Vinci.

In this sentence, the modifier is "because he was one of the greatest thinkers of Renaissance Italy," and the noun it is intended to modify is "Leonardo da Vinci." However, due to the placement of the modifier next to the subject, John, it seems as if the sentence is stating that John was a Renaissance genius, not Da Vinci.

John idolized Leonard da Vinci because he was one of the greatest thinkers of Renaissance Italy.

The modifier is now adjacent to the appropriate noun, clarifying which of the two men in this sentence is the greatest thinker.

Dangling modifiers modify a word or phrase that is not readily apparent in the sentence. That is, they "dangle" because they are not clearly attached to anything:

After getting accepted to college, Amir's parents were proud.

The modifier here, "after getting accepted to college," should modify who got accepted. The noun immediately following the modifier is "Amir's parents"—but they are probably not the ones who are going to college.

After getting accepted to college, Amir made his parents proud.

The subject of the sentence has been changed to Amir himself, and now the subject and its modifier are appropriately matched.

Inconsistent Verb Tense

Verb tense reflects when an action occurred or a state existed. For example, the tense known as **simple present** expresses something that is happening right now or that happens regularly:

She *works* in a hospital.

Present continuous tense expresses something in progress. It is formed by to be + verb + -ing.

Sorry, I can't go out right now. I *am doing* my homework.

Past tense is used to describe events that previously occurred. However, in conversational English, speakers often use present tense or a mix of past and present tense when relating past events because it gives the narrative a sense of immediacy. In formal written English, though, consistency in verb tense is necessary to avoid reader confusion.

I traveled to Europe last summer. As soon as I stepped off the plane, I feel like I'm in a movie! I'm surrounded by quaint cafes and impressive architecture.

The passage above abruptly switches from past tense—*traveled, stepped*—to present tense—*feel, am surrounded*.

I *traveled* to Europe last summer. As soon as I *stepped* off the plane, I *felt* like I was in a movie! I *was surrounded* by quaint cafes and impressive architecture.

All verbs are in past tense, so this passage now has consistent verb tense.

Split Infinitives

The **infinitive form** of a verb consists of "to + base verb"—e.g., to walk, to sleep, to approve. A **split infinitive** occurs when another word, usually an adverb, is placed between *to* and the verb:

I decided *to simply walk* to work to get more exercise every day.

The infinitive *to walk* is split by the adverb *simply*.

It was a mistake *to hastily approve* the project before conducting further preliminary research.

The infinitive *to approve* is split by *hastily*.

Although some grammarians still advise against split infinitives, this syntactic structure is common in both spoken and written English and is widely accepted in standard usage.

Subject-Verb Agreement

In English, verbs must agree with the subject. The form of a verb may change depending on whether the subject is singular or plural, or whether it is first, second, or third person. For example, the verb *to be* has various forms:

I am a student.

You are a student.

She is a student.

We are students.

They are students.

Errors occur when a verb does not agree with its subject. Sometimes, the error is readily apparent:

We is hungry.

Is is not the appropriate form of *to be* when used with the third person plural *we*.

We are hungry.

This sentence now has correct subject-verb agreement.

However, some cases are trickier, particularly when the subject consists of a lengthy noun phrase with many modifiers:

Students who are hoping to accompany the anthropology department on its annual summer trip to Ecuador needs to sign up by March 31st.

The verb in this sentence is *needs*. However, its subject is not the noun adjacent to it—Ecuador. The subject is the noun at the beginning of the sentence—students. Because *students* is plural, *needs* is the incorrect verb form.

Students who are hoping to accompany the anthropology department on its annual summer trip to Ecuador *need* to sign up by March 31st.

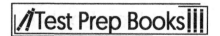

This sentence now uses correct agreement between *students* and *need*.

Another case to be aware of is a collective noun. A **collective noun** refers to a group of many things or people but can be singular in itself—e.g., family, committee, army, pair team, council, jury. Whether or not a collective noun uses a singular or plural verb depends on how the noun is being used. If the noun refers to the group performing a collective action as one unit, it should use a singular verb conjugation:

> The family is moving to a new neighborhood.

The whole family is moving together in unison, so the singular verb form *is* is appropriate here.

> The committee has made its decision.

The verb *has* and the possessive pronoun *its* both reflect the word *committee* as a singular noun in the sentence above; however, when a collective noun refers to the group as individuals, it can take a plural verb:

> The newlywed pair spend every moment together.

This sentence emphasizes the love between two people in a pair, so it can use the plural verb *spend*.

> The council are all newly elected members.

The sentence refers to the council in terms of its individual members and uses the plural verb *are*.

Overall, though, American English is more likely to pair a collective noun with a singular verb, while British English is more likely to pair a collective noun with a plural verb.

Grammar, Usage, Syntax, and Mechanics Choices
Colons and Semicolons
In a sentence, **colons** are used before a list, a summary or elaboration, or an explanation related to the preceding information in the sentence:

> There are two ways to reserve tickets for the performance: by phone or in person.

> One thing is clear: students are spending more on tuition than ever before.

As these examples show, a colon must be preceded by an independent clause. However, the information after the colon may be in the form of an independent clause or in the form of a list.

Semicolons can be used in two different ways—to join ideas or to separate them. In some cases, semicolons can be used to connect what would otherwise be stand-alone sentences. Each part of the sentence joined by a semicolon must be an independent clause. The use of a semicolon indicates that these two independent clauses are closely related to each other:

> The rising cost of childcare is one major stressor for parents; healthcare expenses are another source of anxiety.

> Classes have been canceled due to the snowstorm; check the school website for updates.

Semicolons can also be used to divide elements of a sentence in a more distinct way than simply using a comma. This usage is particularly useful when the items in a list are especially long and complex and contain other internal punctuation.

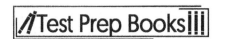

Retirees have many modes of income: some survive solely off their retirement checks; others supplement their income through part time jobs, like working in a supermarket or substitute teaching; and others are financially dependent on the support of family members, friends, and spouses.

Its and It's

These pronouns are the some of the most confused in the English language as most possessives contain the suffix – 's. However, for *it*, it is the opposite. *Its* is a possessive pronoun:

> The government is reassessing *its* spending plan.

It's is a contraction of the words *it is*:

> *It's* snowing outside.

Saw and Seen

Saw and *seen* are both conjugations of the verb *to see*, but they express different verb tenses. *Saw* is used in the simple past tense. *Seen* is the past participle form of *to see* and can be used in all perfect tenses.

> I seen her yesterday.

This sentence is incorrect. Because it expresses a completed event from a specified point in time in the past, it should use simple past tense:

> I *saw* her yesterday.

This sentence uses the correct verb tense. Here's how the past participle is used correctly:

> I *have seen* her before.

The meaning in this sentence is slightly changed to indicate an event from an unspecific time in the past. In this case, present perfect is the appropriate verb tense to indicate an unspecified past experience. Present perfect conjugation is created by combining *to have* + past participle.

Then and Than

Then is generally used as an adverb indicating something that happened next in a sequence or as the result of a conditional situation:

> We parked the car and *then* walked to the restaurant.

> If enough people register for the event, *then* we can begin planning.

Than is a conjunction indicating comparison:

> This watch is more expensive *than* that one.

> The bus departed later *than* I expected.

They're, Their, and There

They're is a contraction of the words *they are*:

> *They're* moving to Ohio next week.

183

Their is a possessive pronoun:

> The baseball players are training for *their* upcoming season.

There can function as multiple parts of speech, but it is most commonly used as an adverb indicating a location:

> Let's go to the concert! Some great bands are playing *there*.

Insure and Ensure

These terms are both verbs. *Insure* means to guarantee something against loss, harm, or damage, usually through an insurance policy that offers monetary compensation:

> The robbers made off with her prized diamond necklace, but luckily it was *insured* for one million dollars.

Ensure means to make sure, to confirm, or to be certain:

> *Ensure* that you have your passport before entering the security checkpoint.

Accept and Except

Accept is a verb meaning to take or agree to something:

> I would like to *accept* your offer of employment.

Except is a preposition that indicates exclusion:

> I've been to every state in America *except* Hawaii.

Affect and Effect

Affect is a verb meaning to influence or to have an impact on something:

> The amount of rainfall during the growing season *affects* the flavor of wine produced from these grapes.

Effect can be used as either a noun or a verb. As a noun, *effect* is synonymous with a result:

> If we implement the changes, what will the *effect* be on our profits?

As a verb, *effect* means to bring about or to make happen:

> In just a few short months, the healthy committee has *effected* real change in school nutrition.

Components of Sentences

Clauses

Clauses contain a subject and a verb. An **independent clause** can function as a complete sentence on its own, but it might also be one component of a longer sentence. **Dependent clauses** cannot stand alone as complete sentences. They rely on independent clauses to complete their meaning. Dependent clauses usually begin with a subordinating conjunction. Independent and dependent clauses are sometimes also referred to as **main clauses** and **subordinate clauses**, respectively. The following structure highlights the differences:

> Apiculturists raise honeybees because they love insects.

Apiculturists raise honeybees is an independent or main clause. The subject is *apiculturists,* and the verb is *raise*. It expresses a complete thought and could be a standalone sentence.

184

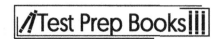

Because they love insects is a dependent or subordinate clause. If it were not attached to the independent clause, it would be sentence fragment. While it contains a subject and verb—*they love*—this clause is dependent because it begins with the subordinate conjunction *because*. Thus, it does not express a complete thought on its own.

Another type of clause is a **relative clause**, and it is sometimes referred to as an **adjective clause** because it gives further description about a noun. A relative clause begins with a **relative pronoun**: *that, which, who, whom, whichever, whomever,* or *whoever.* It may also begin with a **relative adverb**: *where, why,* or *when.* Here's an example of relative clause, functioning as an adjective:

> The strawberries that I bought yesterday are already beginning to spoil.

Here, the relative clause is *that I bought yesterday*; the relative pronoun is *that*. The subject is *I*, and the verb is *bought*. The clause modifies the subject *strawberries* by answering the question, "Which strawberries?" Here's an example of a relative clause with an adverb:

> The tutoring center is a place where students can get help with homework.

The relative clause is *where students can get help with homework*, and it gives more information about a place by describing what kind of place it is. It begins with the relative adverb *where* and contains the noun *students* along with its verb phrase *can get*.

Relative clauses may be further divided into two types: essential or nonessential. **Essential clauses** contain identifying information without which the sentence would lose significant meaning or not make sense. These are also sometimes referred to as **restrictive clauses**. The sentence above contains an example of an essential relative clause. Here is what happens when the clause is removed:

> The tutoring center is a place where students can get help with homework.

> The tutoring center is a place.

Without the relative clause, the sentence loses the majority of its meaning; thus, the clause is essential or restrictive.

Nonessential clauses—also referred to as **non-restrictive clauses**—offer additional information about a noun in the sentence, but they do not significantly control the overall meaning of the sentence. The following example indicates a nonessential clause:

> New York City, which is located in the northeastern part of the country, is the most populated city in America.

> New York City is the most populated city in America.

Even without the relative clause, the sentence is still understandable and continues to communicate its central message about New York City. Thus, it is a nonessential clause.

Punctuation differs between essential and nonessential relative clauses, too. Nonessential clauses are set apart from the sentence using commas whereas essential clauses are not separated with commas. Also, the relative pronoun *that* is generally used for essential clauses, while *which* is used for nonessential clauses. The following examples clarify this distinction:

> *Romeo and Juliet* is my favorite play *that Shakespeare wrote*.

185

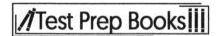

The relative clause *that Shakespeare wrote* contains essential, controlling information about the noun *play*, limiting it to those plays by Shakespeare. Without it, it would seem that *Romeo and Juliet* is the speaker's favorite play out of every play ever written, not simply from Shakespeare's repertoire.

> *Romeo and Juliet, which Shakespeare wrote*, is my favorite play.

Here, the nonessential relative clause—"which Shakespeare wrote"—modifies *Romeo and Juliet*. It doesn't provide controlling information about the play, but simply offers further background details. Thus, commas are needed.

Phrases

Phrases are groups of words that do not contain the subject-verb combination required for clauses. Phrases are classified by the part of speech that begins or controls the phrase.

A **noun phrase** consists of a noun and all its modifiers—adjectives, adverbs, and determiners. Noun phrases can serve many functions in a sentence, acting as subjects, objects, and object complements:

> *The shallow yellow bowl* sits on the top shelf.

> Nina just bought *some incredibly fresh organic produce*.

Prepositional phrases are made up of a preposition and its object. The object of a preposition might be a noun, noun phrase, pronoun, or gerund. Prepositional phrases may function as either an adjective or an adverb:

> Jack picked up the book *in front of him*.

The prepositional phrase *in front of him* acts as an adjective indicating which book Jack picked up.

> The dog ran into the back yard.

The phrase *into the backyard* describes where the dog ran, so it acts as an adverb.

Verb phrases include all of the words in a verb group, even if they are not directly adjacent to each other:

> I *should have woken up* earlier this morning.

> The company **is** now *offering* membership discounts for new enrollers.

This sentence's verb phrase is *is offering*. Even though they are separated by the word *now*, they function together as a single verb phrase.

Structures of Sentences

All sentences contain the same basic elements: a subject and a verb (or **predicate**). The **subject** is who or what the sentence is about; the **verb** describes the subject's action or condition. However, these elements, subjects and verbs, can be combined in different ways. The following graphic describes the different types of sentence structures.

Sentence Structure	Independent Clauses	Dependent Clauses
Simple	1	0
Compound	2 or more	0
Complex	1	1 or more
Compound-Complex	2 or more	1 or more

186

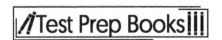

A **simple sentence** expresses a complete thought and consists of one subject and verb combination:

> The children ate pizza.

The subject is *children*. The verb is *ate*.

Either the subject or the verb may be **compound**—that is, it could have more than one element:

> *The children and their parents* ate pizza.

> The children *ate pizza and watched a movie*.

All of these are still simple sentences. Despite having either compound subjects or compound verbs, each sentence still has only one subject and verb combination.

Compound sentences combine two or more simple sentences to form one sentence that has multiple subject-verb combinations:

> *The children ate pizza,* and *their parents watched a movie*.

This structure is comprised of two independent clauses: (1) *the children ate pizza* and (2) *their parents watched a movie*. Compound sentences join different subject-verb combinations using a comma and a coordinating conjunction.

> I called my mom**,** *but* she didn't answer the phone.

> The weather was stormy**,** *so* we canceled our trip to the beach.

A **complex sentence** consists of an independent clause and one or more dependent clauses. Dependent clauses join a sentence using **subordinating conjunctions**. Some examples of subordinating conjunctions are *although, unless, as soon as, since, while, when, because, if,* and *before*.

> I missed class yesterday *because* my mother was ill.

> *Before* traveling to a new country, you need to exchange your money to the local currency.

The order of clauses determines their punctuation. If the dependent clause comes first, it should be separated from the independent clause with a comma. However, if the complex sentence consists of an independent clause followed by a dependent clause, then a comma is not always necessary.

A **compound-complex sentence** can be created by joining two or more independent clauses with at least one dependent clause:

> After the earthquake struck, thousands of homes were destroyed, and many families were left without a place to live.

The first independent clause in the compound structure includes a subordinating clause—*after the earthquake struck*. Thus, the structure is both complex and compound.

Spelling

Spelling might or might not be important to some, or maybe it just doesn't come naturally, but those who are willing to discover some new ideas and consider their benefits can learn to spell better and improve their writing.

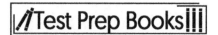

Misspellings reduce a writer's credibility and can create misunderstandings. Spell checkers built into word processors are not a substitute for accuracy. They are neither foolproof nor without error. In addition, a writer's misspelling of one word may also be a word. For example, a writer intending to spell *herd* might accidentally type *s* instead of *d* and unintentionally spell *hers*. Since *hers* is a word, it would not be marked as a misspelling by a spell checker. In short, use spell check, but don't rely on it.

Guidelines for Spelling

Saying and listening to a word serves as the beginning of knowing how to spell it. Keep these subsequent guidelines in mind, remembering there are often exceptions because the English language is replete with them.

Guideline #1: Syllables must have at least one vowel. In fact, every syllable in every English word has a vowel.

- d*o*g
- h*a*yst*a*ck
- *a*nsw*e*r*i*ng
- *a*bstent*iou*s
- s*i*mpl*e*

Guideline #2: The long and short of it. When the vowel has a short vowel sound as in *mad* or *bed,* only the single vowel is needed. If the word has a long vowel sound, add another vowel, either alongside it or separated by a consonant: bed/*bead*; mad/*made.* When the second vowel is separated by two consonants— *madder*—it does not affect the first vowel's sound.

Guideline #3: Suffixes. Refer to the examples listed above.

Guideline #4: Which comes first; the *i* or the *e*? Remember the saying, "*I* before *e* except after *c* or when sounding as *a* as in *neighbor* or *weigh.*" Keep in mind that these are only guidelines and that there are always exceptions to every rule.

Guideline #5: Vowels in the right order. Another helpful rhyme is, "When two vowels go walking, the first one does the talking." When two vowels are in a row, the first one sometimes has a long vowel sound and the other is silent. An example is *team.* This rule is true for about half of the occurrences of two vowels next to each other.

If you have difficulty spelling words, determine a strategy to help. Work on spelling by playing word games like Scrabble or Words with Friends™. Consider using phonics, which is sounding words out by slowly and surely stating each syllable. Try repeating and memorizing spellings as well as picturing words in your head. Try making up silly memory aids. See what works best.

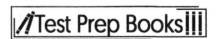

Homophones

Homophones are two or more words that have no particular relationship to one another except their identical pronunciations. Homophones make spelling English words fun and challenging like these:

Common Homophones		
affect, effect	cell, sell	it's, its
allot, a lot	do, due, dew	knew, new
barbecue, barbeque	dual, duel	libel, liable
bite, byte	eminent, imminent	principal, principle
brake, break	flew, flu, flue	their, there, they're
capital, capitol	gauge, gage	to, too, two
cash, cache	holy, wholly	yoke, yolk

Irregular Plurals

Irregular plurals are words that aren't made plural the usual way.

- Most nouns are made plural by adding –s (book*s*, television*s*, skyscraper*s*).

- Most nouns ending in *ch, sh, s, x,* or *z* are made plural by adding –es (church*es*, marsh*es*).

- Most nouns ending in a vowel + *y* are made plural by adding –s (day*s*, toy*s*).

- Most nouns ending in a consonant + *y*, are made plural by the *-y* becoming *-ies* (baby becomes *babies*).

- Most nouns ending in an *o* are made plural by adding –s (piano*s*, photo*s*).

- Some nouns ending in an *o*, though, may be made plural by adding –es (example: potato*es*, volcano*es*), and, of note, there is no known rhyme or reason for this!

- Most nouns ending in an *f* or *fe* are made plural by the *-f* or *-fe* becoming *-ves* (example: wolf becomes *wolves*).

- Some words function as both the singular and plural form of the word (fish, deer).

- Other exceptions include *man* becomes *men, mouse* becomes *mice, goose* becomes *geese,* and *foot* becomes *feet.*

Contractions

The basic rule for making **contractions** is one area of spelling that is pretty straightforward: combine the two words by inserting an apostrophe (') in the space where a letter is omitted. For example, to combine *you* and *are*, drop the *a* and put the apostrophe in its place: *you're.*

> he + is = he's
> you + all = y'all (informal but often misspelled)

Note that *it's*, when spelled with an apostrophe, is always the contraction for *it is*. The possessive form of the word is written without an apostrophe as *its.*

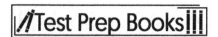
Correcting Misspelled Words

A good place to start looking at commonly misspelled words here is with the word *misspelled*. While it looks peculiar, look at it this way: *mis* (the prefix meaning *wrongly*) + *spelled* = *misspelled*.

Let's look at some commonly misspelled words and see where writers often go wrong with them:

Commonly Misspelled Words					
accept	benign	existence	jewelry	parallel	separate
acceptable	bicycle	experience	judgment	pastime	sergeant
accidentally	brief	extraordinary	library	permissible	similar
accommodate	business	familiar	license	perseverance	supersede
accompany	calendar	February	maintenance	personnel	surprise
acknowledgement	campaign	fiery	maneuver	persuade	symmetry
acquaintance	candidate	finally	mathematics	possess	temperature
acquire	category	forehead	mattress	precede	tragedy
address	cemetery	foreign	millennium	prevalent	transferred
aesthetic	changeable	foremost	miniature	privilege	truly
aisle	committee	forfeit	mischievous	pronunciation	usage
altogether	conceive	glamorous	misspell	protein	valuable
amateur	congratulations	government	mortgage	publicly	vengeance
apparent	courtesy	grateful	necessary	questionnaire	villain
appropriate	deceive	handkerchief	neither	recede	Wednesday
arctic	desperate	harass	nickel	receive	weird
asphalt	discipline	hygiene	niece	recommend	
associate	disappoint	hypocrisy	ninety	referral	
attendance	dissatisfied	ignorance	noticeable	relevant	
auxiliary	eligible	incredible	obedience	restaurant	
available	embarrass	intelligence	occasion	rhetoric	
balloon	especially	intercede	occurrence	rhythm	
believe	exaggerate	interest	omitted	schedule	
beneficial	exceed	irresistible	operate	sentence	

Composition

Forming Paragraphs

A good **paragraph** should have the following characteristics:

- be logical with organized sentences
- have a unified purpose within itself
- use sentences as building blocks
- be a distinct section of a piece of writing

190

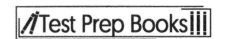

- present a single theme introduced by a topic sentence
- maintain a consistent flow through subsequent, relevant, well-placed sentences
- tell a story of its own or have its own purpose, yet connect with what is written before and after
- enlighten, entertain, and/or inform

Although certainly not set in stone, the length should be a consideration for the reader's sake, not merely for the sake of the topic. When paragraphs are especially short, the reader might experience an irregular, uneven effect; when they're much longer than 250 words, the reader's attention span, and probably their retention, is challenged. While a paragraph can technically be a sentence long, a good rule of thumb is for paragraphs to be at least three sentences long and no more than ten sentence long. An optimal word length is 100 to 250 words.

Coherent Paragraphs

Coherence is simply defined as the quality of being logical and consistent. In order to have coherent paragraphs, therefore, authors must be logical and consistent in their writing, whatever the document might be. Two words are helpful to understanding coherence: flow and relationship. Earlier, transitions were referred to as being the "glue" to put organized thoughts together. Now, let's look at the topic sentence from which flow and relationship originate.

The topic sentence, usually the first in a paragraph, holds the essential features that will be brought forth in the paragraph. Not only is it important because of what it is and contains but also because it is here that authors either grab or lose readers. It also may be the only piece that a reader encounters from that writer, so it is a good idea to summarize and represent ideas accurately.

The coherent paragraph has a logical order. It utilizes transitional words and phrases, parallel sentence structure, clear pronoun references, and reasonable repetition of key words and phrases. Use common sense for repetition. Consider synonyms for variety. Be consistent in verb tense whenever possible.

When writers have accomplished their paragraph's purpose, they prepare it to receive the next. While writing, read the paragraph over, edit, examine, evaluate, and make changes accordingly. Possibly, a paragraph has gone on too long. If that occurs, it needs to be broken up into other paragraphs, or the length should be reduced. If a paragraph didn't fully accomplish its purpose, consider it a chance for revisions. One might simply say, "Ah, that is good."

Main Point of a Paragraph

What is the main point of a paragraph? It is *the* point all of the other important and lesser important points should lead up to, and it should be summed up in the topic sentence.

Sometimes there is a fine line of difference to distinguish between a paragraph's topic sentence and its main point because of their relationship. In fact, they actually might be one and the same. Often, though, they are two separate but closely related aspects of the same paragraph.

Depending upon writers' purposes, they might not fully reveal the topic sentence or the paragraph's main point until the paragraph's conclusion.

Sometimes, while developing paragraphs, authors deviate from the main point, which means they have to delete and rework their materials to stay on point.

191

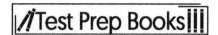

Examining Paragraphs

Throughout this text, composing and combining sentences, using basic grammar skills, employing rules and guidelines, identifying differing points of view, using appropriate context, constructing accurate word usage, and discerning correct punctuation have all been discussed. Whew! The types of sentences, patterns, transitions, and overall structure have been covered as well.

While authors write, thoughts coalesce to form words on "paper" (aka a computer screen). Authors strategically place those thoughts in sentences to give them "voice" in an orderly manner, and then they manipulate them into cohesive sentences for cohesion to express ideas. Like a hunk of modeling clay (thanks to computers, people are no longer bound to erasers and whiteout), sentences can be worked and reworked until they cooperate and say what was originally intended.

Before calling a paragraph complete, identify its main point, making sure that related sentences stay on point. Pose questions such as, "Did I sufficiently develop the main point by the other points pointing to it? Did I say it succinctly enough? Did I give it time to develop? *Is* it developed?"

Let's examine the following two paragraphs, each an example of a movie review. Read them and form a critique.

Example 1: *Eddie the Eagle* is a movie about a struggling athlete. Eddie was crippled at birth. He had a lot of therapy and he had a dream. Eddie trained himself for the Olympics. He went far away to learn how to ski jump. It was hard for him, but he persevered. He got a coach and kept trying. He qualified for the Olympics. He was the only one from Britain who could jump. When he succeeded, they named him, "Eddie the Eagle."

Example 2: The last movie I saw in the theater was *Eddie the Eagle,* a story of extraordinary perseverance inspired by real life events. Eddie was born in England with a birth defect that he slowly but surely overcame, but not without trial and error (not the least of which was his father's perpetual *dis*couragement). In fact, the old man did everything to get him to give up, but Eddie was dogged beyond anyone in the neighborhood; in fact, maybe beyond anyone in the whole town or even the whole world! Eddie, simply, did not know to quit. As he grew up, so did his dream; a strange one, indeed, for someone so unaccomplished: to compete in the Winter Olympics as a ski jumper (which he knew absolutely nothing about). Eddie didn't just keep on dreaming about it. He actually went to Germany and *worked* at it, facing unbelievable odds, defeats, and put-downs by Dad and the other Men in Charge, aka the Olympic decision-makers. Did that stop him? No way! Eddie got a coach and persevered. Then, when he failed, he persevered some more, again and again. You should be able to open up a dictionary, look at the word "persevere," and see a picture of Eddie the Eagle because, when everybody told him he couldn't, he did. The result? He is forever dubbed, "Eddie the Eagle."

Both reviews tell something about the movie *Eddie the Eagle*. Does one motivate the reader to want to see the movie more than the other? Does one just provide a few facts while the other paints a virtual picture of the movie? Does one give a carrot and the other a rib eye steak, mashed potatoes, and chocolate silk pie?

Paragraphs sometimes only give facts. Sometimes that's appropriate and all that is needed. Sometimes, though, writers want to use the blank documents on their computer screens to paint a picture. Writers must "see" the painting come to life. To do so, pick a familiar topic, write a simple sentence, and add to it. Pretend, for instance, there's a lovely view. What does one see? Is it a lake? Try again – picture it as though it were the sea! Visualize a big ship sailing out there. Is it sailing away or approaching? Who is on it? Is it dangerous? Is it night and are there crazy pirates on board? Uh-oh! Did one just jump ship and start swimming toward shore?

Verbal Skills

Verbal Analogies

The questions below ask you to find relationships between words. For each question, select the answer that best completes the meaning of the sentence.

1. Wheel is to truck as:
   a. Foot is to body
   b. Steering wheel is to car
   c. Truck is to road
   d. Head is to body

2. Wire is to electricity as:
   a. Power is to lamp
   b. Pipe is to water
   c. Fire is to heat
   d. Heat is to fire

3. Cow is to milk as:
   a. Horse is to cow
   b. Egg is to chicken
   c. Bee is to honey
   d. Glass is to milk

4. Web is to spider as den is to:
   a. Living room
   b. Eagle
   c. Fox
   d. Dog

5. Sad is to blue as happy is to:
   a. Glad
   b. Yellow
   c. Smiling
   d. Laugh

6. Door is to store as deal is to:
   a. Money
   b. Purchase
   c. Sell
   d. Wheel

193

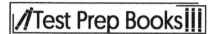
7. Falcon is to mice as giraffe is to
   a. Leaves
   b. Rocks
   c. Antelope
   d. Grasslands

8. Clock is to time as:
   a. Ruler is to length
   b. Jet is to speed
   c. Alarm is to sleep
   d. Drum is to beat

9. Ice is to slippery as rug is to:
   a. Soft
   b. Carpet
   c. Floor
   d. Hard

10. Calf is to cow as foal is to:
    a. Gerbil
    b. Monkey
    c. Horse
    d. Goat

Synonyms

Each of the questions below has one word. The one word is followed by four words or phrases. Please select one answer whose meaning is closest to the word in capital letters.

11. DEDUCE
    a. Explain
    b. Win
    c. Reason
    d. Gamble

12. ELUCIDATE
    a. Learn
    b. Enlighten
    c. Plan
    d. Corroborate

13. VERIFY
    a. Criticize
    b. Change
    c. Teach
    d. Substantiate

14. INSPIRE
    a. Motivate
    b. Impale
    c. Exercise
    d. Patronize

15. MENDACIOUS
    a. Earnest
    b. Bold
    c. Criminal
    d. Liar

16. NOMAD
    a. Munching
    b. Propose
    c. Wanderer
    d. Conscientious

17. MALEVOLENT
    a. Evil
    b. Concerned
    c. Maximum
    d. Cautious

18. PERPLEXED
    a. Annoyed
    b. Vengeful
    c. Injured
    d. Confused

19. LYRICAL
    a. Whimsical
    b. Playful
    c. Fruitful
    d. Expressive

20. BREVITY
    a. Dullness
    b. Dangerous
    c. Brief
    d. Ancient

21. IRATE
    a. Anger
    b. Knowledge
    c. Tired
    d. Confused

22. LUXURIOUS
   a. Faded
   b. Bright
   c. Lavish
   d. Inconsiderate

23. RETORT
   a. Conversation
   b. Jest
   c. Counter
   d. Flexible

24. SUBLIMINAL
   a. Subconscious
   b. Transportation
   c. Underground
   d. Substitute

25. INCITE
   a. Understanding
   b. Illumination
   c. Rally
   d. Judgment

Logic

Answer the following logical questions either "true," "false," or "uncertain" relating to the third statement.

26. Nocturnal animals are active mostly during the night. Squirrels are active mostly during the day. Squirrels are considered nocturnal animals. If the first two statements are true, the third is:
   a. true
   b. false
   c. uncertain

27. Katie runs faster than Celia. Celia runs faster than John. John runs faster than Katie. If the first two statements are true, the third is:
   a. true
   b. false
   c. uncertain

28. Mint is better than strawberry. Chocolate is not as good as mint. Chocolate is better than strawberry. If the first two statements are true, the third is:
   a. true
   b. false
   c. uncertain

29. Cup A contains orange juice. Cup B contains lemonade. Cup C contains milk. If the first two statements are true, the third is:
   a. true
   b. false
   c. uncertain

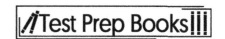

30. Some poems are considered literature. All literature is important. Some poems are important. If the first two statements are true, the third is:
    a. true
    b. false
    c. uncertain

31. Red boxes are heavier than green boxes. Blue boxes are heavier than red boxes. Green boxes are not as heavy as blue boxes. If the first two statements are true, the third is:
    a. true
    b. false
    c. uncertain

32. Some goldfish are red. All goldfish have gold specks. Some goldfish are red with gold specks. If the first two statements are true, the third is:
    a. true
    b. false
    c. uncertain

33. No sports are entertaining. Baseball is a sport. Baseball is not entertaining. If the first two statements are true, the third is:
    a. true
    b. false
    c. uncertain

34. All shampoos contain parabens. All parabens are considered synthetic. Only some shampoos contain synthetic ingredients. If the first two statements are true, the third is:
    a. true
    b. false
    c. uncertain

35. Jordan is not funny. Jordan is a comedian. No comedians are funny. If the first two statements are true, the third is:
    a. true
    b. false
    c. uncertain

Verbal Classifications

In the following questions, one word does not belong with the others. Your answer choice will reflect the word that is the "odd one out."

36. Which word does *not* belong with the others?
    a. Mountain
    b. Canyon
    c. Gorge
    d. Ravine

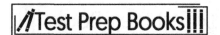

37. Which word does *not* belong with the others?
    a. Bright
    b. Dazzling
    c. Luminous
    d. Lackluster

38. Which word does *not* belong with the others?
    a. Apathetic
    b. Vigorous
    c. Lethargic
    d. Indifferent

39. Which word does *not* belong with the others?
    a. Exuberant
    b. Morose
    c. Festive
    d. Upbeat

40. Which word does *not* belong with the others?
    a. Vacation
    b. Sabbatical
    c. Assignment
    d. Intermission

41. Which word does *not* belong with the others?
    a. Origin
    b. Source
    c. Derivation
    d. Declaration

42. Which word does *not* belong with the others?
    a. Amplify
    b. Development
    c. Evolution
    d. Migration

43. Which word does *not* belong with the others?
    a. Guppy
    b. Trout
    c. Penguin
    d. Swordfish

44. Which word does *not* belong with the others?
    a. Antibiotic
    b. Prescription
    c. Pharmaceutical
    d. Injury

45. Which word does *not* belong with the others?
   a. Blandishment
   b. Fulfillment
   c. Gratification
   d. Contentment

46. Which word does *not* belong with the others?
   a. Tent
   b. Office
   c. House
   d. Camper

47. Which word does *not* belong with the others?
   a. Lamp
   b. Sun
   c. Tree
   d. Firecracker

48. Which word does *not* belong with the others?
   a. Cedar
   b. Maple
   c. Moss
   d. Mahogany

49. Which word does *not* belong with the others?
   a. Distinguished
   b. Exceptional
   c. Phenomenal
   d. Cooperation

50. Which word does *not* belong with the others?
   a. Valley
   b. Stream
   c. River
   d. Ocean

51. Which word does *not* belong with the others?
   a. Farmer
   b. Ranger
   c. Lifeguard
   d. Editor

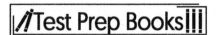

Antonyms

These questions ask you to find the antonym, or the opposite, of the given word. Choose only one answer choice per question.

52. Integral means the opposite of
    a. component
    b. nonessential
    c. parched
    d. tactful

53. Tangible means the opposite of
    a. abstract
    b. spurious
    c. sallow
    d. radical

54. Abandon means the opposite of
    a. clamorous
    b. pensive
    c. wary
    d. restraint

55. Nonchalant means the opposite of
    a. elicit
    b. callous
    c. banal
    d. enthusiastic

56. Latent means the opposite of
    a. impeccable
    b. vanquish
    c. obvious
    d. prosaic

57. Macabre means the opposite of
    a. palpable
    b. cheerful
    c. sanitation
    d. abrupt

58. Audacity means the opposite of
    a. oblivious
    b. refute
    c. timidity
    d. reverence

200

59. Superficial means the opposite of
    a. authentic
    b. pretentious
    c. transient
    d. intrepid

60. Subside means the opposite of
    a. aloof
    b. ruminate
    c. nomadic
    d. develop

Quantitative Skills

Number Series

1. Examine this series: 4, 7, 10, 13, 16 ...

What number should come next?
    a. 18
    b. 19
    c. 21
    d. 23

2. Examine this series: 2, 3, 5, 9, 17 ...

What number should come next?
    a. 21
    b. 27
    c. 29
    d. 33

3. Examine this series: 1, -2, 3, -4, 5 ...

What number should come next?
    a. -6
    b. -5
    c. 6
    d. 7

4. Examine this series: 2, 2, 4, 6, 10, 16 ...

What number should come next?
    a. 18
    b. 20
    c. 22
    d. 26

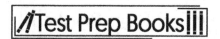

5. Examine this series: 18, 9, 14, 7, 12 …

What number should come next?
   a. 15
   b. 10
   c. 8
   d. 6

6. Examine this series: 2, 4, 8, 16, 32 …

What number should come next?
   a. 54
   b. 40
   c. 64
   d. 36

7. Examine this series: $\frac{1}{2}, \frac{3}{5}, \frac{5}{8}, \frac{7}{11}, \frac{9}{14}$ …

What number should come next?
   a. $\frac{12}{14}$

   b. $\frac{11}{17}$

   c. $\frac{11}{16}$

   d. $\frac{12}{16}$

8. What are the first four terms of the sequence $\left\{ \frac{(-1)^{n+1}}{n^2+5} \right\}_{n=0}^{\infty}$?
   a. $\frac{1}{6}, \frac{1}{9}, \frac{1}{14}, \frac{1}{19}$

   b. $\frac{1}{6}, \frac{-1}{9}, \frac{1}{14}, \frac{-1}{19}$

   c. $\frac{-1}{5}, \frac{1}{6}, \frac{-1}{9}, \frac{1}{14}$

   d. $\frac{1}{5}, \frac{1}{6}, \frac{1}{9}, \frac{1}{14}$

9. Examine this series: 55, 53, 49, 43, 35 …

What number should come next?
   a. 25
   b. 23
   c. 31
   d. 27

10. Examine this series: 144, 121, 100, 81, 64 ...

What number should come next?
    a. 51
    b. 49
    c. 36
    d. 25

11. Examine this series: 14, 11, 21, 18, 28 ...

What number should come next?
    a. 25
    b. 26
    c. 31
    d. 38

12. Examine this series: 5, -15, 45, -135, 405 ...

What number should come next?
    a. 1215
    b. 910
    c. -1215
    d. -910

13. Examine this series: 48, 24, 12, 6, 3 ...

What number should come next?
    a. 1.5
    b. 1
    c. 0
    d. -3

14. Examine this series: 0.5, 0, 0.1, -0.4, -0.3 ...

What number should come next?
    a. -0.8
    b. 0.1
    c. 0.2
    d. -0.2

15. Examine this series: 3, 9, 15, 21, 27 ...

What number should come next?
    a. 29
    b. 31
    c. 33
    d. 37

16. Examine this series: 1.5, 4.5, 13.5, ___, 121.5 ...

What number should fill in the blank?
- a. 29.5
- b. 40.5
- c. 31.5
- d. 35.5

17. Examine this series: 5, 6, 11, 17, 28 ...

What number should come next?
- a. 37
- b. 39
- c. 43
- d. 45

18. Examine this series: 30, 29, 27, ___, 20, 15 ...

What number should fill in the blank?
- a. 25
- b. 24
- c. 23
- d. 22

Geometric Comparison

19. Examine I, II, and III and select the best answer.

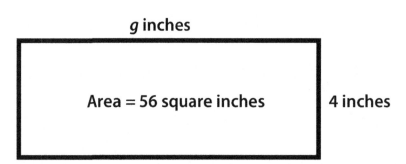

g inches

Area = 56 square inches   4 inches

I. The value of g
II. The length of the base of a triangle with a height of 8 in. and an area of 52 sq. inches
III. The side length of a cube with a volume of 1728 cubic inches

- a. III > II
- b. II < I = III
- c. I > II > III
- d. I > II = III

20. Examine I, II, and III and select the best answer.

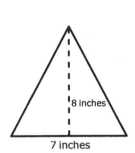
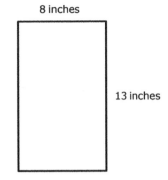

8 inches

13 inches

8 inches

7 inches

     I. 7 times the area of the triangle
     II. 2 times the area of the rectangle
     III. The area of the rectangle plus 3 times the area of the triangle

    a.   I = II = III
    b.   II > I > III
    c.   I > III > II
    d.   III > II = I

21. Examine I, II, and III and select the best answer.

     I. A sphere with a volume of 288π cubic meters
     II. A sphere with a radius of 6 meters
     III. A sphere with a surface area of 144π square meters

    a.   I = II = III
    b.   I > II > III
    c.   I < II < III
    d.   I = II < III

205

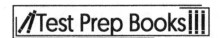

22. Examine I, II, and III and select the best answer.

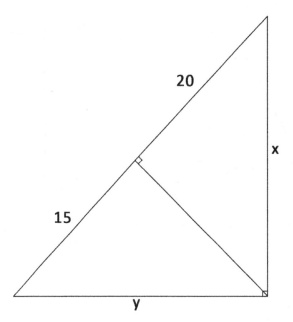

I. In the triangle above, the value of x if $y = 21$ cm.

II. The length of the line drawn on the triangle above that bisects the right angle in the lower right corner and forms a right angle between the 15 and 20 when $y = 21$ cm.

III. The length of a rectangle with a perimeter of 90 cm. that has a length that is 5 cm. longer than three times its width.

a. III > I > II
b. III = I > II
c. I > III > I
d. I > II > III

23. Examine I, II, and III and select the best answer.
   I. The value of x in the image below

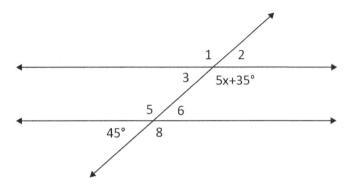

   II. The value of angle z when angle y measures 48° and angle x measures twice the value of angle y

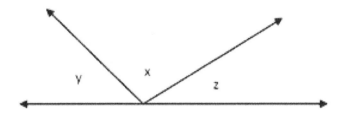

   III. One fourth of the measurement of angle f in the following picture assuming the lines are parallel

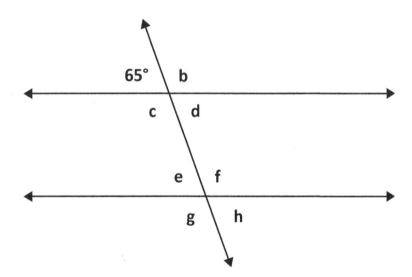

   a.   I =II > III
   b.   II = III > I
   c.   III > II > I
   d.   II > III > I

207

24. Examine I, II, and III and select the best answer.

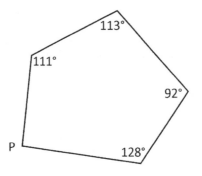

    I. Angle P above
    II. The measure of an angle on a regular pentagon
    III. The measure of an angle on a regular hexagon

a.   I = II > III
b.   II = III > I
c.   III > II > I
d.   II > III > I

25. Examine I, II, and III and select the best answer.

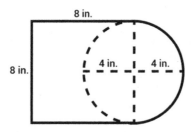

    I. The perimeter of the figure above (Note that the solid outer line is the perimeter.)
    II. The circumference of the entire circle
    III. The perimeter of the entire square minus the radius of the circle in the image above

a.   II < I = III
b.   II < III < I
c.   III < II < I
d.   II = III < I

208

26. Examine I, II, and III and select the best answer.

    I. The total volume of three cylindrical oil barrels that have bases with a diameter of 2 feet and a height of 3 feet.
    II. The volume of a truck bed with a length of 3 feet, a width of 2.5 feet, and a height of 4 feet
    III. The total volume of 8 traffic cones with a radius of 1 foot and a height of 3 feet

  a. II > III > I
  b. I = III > II
  c. II = III < I
  d. II > I > III

27. Examine I, II, and III and select the best answer.

An angle measures 54 degrees.

    I. The measure of a complementary angle
    II. The measure of a supplementary angle
    III. A right angle

  a. II > III > I
  b. I = III > II
  c. II = III < I
  d. II > I > II

Non-Geometric Comparison

28. Examine I, II, and III and select the best answer.

h is an integer in the following mathematical series: 4, h, 19, 39, 79

    I. $\sqrt{(99-18)}$
    II. The value of h
    III. 2^3

  a. I > II > III
  b. I = II = III
  c. I = II > III
  d. II > I > III

29. Examine I, II, and III and select the best answer.

    I. x, if $3x - 4 + 5x = 8 - 10x$
    II. b, if $4b - 12 = -2b$
    III. c, if $\frac{4}{5}c + \frac{2}{3}c = 3$

  a. III < I < II
  b. I < III < II
  c. I < II = III
  d. III > II > I

30. Examine I, II, and III and select the best answer.

    I. $4 \times 7 + (25 - 21)^2 \div 2$
    II. $7^2 - 3 \times (4 + 2) + 15 \div 5$
    III. $9 \times 9 \div 9 + 9 - 9 \div 9$

    a. III > I > II
    b. II > I > III
    c. I > II > III
    d. I = II > III

31. Examine I, II, and III and select the best answer.

    I. The fraction of the bill that the fourth person pays if the first person pays for $\frac{1}{6}$, the second person pays for $\frac{1}{4}$, and the third person pays for $\frac{1}{3}$

    II. The fraction of blue shirts in a closet if it contains just red, blue, and green shirts, and $\frac{1}{3}$ of the shirts are green and $\frac{2}{5}$ are red

    III. $3\frac{2}{3} - 2\frac{4}{5}$

    a. I > III > II
    b. I > II > III
    c. III > II > I
    d. II > III > I

32. Examine I, II, and III and select the best answer.

    I. x, if $\frac{x+2}{x} = 2$
    II. t, if $6t + 4 = 16$
    III. a, if $2a^2 - 4 = 14$, and a is positive

    a. I = II = III
    b. III > II = I
    c. III = II > I
    d. III > II > I

33. Examine I, II, and III and select the best answer.

    I. The value of y when $x = 20$ if the variable y is directly proportional to x and $y = 3$ when $x = 5$.
    II. The value of the sixth number if five of six numbers have a sum of 25 and the average of all six numbers is 6.
    III. The number of workers wearing skirts in an office where there are 50 workers, of whom a total of 60% of the workers are women, and the chances of a woman wearing a skirt is 50%, and no men wear skirts.

    a. III > I > II
    b. III > II > I
    c. III > II = I
    d. I = III > II

34. Examine I, II, and III and select the best answer.

    I. The amount of paint left if Shawna buys $2\frac{1}{2}$ gallons of paint and uses $\frac{1}{3}$ of it on the first day

    II. The amount of milk Tom drank if he had $\frac{1}{3}$ of a gallon Tuesday, $\frac{1}{5}$ of a gallon Wednesday, and $\frac{3}{4}$ of a gallon this morning.

    III. $\frac{2}{5}$ of 4 gallons

  a.   III = I > II
  b.   III > I > II
  c.   I > II > III
  d.   I > III > II

35. Examine I, II, and III and select the best answer.

A data set is comprised of the following values: 30, 33, 33, 26, 27, 32, 33, 35, 29, 27

    I. Mean of the data set
    II. Median of the data set
    III. Mode of the data set

  a.   I > II > III
  b.   III > II > I
  c.   III > II = I
  d.   II < III = I

Number Manipulation

36. Simplify:

$$\frac{4a^{-1}b^3}{a^4b^{-2}} \times \frac{3a}{b}$$

  a. $12a^3b^5$

  b. $12\frac{b^4}{a^4}$

  c. $\frac{12}{a^4}$

  d. $7\frac{b^4}{a}$

37. What are the zeros of the function: $f(x) = x^3 + 4x^2 + 4x$?
  a.   -2
  b.   0, -2
  c.   2
  d.   0, 2

38. $(2x - 4y)^2 =$
    a. $4x^2 - 16xy + 16y^2$
    b. $4x^2 - 8xy + 16y^2$
    c. $4x^2 - 16xy - 16y^2$
    d. $2x^2 - 8xy + 8y^2$

39. If x is not zero, then $\frac{3}{x} + \frac{5u}{2x} - \frac{u}{4} =$
    a. $\frac{12 + 10u - ux}{4x}$

    b. $\frac{3 + 5u - ux}{x}$

    c. $\frac{12x + 10u + ux}{4x}$

    d. $\frac{12 + 10u - u}{4x}$

40. What is the product of the following expression?

$$(4x - 8)(5x^2 + x + 6)$$

    a. $20x^3 - 36x^2 + 16x - 48$
    b. $6x^3 - 41x^2 + 12x + 15$
    c. $20x^4 + 11x^2 - 37x - 12$
    d. $2x^3 - 11x^2 - 32x + 20$

41. How could the following equation be factored to find the zeros?

$$y = x^3 - 3x^2 - 4x$$

    a. $0 = x^2(x - 4), x = 0, 4$
    b. $0 = 3x(x + 1)(x + 4), x = 0, -1, -4$
    c. $0 = x(x + 1)(x + 6), x = 0, -1, -6$
    d. $0 = x(x + 1)(x - 4), x = 0, -1, 4$

42. What is the simplified quotient of $\frac{5x^3}{3x^2y} \div \frac{25}{3y^9}$?
    a. $\frac{125x}{9y^{10}}$

    b. $\frac{x}{5y^8}$

    c. $\frac{5}{xy^8}$

    d. $\frac{xy^8}{5}$

43. What is the solution for the following equation?

$$\frac{x^2 + x - 30}{x - 5} = 11$$

    a. $x = -6$
    b. There is no solution.
    c. $x = 16$
    d. $x = 5$

44. Mom's car drove 72 miles in 90 minutes. How fast did she drive in feet per second?
    a. 0.8 feet per second
    b. 48.9 feet per second
    c. 0.009 feet per second
    d. 70.4 feet per second

45. How do you solve $V = lwh$ for h?
    a. $lwV = h$

    b. $h = \dfrac{V}{lw}$

    c. $h = \dfrac{Vl}{w}$

    d. $h = \dfrac{Vw}{l}$

46. If Sarah reads at an average rate of 21 pages in 4 nights, how long will it take her to read 140 pages?
    a. 6 nights
    b. 26 nights
    c. 8 nights
    d. 27 nights

47. The phone bill is calculated each month using the equation $c = 50g + 75$. The cost of the phone bill per month is represented by c, and g represents the gigabytes of data used that month. What is the value and interpretation of the slope of this equation?
    a. 75 dollars per day
    b. 75 gigabytes per day
    c. 50 dollars per day
    d. 50 dollars per gigabyte

48. What is the y-intercept for $y = x^2 + 3x - 4$?
    a. $y = 1$
    b. $y = -4$
    c. $y = 3$
    d. $y = 4$

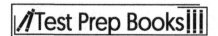
49. On Monday, Robert mopped the floor in 4 hours. On Tuesday, he did it in 3 hours. If on Monday, his average rate of mopping was p sq. ft. per hour, what was his average rate on Tuesday?

    a. $\frac{4}{3} p$ sq. ft. per hour

    b. $\frac{3}{4} p$ sq. ft. per hour

    c. $\frac{5}{4} p$ sq. ft. per hour

    d. $p + 1$ sq. ft. per hour

50. Which of the following is NOT a way to write 40 percent of N?

    a. $(0.4)N$

    b. $\frac{2}{5}N$

    c. $40N$

    d. $\frac{4}{10}N$

51. Which is closest to 17.8×9.9?

    a. 140
    b. 180
    c. 200
    d. 350

52. If $\frac{5}{2} \div \frac{1}{3} = n$, then n is between:

    a. 5 and 7
    b. 7 and 9
    c. 9 and 11
    d. 3 and 5

Reading

Comprehension

The next six questions are based on the following passage:

What's About to Happen to Mr. Button?

As long ago as 1860 it was the proper thing to be born at home. At present, so I am told, the high gods of medicine have decreed that the first cries of the young shall be uttered upon the anesthetic air of a hospital, preferably a fashionable one. So young Mr. and Mrs. Roger Button were fifty years ahead of style when they decided, one day in the summer of 1860, that their first baby should be born in a hospital. Whether this anachronism had any bearing upon the astonishing history I am about to set down will never be known.

I shall tell you what occurred, and let you judge for yourself.

The Roger Buttons held an enviable position, both social and financial, in ante-bellum Baltimore. They were related to the This Family and the That Family, which, as every Southerner knew, entitled them to membership in that enormous peerage which largely populated the Confederacy.

214

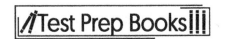

This was their first experience with the charming old custom of having babies—Mr. Button was naturally nervous. He hoped it would be a boy so that he could be sent to Yale College in Connecticut, at which institution Mr. Button himself had been known for four years by the somewhat obvious nickname of "Cuff."

On the September morning consecrated to the enormous event he arose nervously at six o'clock, dressed himself, adjusted an impeccable stock, and hurried forth through the streets of Baltimore to the hospital, to determine whether the darkness of the night had borne in new life upon its bosom.

When he was approximately a hundred yards from the Maryland Private Hospital for Ladies and Gentlemen he saw Doctor Keene, the family physician, descending the front steps, rubbing his hands together with a washing movement—as all doctors are required to do by the unwritten ethics of their profession.

Mr. Roger Button, the president of Roger Button & Co., Wholesale Hardware, began to run toward Doctor Keene with much less dignity than was expected from a Southern gentleman of that picturesque period. "Doctor Keene!" he called. "Oh, Doctor Keene!"

The doctor heard him, faced around, and stood waiting, a curious expression settling on his harsh, medicinal face as Mr. Button drew near.

"What happened?" demanded Mr. Button, as he came up in a gasping rush. "What was it? How is she? A boy? Who is it? What—"

"Talk sense!" said Doctor Keene sharply. He appeared somewhat irritated.

"Is the child born?" begged Mr. Button.

Doctor Keene frowned. "Why, yes, I suppose so—after a fashion." Again he threw a curious glance at Mr. Button.

Excerpt from *The Curious Case of Benjamin Button*, F. S. Fitzgerald, 1922

1. What major event is about to happen in this story?
   a. Mr. Button is about to go to a funeral.
   b. Mr. Button's wife is about to have a baby.
   c. Mr. Button is getting ready to go to the doctor's office.
   d. Mr. Button is about to go shopping for new clothes.

2. What kind of tone does the above passage have?
   a. Nervous and excited
   b. Sad and angry
   c. Shameful and confused
   d. Grateful and joyous

3. What is the meaning of the word "consecrated" in paragraph 4?
   a. Numbed
   b. Chained
   c. Dedicated
   d. Moved

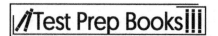

4. What does the author mean to do by adding the following description?

> rubbing his hands together with a washing movement—as all doctors are required to do by the unwritten ethics of their profession.

  a. Suggest that Mr. Button is tired of the doctor
  b. Try to explain the details of the doctor's profession
  c. Hint to readers that the doctor is an unethical man
  d. Give readers a visual picture of what the doctor is doing

5. Which of the following best describes the development of this passage?
  a. It starts in the middle of a narrative in order to transition smoothly to a conclusion.
  b. It is a chronological narrative from beginning to end.
  c. The sequence of events is backwards—we go from future events to past events.
  d. It introduces the setting of the story and its characters.

6. Which of the following is an example of an imperative sentence?
  a. "Oh, Doctor Keene!"
  b. "Talk sense!"
  c. "Is the child born?"
  d. "Why, yes, I suppose so—"

Questions 7-12 are based on the following passage:

Death or Freedom?

Knowing that Mrs. Mallard was afflicted with heart trouble, great care was taken to break to her as gently as possible the news of her husband's death.

It was her sister Josephine who told her, in broken sentences; veiled hints that revealed in half concealing. Her husband's friend Richards was there, too, near her. It was he who had been in the newspaper office when intelligence of the railroad disaster was received, with Brently Mallard's name leading the list of "killed." He had only taken the time to assure himself of its truth by a second telegram, and had hastened to forestall any less careful, less tender friend in bearing the sad message.

She did not hear the story as many women have heard the same, with a paralyzed inability to accept its significance. She wept at once, with sudden, wild abandonment, in her sister's arms. When the storm of grief had spent itself she went away to her room alone. She would have no one follow her.

There stood, facing the open window, a comfortable, roomy armchair. Into this she sank, pressed down by a physical exhaustion that haunted her body and seemed to reach into her soul.

She could see in the open square before her house the tops of trees that were all aquiver with the new spring life. The delicious breath of rain was in the air. In the street below a peddler was crying his wares. The notes of a distant song which some one was singing reached her faintly, and countless sparrows were twittering in the eaves.

There were patches of blue sky showing here and there through the clouds that had met and piled one above the other in the west facing her window.

216

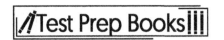

She sat with her head thrown back upon the cushion of the chair, quite motionless, except when a sob came up into her throat and shook her, as a child who has cried itself to sleep continues to sob in its dreams.

She was young, with a fair, calm face, whose lines bespoke repression and even a certain strength. But now there was a dull stare in her eyes, whose gaze was fixed away off yonder on one of those patches of blue sky. It was not a glance of reflection, but rather indicated a suspension of intelligent thought.

There was something coming to her and she was waiting for it, fearfully. What was it? She did not know; it was too subtle and elusive to name. But she felt it, creeping out of the sky, reaching toward her through the sounds, the scents, the color that filled the air.

Now her bosom rose and fell tumultuously. She was beginning to recognize this thing that was approaching to possess her, and she was striving to beat it back with her will—as powerless as her two white slender hands would have been. When she abandoned herself a little whispered word escaped her slightly parted lips. She said it over and over under her breath: "free, free, free!" The vacant stare and the look of terror that had followed it went from her eyes. They stayed keen and bright. Her pulses beat fast, and the coursing blood warmed and relaxed every inch of her body.

She did not stop to ask if it were or were not a monstrous joy that held her. A clear and exalted perception enabled her to dismiss the suggestion as trivial. She knew that she would weep again when she saw the kind, tender hands folded in death; the face that had never looked save with love upon her, fixed and gray and dead. But she saw beyond that bitter moment a long procession of years to come that would belong to her absolutely. And she opened and spread her arms out to them in welcome.

Excerpt from *The Story of an Hour*, Kate Chopin, 1894

7. The passage is told in which of the following points of view?
    a. First person
    b. Second person
    c. Third person omniscient
    d. Third person limited

8. What kind of irony are readers presented with in this story?
    a. The way Mrs. Mallard reacted to her husband's death
    b. The way in which Mr. Mallard died
    c. The way in which the news of her husband's death was presented to Mrs. Mallard
    d. The way in which nature is compared with death in the story

9. What is the meaning of the word *elusive* in paragraph 9?
    a. Horrible
    b. Indefinable
    c. Quiet
    d. Joyful

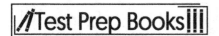

10. What is the best summary of the passage above?
   a. Mr. Mallard, a soldier during World War I, is killed by the enemy and leaves his wife widowed.
   b. Mrs. Mallard understands the value of friendship when her friends show up for her after her husband's death.
   c. Mrs. Mallard combats mental illness daily and will perhaps be sent to a mental institution soon.
   d. Mrs. Mallard, a newly widowed woman, finds unexpected relief in her husband's death.

11. What is the tone of this story?
   a. Confused
   b. Joyful
   c. Depressive
   d. All of the above

12. What is the meaning of the word *tumultuously* in paragraph 10?
   a. Orderly
   b. Unashamedly
   c. Violently
   d. Calmly

Question 13 is based on the following passage:

Which Statement is Correct?

In 2015, 28 countries, including Estonia, Portugal, Slovenia, and Latvia, scored significantly higher than the United States on standardized high school math tests. In the 1960s, the United States consistently ranked first in the world. Today, the United States spends more than $800 billion on education, which exceeds the next highest country by more than $600 billion. The United States also leads the world in spending per school-aged child by an enormous margin.

13. If the statements above are true, which of the following statements must be correct?
   a. Outspending other countries on education has benefits beyond standardized math tests.
   b. The United States' education system is corrupt and broken.
   c. The standardized math tests are not representative of American academic prowess.
   d. Spending more money does not guarantee success on standardized math tests.

Questions 14-17 are based on the following passage:

This article discusses the famous poet and playwright William Shakespeare.

Who Wrote Shakespeare's Plays?

People who argue that William Shakespeare is not responsible for the plays attributed to his name are known as anti-Stratfordians (from the name of Shakespeare's birthplace, Stratford-upon-Avon). The most common anti-Stratfordian claim is that William Shakespeare simply was not educated enough or from a high enough social class to have written plays overflowing with references to such a wide range of subjects like history, the classics, religion, and international culture. William Shakespeare was the son of a glove-maker, he only had a basic grade-school education, and he never set foot outside of England—so how could he have produced plays of such sophistication and imagination? How could he have written in such detail about historical figures and events, or about different cultures and locations around Europe? According to anti-Stratfordians, the depth of knowledge contained in Shakespeare's plays suggests a well-traveled writer from a wealthy

218

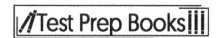

background with a university education, not a countryside writer like Shakespeare. But in fact, there is not much substance to such speculation, and most anti-Stratfordian arguments can be refuted with a little background about Shakespeare's time and upbringing.

First of all, those who doubt Shakespeare's authorship often point to his common birth and brief education as stumbling blocks to his writerly genius. Although it is true that Shakespeare did not come from a noble class, his father was a very *successful* glove-maker and his mother was from a very wealthy landowning family—so while Shakespeare may have had a country upbringing, he was certainly from a well-off family and would have been educated accordingly. Also, even though he did not attend university, grade-school education in Shakespeare's time was actually quite rigorous and exposed students to classic drama through writers like Seneca and Ovid. It is not unreasonable to believe that Shakespeare received a very solid foundation in poetry and literature from his early schooling.

Next, anti-Stratfordians tend to question how Shakespeare could write so extensively about countries and cultures he had never visited before. For instance, several of his most famous works like *Romeo and Juliet* and *The Merchant of Venice* were set in Italy, which is located on the opposite side of Europe from England. But again, this criticism does not hold up under scrutiny. For one thing, Shakespeare was living in London, a bustling metropolis of international trade, the most populous city in England, and a political and cultural hub of Europe. In the daily crowds of people, Shakespeare would certainly have been able to meet travelers from other countries and hear firsthand accounts of life in their home country. And, in addition to the influx of information from world travelers, this was also the age of the printing press. This jump in technology made it possible to print and circulate books much more easily than in the past. This also facilitated a freer flow of information across different countries, allowing people to read about life and ideas from all over Europe. One needn't travel the continent in order to learn and write about its different cultures.

14. Which sentence best captures the author's thesis?
   a. People who argue that William Shakespeare is not responsible for the plays attributed to his name are known as anti-Stratfordians.
   b. But in fact, there is not much substance to such speculation, and most anti-Stratfordian arguments can be refuted with a little background about Shakespeare's time and upbringing.
   c. It is not unreasonable to believe that Shakespeare received a very solid foundation in poetry and literature from his early schooling.
   d. Next, anti-Stratfordians tend to question how Shakespeare could write so extensively about countries and cultures he had never visited before.

15. In the first paragraph, "How could he have written in such detail about historical figures and events, or about different cultures and locations around Europe?" is an example of which of the following?
   a. Hyperbole
   b. Onomatopoeia
   c. Rhetorical question
   d. Appeal to authority

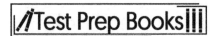

16. How does the author respond to the claim that Shakespeare was not well-educated because he did not attend university?
    a. By insisting upon Shakespeare's natural genius
    b. By explaining grade-school curriculum in Shakespeare's time
    c. By comparing Shakespeare with other uneducated writers of his time
    d. By pointing out that Shakespeare's wealthy parents probably paid for private tutors

17. The word *bustling* in the third paragraph most nearly means which of the following?
    a. Busy
    b. Foreign
    c. Expensive
    d. Undeveloped

Questions 18-23 are based on the following passage:

This article discusses NASA technology.

What Is Spinoff Technology?

When researchers and engineers undertake a large-scale scientific project, they may end up making discoveries and developing technologies that have far wider uses than originally intended. This is especially true at NASA, one of the most influential and innovative scientific organizations in America. NASA spinoff technology refers to innovations originally developed for NASA space projects that are now used in a wide range of different commercial fields. Many consumers are unaware that products they are buying are based on NASA research! Spinoff technology proves that it is worthwhile to invest in scientific research because it could enrich people's lives in unexpected ways.

The first spinoff technology worth mentioning is baby food. In space, where astronauts have limited access to fresh food and fewer options with their daily meals, malnutrition is a serious concern. Consequently, NASA researchers were looking for ways to enhance the nutritional value of astronauts' food. Scientists found that a certain type of algae could be added to food to improve the food's neurological benefits. When experts in the commercial food industry learned of this algae's potential to boost brain health, they were quick to begin their own research. The nutritional substance from algae then developed into a product called life's DHA, which can be found in over 90 percent of infant food sold in America.

Another intriguing example of a spinoff technology can be found in fashion. People who are always dropping their sunglasses may have invested in a pair of sunglasses with scratch-resistant lenses, which are made of glass that is impossible to scratch, even when dropped on an abrasive surface. This innovation is incredibly advantageous for people who are clumsy, but most shoppers don't know that this technology was originally developed by NASA. Scientists first created scratch-resistant glass to help protect costly and crucial equipment from getting scratched in space, especially the helmet visors in space suits. However, sunglass companies later realized that this technology could be profitable for their products, and they licensed the technology from NASA.

18. What is the main purpose of this article?
    a. To advise consumers to do more research before making a purchase
    b. To persuade readers to support NASA's research
    c. To tell a narrative about the history of space technology
    d. To define and describe instances of spinoff technology

This material is provided for exam preparation purposes only and does not indicate an endorsement of any specific scientific, political, or religious point of view. © TPB Publishing. You have been licensed one copy of this document for personal use only. Any other reproduction or redistribution is strictly prohibited. All rights reserved.

19. What is the organizational structure of this article?
    a. A general definition followed by more specific examples
    b. A general opinion followed by supporting evidence
    c. An important moment in history followed by chronological details
    d. A popular misconception followed by counterevidence

20. Why did NASA scientists research algae?
    a. They already knew algae was healthy for babies.
    b. They were interested in how to grow food in space.
    c. They were looking for ways to add health benefits to food.
    d. They hoped to use it to protect expensive research equipment.

21. What does the word *neurological* mean in the second paragraph?
    a. Related to the body
    b. Related to the brain
    c. Related to vitamins
    d. Related to technology

22. Why does the author mention space suit helmets?
    a. To give an example of astronaut fashion
    b. To explain where sunglasses got their shape from
    c. To explain how astronauts protect their eyes
    d. To give an example of valuable space equipment

23. Which statement would the author probably NOT agree with?
    a. Consumers don't always know the history of the products they are buying.
    b. Sometimes new innovations have unexpected applications.
    c. It is difficult to make money from scientific research.
    d. Space equipment is often very expensive.

Questions 24-28 are based on the following passage:

How Can We Honor Them?

Four score and seven years ago our fathers brought forth on this continent, a new nation, conceived in Liberty, and dedicated to the proposition that all men are created equal.

Now we are engaged in a great civil war, testing whether that nation, or any nation so conceived and so dedicated, can long endure. We are met on a great battle-field of that war. We have come to dedicate a portion of that field, as a final resting place for those who here gave their lives that that nation might live. It is altogether fitting and proper that we should do this.

But, in a larger sense, we cannot dedicate—we cannot consecrate—we cannot hallow—this ground. The brave men, living and dead, who struggled here, have consecrated it, far above our poor power to add or detract. The world will little note, nor long remember what we say here, but it can never forget what they did here. It is for us the living, rather, to be dedicated here to the unfinished work which they who fought here have thus far so nobly advanced. It is rather for us to be here dedicated to the great task remaining before us—that from these honored dead we take increased devotion to that cause for which they gave the last full measure of devotion—that we here highly resolve that these dead shall not have died in vain—that this nation, under God, shall

221

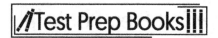

have a new birth of freedom—and that government of the people, by the people, for the people, shall not perish from the earth.

Excerpt from an adaptation of Abraham Lincoln's *Address Delivered at the Dedication of the Cemetery at Gettysburg,* November 19, 1863

24. The best description for the phrase "Four score and seven years ago" is:
    a. A unit of measurement
    b. A period of time
    c. A literary movement
    d. A statement of political reform

25. What is the setting of this text?
    a. A battleship off of the coast of France
    b. A desert plain on the Sahara Desert
    c. A battlefield in a North American town
    d. The residence of Abraham Lincoln

26. Which war is Abraham Lincoln referring to in the following sentence?

    Now we are engaged in a great civil war, testing whether that nation, or any nation so conceived and so dedicated, can long endure.

    a. World War I
    b. The War of Spanish Succession
    c. World War II
    d. The American Civil War

27. What message is the speaker trying to convey through this address?
    a. The audience should perpetuate the ideals of freedom that the soldiers died fighting for.
    b. The audience should honor the dead by establishing an annual memorial service.
    c. The audience should form a militia that would overturn the current political structure.
    d. The audience should forget the lives that were lost and discredit the soldiers.

28. What is the effect of Lincoln's statement in the following passage?

    But, in a larger sense, we cannot dedicate—we cannot consecrate—we cannot hallow—this ground. The brave men, living and dead, who struggled here, have consecrated it, far above our poor power to add or detract.

    a. His comparison emphasizes the great sacrifice of the soldiers who fought in the war.
    b. His comparison serves as a reminder of the inadequacies of his audience.
    c. His comparison serves as a catalyst for guilt and shame among audience members.
    d. His comparison suggests that the dedication ceremony was inappropriate.

Questions 29-30 are based on the following passage:

To Whom It May Concern:

I'm writing in regard to the Writer/Producer position at Shadow Heat. I graduated with my MA degree in English in May 2016 at the University of Texas, where I taught technical writing and writing arguments for my fellowship. My years taking and teaching English courses have enabled

222

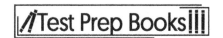

me to develop strong writing skills, which I believe will contribute greatly to the position in question.

Although a work in progress, my website, linked below, features technical writing, graphic design, blog writing, and creative writing samples. My passion for using writing to connect with a specific audience is demonstrated by my various publications as well as my degrees, which focus heavily on academic and creative writing. I would love to write for your company and hope you'll consider me for this position.

I'm highly motivated, carrying energy and creativity into my work. My nine years' experience in higher education enables me to adapt to changing ideals and trends while also maintaining personal values. I hope that you'll consider me for this position. I look forward to hearing from you!

Thanks!

29. What type of writing is this passage?
    a. A how-to document on teaching
    b. A consumer email to a corporation
    c. A cover letter for a resume
    d. A memo concerning employees in the workplace

30. Which of the following is correct?
    a. The writer of the letter is a writer/producer at Shadow Heat.
    b. The writer of the letter has a master's degree in English.
    c. The writer of the letter has ten years' experience in higher education.
    d. The writer of the letter is applying to be a website designer.

Questions 31-33 are based on the following passage:

Who Was George Washington?

George Washington emerged out of the American Revolution as an unlikely champion of liberty. On June 14, 1775, the Second Continental Congress created the Continental Army, and John Adams, serving in the Congress, nominated Washington to be its first commander. Washington had fought under the British during the French and Indian War, and his experience and prestige proved instrumental to the American war effort. Washington provided invaluable leadership, training, and strategy during the Revolutionary War. He emerged from the war as the embodiment of liberty and freedom from tyranny.

After vanquishing the heavily favored British forces, Washington could have pronounced himself the autocratic leader of the former colonies without any opposition, but he famously refused and returned to his Mount Vernon plantation. His restraint proved his commitment to the fledgling state's republicanism. Washington was later unanimously elected as the first American president. But it is Washington's farewell address that cemented his legacy as a visionary worthy of study.

In 1796, President Washington issued his farewell address by public letter. Washington enlisted his good friend, Alexander Hamilton, in drafting his most famous address. The letter expressed Washington's faith in the Constitution and rule of law. He encouraged his fellow Americans to put aside partisan differences and establish a national union. Washington warned Americans against meddling in foreign affairs and entering military alliances. Additionally, he stated his opposition to national political parties, which he considered partisan and counterproductive.

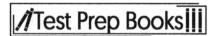

Americans would be wise to remember Washington's farewell, especially during presidential elections, when politics hit a fever pitch. They might want to question the political institutions that were not planned by the Founding Fathers, such as the nomination process and political parties themselves.

31. Which of the following statements is logically based on the information contained in the passage above?
   a. George Washington's background as a wealthy landholder directly led to his faith in equality, liberty, and democracy.
   b. George Washington would have opposed America's involvement in the Second World War.
   c. George Washington would not have been able to write as great a farewell address without the assistance of Alexander Hamilton.
   d. George Washington would probably not approve of modern political parties.

32. Which of the following is the best description of the author's purpose in writing this passage about George Washington?
   a. To inform American voters about a Founding Father's sage advice on a contemporary issue and explain its applicability to modern times
   b. To introduce George Washington to readers as a historical figure worthy of study
   c. To note that George Washington was more than a famous military hero
   d. To convince readers that George Washington is a hero of republicanism and liberty

33. In which of the following materials would the author be the most likely to include this passage?
   a. A history textbook
   b. An obituary
   c. A fictional story
   d. A newspaper editorial

Questions 34-38 are based on the following passage:

Who First Came to the New World?

Christopher Columbus is often credited with discovering America. This is a matter of perspective; America was unknown to fifteenth-century Europe, but bear in mind that the places he "discovered" were already filled with people who had been living there for centuries. What's more, Christopher Columbus was not the first European explorer to reach the Americas! Rather, it was Leif Erikson who first came to the New World and contacted the natives nearly 500 years before Christopher Columbus.

Leif Erikson, the son of Erik the Red (a famous Viking outlaw and explorer in his own right), was born in either 970 or 980, depending on which historian you read. His own family, though, did not raise Leif, which was a Viking tradition. Instead, one of Erik's prisoners taught Leif reading and writing, languages, sailing, and weaponry. At age 12, Leif was considered a man and returned to his family. He killed a man during a dispute shortly after his return, and the council banished the Erikson clan to Greenland.

In 999, Leif left Greenland and traveled to Norway, where he would serve as a guard to King Olaf Tryggvason. It was there that he became a convert to Christianity. Leif later tried to return home with the intention of taking supplies and spreading Christianity to Greenland, but his ship was blown off course and he arrived in a strange new land: present-day Newfoundland, Canada.

224

When he finally returned to his adopted homeland of Greenland, Leif consulted with a merchant who had also seen the shores of this previously unknown land. The son of the legendary Viking explorer then gathered a crew of 35 men and set sail. Leif became the first European to set foot in the New World as he explored present-day Baffin Island and Labrador, Canada. His crew called the land Vinland since it was plentiful with grapes.

During their time in present-day Newfoundland, Leif's expedition made contact with the natives, whom they referred to as Skraelings (which translates to "wretched ones" in Norse). There are several secondhand accounts of their meetings. Some contemporaries described trade between the peoples. Other accounts describe clashes where the Skraelings defeated the Viking explorers with long spears, while still others claim the Vikings dominated the natives. Regardless of the circumstances, it seems that the Vikings made contact of some kind. This happened around the year 1000, nearly five hundred years before Columbus famously sailed the ocean blue.

Eventually, in 1003, Leif set sail for home and arrived at Greenland with a ship full of timber.

In 1020, 17 years later, the legendary Viking died. Many believe that Leif Erikson should receive more credit for his contributions in exploring the New World.

34. Which of the following best describes how the author generally presents the information?
   a. Chronological order
   b. Comparison-contrast
   c. Cause-effect
   d. Conclusion-premises

35. Which of the following is an opinion, rather than a historical fact, expressed by the author?
   a. Leif Erikson was definitely the son of Erik the Red; however, historians debate the year of his birth.
   b. Leif Erikson's crew called the land Vinland since it was plentiful with grapes.
   c. Leif Erikson deserves more credit for his contributions in exploring the New World.
   d. Leif Erikson explored the Americas nearly 500 years before Christopher Columbus.

36. Which of the following most accurately describes the author's main conclusion?
   a. Leif Erikson is a legendary Viking explorer.
   b. Leif Erikson deserves more credit for exploring America hundreds of years before Columbus.
   c. Spreading Christianity motivated Leif Erikson's expeditions more than any other factor.
   d. Leif Erikson contacted the natives nearly five hundred years before Columbus.

37. Which of the following best describes the author's intent in the passage?
   a. To entertain
   b. To inform
   c. To alert
   d. To suggest

38. Which of the following can be logically inferred from the passage?
   a. The Vikings disliked exploring the New World.
   b. Leif Erikson's banishment from Iceland led to his exploration of present-day Canada.
   c. Leif Erikson never shared his stories of exploration with the King of Norway.
   d. Historians have difficulty definitively pinpointing events in the Vikings' history.

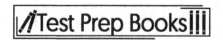

Questions 39-40 are based on the following passage:

Why Should I Stop Smoking?

Smoking tobacco products is terribly destructive. A single cigarette contains over 4,000 chemicals, including 43 known carcinogens and 400 deadly toxins. Some of the most dangerous ingredients include tar, carbon monoxide, formaldehyde, ammonia, arsenic, and DDT. Smoking can cause numerous types of cancer, including throat, mouth, nasal cavity, esophageal, gastric, pancreatic, renal, bladder, and cervical cancer.

Cigarettes contain a drug called nicotine, one of the most addictive substances known. Addiction is defined as a compulsion to seek the substance despite negative consequences. According to the National Institute on Drug Abuse, nearly 35 million smokers expressed a desire to quit smoking in 2015; however, more than 85 percent of those addicts will not achieve their goal. Almost all smokers regret picking up that first cigarette. You would be wise to learn from their mistake if you have not yet started smoking.

According to the US Department of Health and Human Services, 16 million people in the United States presently suffer from a smoking-related condition, and nearly nine million suffer from a serious smoking-related illness. According to the Centers for Disease Control and Prevention (CDC), tobacco products cause nearly six million deaths per year. This number is projected to rise to over eight million deaths by 2030. Smokers, on average, die ten years earlier than their nonsmoking peers.

In the United States, local, state, and federal governments typically tax tobacco products, which leads to high prices. Nicotine addicts sometimes pay more for a pack of cigarettes than for a few gallons of gas. Additionally, smokers tend to stink. The smell of smoke is all-consuming and creates a pervasive nastiness. Smokers also risk staining their teeth and fingers with yellow residue from the tar.

Smoking is deadly, expensive, and socially unappealing. Clearly, smoking is not worth the risks.

39. Which of the following best describes the passage?
    a. Narrative
    b. Persuasive
    c. Expository
    d. Technical

40. Which of the following statements most accurately summarizes the passage?
    a. Tobacco is less healthy than many alternatives.
    b. Tobacco is deadly, expensive, and socially unappealing, and smokers would be much better off kicking the addiction.
    c. In the United States, local, state, and federal governments typically tax tobacco products, which leads to high prices.
    d. Tobacco products shorten smokers' lives by ten years and kill more than six million people per year.

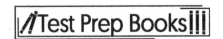

Vocabulary

Select the word or phrase that most correctly completes the sentence.

41. When the baseball game was over, the first thing Jackson did was run towards the dugout to grab his water bottle to relieve his _____ throat.
    a. humid
    b. scorched
    c. parched
    d. dusty

42. Driving across the United States, the two friends became _____ each time they arrived in a new state. They shared many good memories on that trip they would remember for the rest of their lives.
    a. closer
    b. distant
    c. suffering
    d. irritable

43. After Kira wrote her first book, she _____ her fans the sequel would be just as exciting as the first.
    a. denied
    b. promised
    c. invigorated
    d. germinated

44. When I heard the wolf howl from my tent, my hands started _____ and my heart stopped ... hopefully I would make it through this night alive!
    a. dancing
    b. glowing
    c. shaking
    d. throbbing

45. Unlike Leo, who always played basketball in the park after school, Gabriel would usually go to the _____ and study after school.
    a. park
    b. library
    c. mall
    d. arcade

46. As soon as the shot rang out, the runners _____ toward the finish line.
    a. sprinted
    b. skipped
    c. rejoiced
    d. herded

47. Determined to get an *A* on her paper, LaShonda _____ to write it two weeks before it was due.
    a. refused
    b. located
    c. procrastinated
    d. vowed

227

48. After Colby's mom picked him up from school, they went to the bank to _____ a check.
   a. celebrate
   b. neutralize
   c. eliminate
   d. deposit

49. The sale at the grocery store _____ my dad to buy four avocados instead of two.
   a. intimidated
   b. inspired
   c. dismayed
   d. berated

50. My mom recently started drinking fruit and vegetable smoothies in order to increase the _____ of her health.
   a. quality
   b. roots
   c. tools
   d. posterity

51. When Lindsay asked me to _____ her party, I immediately began writing a list of the birthday presents she might like to receive.
   a. acclaim
   b. astound
   c. attend
   d. amend

52. Cooking dinner was her favorite activity until she _____ the fire alarm by burning the casserole in the oven.
   a. activated
   b. offended
   c. unplugged
   d. disbanded

53. Before she arrived at the _____ dentist's office to take care of a cavity, she did some breathing exercises and made sure her teeth were clean.
   a. refreshing
   b. creative
   c. rapturous
   d. dreaded

54. The yellow feathers and purple markings told us that this bird was _____ to the southeast part of the United States.
   a. entertaining
   b. indigenous
   c. impudent
   d. monotonous

55. Ever since the bus changed its _____ from Anna's house to the other side of town, Anna began riding her bike to school.
    a. entrance
    b. portico
    c. route
    d. emergence

56. When we caught the eels, their bodies _____ out of our hands and back into the water.
    a. exploded
    b. deteriorated
    c. thundered
    d. slithered

57. Even though at the restaurant my mom _____ the eggplant with no cheese, she received a huge serving of parmesan on top.
    a. requested
    b. directed
    c. mourned
    d. endorsed

58. The _____ into the museum was fifteen dollars per person, but when we came up short five dollars, the employees let us in anyway.
    a. admittance
    b. annex
    c. disjunction
    d. occult

59. Planning a trip to the Great Smoky Mountains taught me to be _____ about saving money.
    a. delirious
    b. superfluous
    c. diligent
    d. reticent

60. Our friendship was growing _____ due to my move to Italy and her brand new family.
    a. elegant
    b. loquacious
    c. mingling
    d. distant

61. Although the patient's _____ was a long one, the gradual restoration to health surprised even his friends and family.
    a. transaction
    b. convalescence
    c. reverberation
    d. consciousness

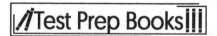

62. Luckily, soon after the truck slammed on the breaks, the deer jumped _____ out of the way.
   a. wistfully
   b. hastily
   c. vivaciously
   d. augustly

Mathematics

1. Which of the following numbers has the greatest value?
   a. 1.43785
   b. 1.07548
   c. 1.43592
   d. 0.89409

2. The value of 6×12 is the same as:
   a. $2 \times 4 \times 4 \times 2$
   b. $7 \times 4 \times 3$
   c. $6 \times 6 \times 3$
   d. $3 \times 3 \times 4 \times 2$

3. This chart indicates how many sales of CDs, vinyl records, and MP3 downloads occurred over the last year. Approximately what percentage of the total sales was from CDs?

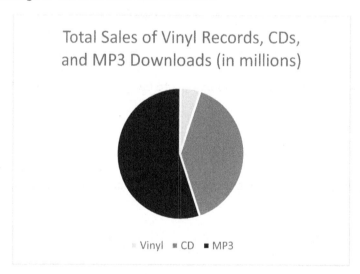

Total Sales of Vinyl Records, CDs, and MP3 Downloads (in millions)

Vinyl ▪ CD ▪ MP3

   a. 55%
   b. 25%
   c. 40%
   d. 5%

4. After a 20% sale discount, Frank purchased a new refrigerator for $850. How much money did he save off of the original price?
   a. $170
   b. $212.50
   c. $105.75
   d. $200

5. The graph of which function has an x-intercept of -2?
   a. $y = 2x - 3$
   b. $y = 4x + 2$
   c. $y = x^2 + 5x + 6$
   d. $y = 2x^2 + 3x - 1$

6. Karen gets paid a weekly salary and a commission for every sale that she makes. The table below shows the number of sales and her pay for different weeks.

Sales	2	7	4	8
Pay	$380	$580	$460	$620

Which of the following equations represents Karen's weekly pay?
   a. $y = 90x + 200$
   b. $y = 90x - 200$
   c. $y = 40x + 300$
   d. $y = 40x - 300$

7. A school's faculty consists of 15 teachers and 20 teaching assistants. They have 200 students. What is the ratio of faculty to students?
   a. $3 : 20$
   b. $4 : 17$
   c. $3 : 2$
   d. $7 : 40$

8. Express the following in decimal form:

$$\frac{3}{5} \times \frac{7}{10} \div \frac{1}{2}$$

   a. 0.042
   b. 84%
   c. 0.84
   d. 0.42

9. A student gets an 85% on a test with 20 questions. How many questions did the student solve correctly?
   a. 15 questions
   b. 16 questions
   c. 17 questions
   d. 18 questions

10. Write the following number in standard form:

$$(1 \times 10^4) + (3 \times 10^3) + (7 \times 10^1) + (8 \times 10^0)$$

   a. 137
   b. 13,078
   c. 1,378
   d. 8,731

231

11. Alan currently weighs 200 pounds, but he wants to lose weight to get down to 175 pounds. What is this difference in kilograms? (1 pound is approximately equal to 0.45 kilograms.)
   a. 9 kg
   b. 11.25 kg
   c. 78.75 kg
   d. 90 kg

12. Johnny earns $2,334.50 from his job each month. He pays $1,437 for monthly expenses and saves the rest. Johnny is planning a vacation in 3 months that he estimates will cost $1,750 total. How much will Johnny have left over from 3 months of saving once he pays for his vacation?
   a. $948.50
   b. $584.50
   c. $852.50
   d. $942.50

13. What is $\frac{420}{98}$ rounded to the nearest integer?
   a. 3
   b. 4
   c. 5
   d. 6

14. Which graph will be a line parallel to the graph of $y = 3x - 2$?
   a. $6x - 2y = -2$
   b. $4x - y = -4$
   c. $3y = x - 2$
   d. $2x - 2y = 2$

15. The total perimeter of a rectangle is 36 cm. If the length is 12 cm, what is the width?
   a. 3 cm
   b. 12 cm
   c. 6 cm
   d. 8 cm

16. Dwayne has received the following scores on his math tests: 78, 92, 83, 97. What score must Dwayne get on his next math test to have an overall average of 90?
   a. 89
   b. 98
   c. 95
   d. 100

17. What is the overall median of Dwayne's current scores: 78, 92, 83, 97?
   a. 80.5
   b. 85
   c. 90
   d. 87.5

232

18. Simplify the following:

$$(\sqrt{36} \times \sqrt{16}) - 3^2$$

a. 30
b. 21
c. 15
d. 13

19. In Jim's school, there are a total of 650 students. There are three girls for every two boys. How many students are girls?
a. 260 girls
b. 130 girls
c. 65 girls
d. 390 girls

20. A company invests $50,000 in a building where they can produce saws. If the cost of producing one saw is $40, then which function expresses the total amount of money the company spends on producing saws? The variable y is the money paid, and x is the number of saws produced.
a. $y = 50{,}000x + 40$
b. $y + 40 = x - 50{,}000$
c. $y = 40x - 50{,}000$
d. $y = 40x + 50{,}000$

21. Kimberley earns $10 an hour babysitting, and after 10 p.m., she earns $12 an hour. The time she works is rounded to the nearest hour for pay purposes. On her last job, she worked from 5:30 p.m. to 11:00 p.m. In total, how much did Kimberley earn on her last job?
a. $45
b. $57
c. $62
d. $42

22. What value of x would solve the following equation?

$$9x + x - 7 = 16 + 2x$$

a. $x = -4$
b. $x = 3$
c. $x = \frac{9}{8}$
d. $x = \frac{23}{8}$

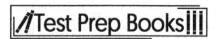

23. Arrange the following numbers from least to greatest value:

$$0.85, \frac{4}{5}, \frac{2}{3}, \frac{91}{100}$$

   a. $0.85, \frac{4}{5}, \frac{2}{3}, \frac{91}{100}$

   b. $\frac{4}{5}, 0.85, \frac{91}{100}, \frac{2}{3}$

   c. $\frac{2}{3}, \frac{4}{5}, 0.85, \frac{91}{100}$

   d. $0.85, \frac{91}{100}, \frac{4}{5}, \frac{2}{3}$

24. Keith's bakery had 252 customers go through its doors last week. This week, that number increased to 378. Express this increase as a percentage.
   a.   26%
   b.   50%
   c.   35%
   d.   12%

25. The table below displays the number of three-year-olds at Kids First Daycare who are potty-trained and those who still wear diapers.

	Potty-trained	Wear diapers	
Boys	26	22	48
Girls	34	18	52
	60	40	

If a three-year-old girl is randomly selected from this school, what is the probability that she is potty-trained?
   a.   52%
   b.   34%
   c.   65%
   d.   57%

26. Simplify the following fraction:

$$\frac{\left(\frac{5}{7}\right)}{\left(\frac{9}{11}\right)}$$

   a. $\frac{55}{63}$

   b. $\frac{7}{1,000}$

   c. $\frac{13}{15}$

   d. $\frac{5}{11}$

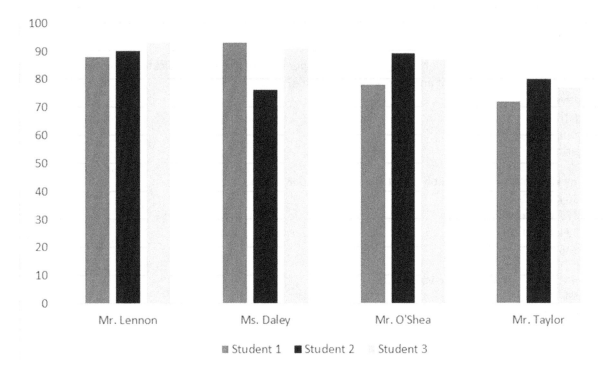

27. The following graph compares the various test scores of the top three students in each of these teachers' classes. Based on the graph, which teacher's students had the lowest range of test scores?

■ Student 1   ■ Student 2   Student 3

a. Mr. Lennon
b. Mr. O'Shea
c. Mr. Taylor
d. Ms. Daley

28. Bernard can make $80 per day. If he needs to make $300 and only works full days, how many days will this take?
a. 2 days
b. 3 days
c. 4 days
d. 5 days

29. Using the following diagram, calculate the total circumference, rounding to the nearest tenths place.

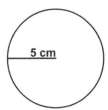

5 cm

a. 25.0 cm
b. 15.7 cm
c. 78.5 cm
d. 31.4 cm

235

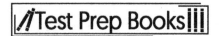

30. Which measure for the center of a small sample set would be most affected by outliers?
   a. Mean
   b. Median
   c. Mode
   d. None of the above

31. A line that travels from the lower left of a graph to the upper right of the graph indicates what kind of relationship between an independent and a dependent variable?
   a. Positive
   b. Negative
   c. Exponential
   d. Logarithmic

32. How many kilometers is 4,382 feet if 1 foot is equal to 0.3048 meters?
   a. 1.336 kilometers
   b. 14,376 kilometers
   c. 1.437 kilometers
   d. 13,336 kilometers

33. If $-3(x + 4) \geq x + 8$, what is the value of x?
   a. $x = 4$
   b. $x \geq 2$
   c. $x \geq -5$
   d. $x \leq -5$

34. Five students take a test. The scores of the first four students are 80, 85, 75, and 60. If the median score is 80, which of the following could NOT be the score of the fifth student?
   a. 60
   b. 80
   c. 85
   d. 100

35. Ten students take a test. Five students get a 50. Four students get a 70. If the average score is 55, what was the last student's score?
   a. 20
   b. 40
   c. 50
   d. 60

36. Given the value of a particular stock at monthly intervals, which graph should be used to best represent the trend of the stock?
   a. Box plot
   b. Line plot
   c. Line graph
   d. Circle graph

37. Simplify the equation:

$$4\frac{1}{3} + 3\frac{3}{4}$$

a. $6\frac{5}{12}$

b. $8\frac{1}{12}$

c. $8\frac{2}{3}$

d. $7\frac{7}{12}$

38. Before a race of 4 horses, you make a random guess of which horse will get first place and which will get second place. What is the probability that both your guesses will be correct?

a. $\frac{1}{4}$

b. $\frac{1}{2}$

c. $\frac{1}{16}$

d. $\frac{1}{12}$

39. What is the 42nd item in the pattern: ▲○○□ ▲○○□ ▲...?

a. ○

b. ▲

c. □

d. None of the above

40. What is the solution to the following system of equations?

$$x^2 - 2x + y = 8$$

$$x - y = -2$$

a. $(-2, 3)$

b. There is no solution.

c. $(-2, 0) \ (1, 3)$

d. $(-2, 0) \ (3, 5)$

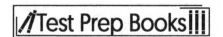

41. Which of the following statements is true about the two lines below?

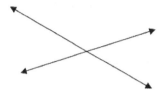

   a. The two lines are parallel but not perpendicular.
   b. The two lines are perpendicular but not parallel.
   c. The two lines are both parallel and perpendicular.
   d. The two lines are neither parallel nor perpendicular.

42. What is the equation of a circle whose center is (0, 0) and whose radius is 5?
   a. $(x - 5)^2 + (y - 5)^2 = 25$
   b. $(x)^2 + (y)^2 = 5$
   c. $(x)^2 + (y)^2 = 25$
   d. $(x + 5)^2 + (y + 5)^2 = 25$

43. How would $\frac{4}{5}$ be written as a percent?
   a. 40%
   b. 125%
   c. 90%
   d. 80%

44. A traveler takes an hour to drive to a museum, spends three hours and 30 minutes there, and takes half an hour to drive home. What percentage of their time was spent driving?
   a. 15%
   b. 30%
   c. 40%
   d. 60%

45. At the beginning of the day, Xavier has 20 apples. At lunch, he meets his sister Emma and gives her half of his apples. After lunch, he stops by his neighbor Jim's house and gives him six of his apples. He then uses $\frac{3}{4}$ of his remaining apples to make an apple pie for dessert at dinner. At the end of the day, how many apples does Xavier have left?
   a. 4
   b. 6
   c. 2
   d. 1

46. How would the number 847.89632 be written if rounded to the nearest hundredth?
   a. 847.90
   b. 900
   c. 847.89
   d. 847.896

238

47. What is the sum of $\frac{1}{3}$ and $\frac{2}{5}$?
    a. $\frac{3}{8}$
    b. $\frac{11}{15}$
    c. $\frac{11}{30}$
    d. $\frac{4}{5}$

48. A ball is drawn at random from a ball pit containing 8 red balls, 7 yellow balls, 6 green balls, and 5 purple balls. What's the probability that the ball drawn is yellow?
    a. $\frac{1}{26}$
    b. $\frac{19}{26}$
    c. $\frac{7}{26}$
    d. 1

49. Divide and reduce $\frac{4}{13} \div \frac{27}{169}$.
    a. $\frac{52}{27}$
    b. $\frac{51}{27}$
    c. $\frac{52}{29}$
    d. $\frac{51}{29}$

50. Express $\frac{54}{15}$ as a mixed number, reduced to lowest terms.
    a. $3\frac{3}{5}$
    b. $3\frac{1}{15}$
    c. $3\frac{3}{54}$
    d. $3\frac{1}{54}$

51. In the problem $5 \times 6 + 4 \div 2 - 1$, which operation should be completed first?
    a. Multiplication
    b. Addition
    c. Division
    d. Subtraction

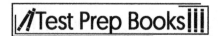

52. A pizzeria owner regularly creates jumbo pizzas, each with a radius of 9 inches. She is mathematically inclined, and wants to know the area of the pizza to purchase the correct boxes and know how much she is feeding her customers. What is the area of a circle with a radius of 9 inches, in terms of π?
    a. $81\pi\ \text{in}^2$
    b. $18\pi\ \text{in}^2$
    c. $90\pi\ \text{in}^2$
    d. $9\pi\ \text{in}^2$

53. A shipping box has a length of 8 inches, a width of 14 inches, and a height of 4 inches. If all three dimensions are doubled, what is the relationship between the volume of the new box and the volume of the original box?
    a. The volume of the new box is double the volume of the original box.
    b. The volume of the new box is four times as large as the volume of the original box.
    c. The volume of the new box is six times as large as the volume of the original box.
    d. The volume of the new box is eight times as large as the volume of the original box.

54. What is the equation of a circle whose center is (1, 5) and whole radius is 4?
    a. $(x - 1)^2 + (y - 25)^2 = 4$
    b. $(x - 1)^2 + (y - 25)^2 = 16$
    c. $(x + 1)^2 + (y + 5)^2 = 16$
    d. $(x - 1)^2 + (y - 5)^2 = 16$

55. When rounding 245.2678 to the nearest thousandth, which place value would be used to decide whether to round up or round down?
    a. Ten-thousandths
    b. Thousandths
    c. Hundredths
    d. Thousands

56. The perimeter of a 6-sided polygon is 56 cm. The lengths of 3 sides are 9 cm each. The lengths of 2 other sides are 8 cm each. What is the length of the final side?
    a. 11 cm
    b. 12 cm
    c. 13 cm
    d. 10 cm

57. An equilateral triangle has a perimeter of 18 feet. The sides of a square have the same length as the triangle's sides. What is the area of the square?
    a. 6 square feet
    b. 36 square feet
    c. 256 square feet
    d. 1,000 square feet

58. The area of a given rectangle is 24 cm^2. If the measure of each side is multiplied by 3, what is the area of the new figure?
    a. 48 cm^2
    b. 72 cm^2
    c. 216 cm^2
    d. 13,824 cm^2

59. Apples cost $2 each, while bananas cost $3 each. Maria purchased a total of 10 pieces of fruit and spent $22. How many apples did she buy?

    a. 5
    b. 6
    c. 7
    d. 8

60. Simplify the equation:

$$3\frac{2}{3} - 1\frac{4}{5}$$

    a. $1\frac{13}{15}$

    b. $\frac{14}{15}$

    c. $2\frac{2}{3}$

    d. $\frac{4}{5}$

61. 20 is 40% of what number?

    a. 50
    b. 8
    c. 200
    d. 5,000

62. $(4x^2y^4)^{\frac{3}{2}}$ can be simplified to which of the following?

    a. $8x^3y^6$

    b. $4x^{\frac{5}{2}}y$

    c. $4xy$

    d. $32x^{\frac{7}{2}}y^{\frac{11}{2}}$

63. A line passes through the origin and through the point $(-3, 4)$. What is the slope of the line?

    a. $-\frac{4}{3}$

    b. $-\frac{3}{4}$

    c. $\frac{4}{3}$

    d. $\frac{3}{4}$

64. Jessica buys 10 cans of paint. Red paint costs $1 per can, and blue paint costs $2 per can. In total, she spends $16. How many red cans did she buy?

    a. 2
    b. 3
    c. 4
    d. 5

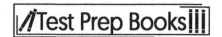

Language

Punctuation and Capitalization

1. Choose the sentence that contains an error in punctuation or capitalization. If there are no errors, select Choice *D*.
   a. "The show is on," Jackson said.
   b. The Grand Canyon is a national park.
   c. Lets celebrate tomorrow.
   d. No errors

2. Choose the sentence that contains an error in punctuation or capitalization. If there are no errors, select Choice *D*.
   a. It was true, Lyla ate the last cupcake.
   b. According to the news, Florida will get heavy rain today.
   c. Chicago, Illinois is a beautiful city.
   d. No errors

3. Choose the sentence that contains an error in punctuation or capitalization If there are no errors, select Choice *D*.
   a. Marcie went to the wrong building yesterday.
   b. Oliver, a social worker, got a new job this month.
   c. My cat's name is River.
   d. No errors

4. Choose the sentence that contains an error in punctuation or capitalization. If there are no errors, select Choice *D*.
   a. Matthew got married to his best friend, Maria.
   b. The Titanic sank on April 14, 1912.
   c. Did you water the plants? Sierra asked.
   d. No errors

5. Choose the sentence that contains an error in punctuation or capitalization. If there are no errors, select Choice *D*.
   a. We studied geology, philosophy, and engineering.
   b. The great depression was the worst disaster in American history.
   c. We kept the journal and locket in a safe place.
   d. No errors

6. Choose the sentence that contains an error in punctuation or capitalization. If there are no errors, select Choice *D*.
   a. Stacey's shoes were the problem, according to Lorraine.
   b. When I was a kid, we lived on evergreen road.
   c. His new truck fit his lifestyle perfectly.
   d. No errors

7. Choose the sentence that contains an error in punctuation or capitalization. If there are no errors, select Choice *D*.
- a. We were the lucky ones.
- b. It was certain; Leroy got accepted to University of Texas.
- c. No one knew what to make of Aunt Linda's new haircut.
- d. No errors

8. Choose the sentence that contains an error in punctuation or capitalization. If there are no errors, select Choice *D*.
- a. Afterwards, we got ice cream down the road.
- b. The word "slacken" means to decrease.
- c. They started building the Hoover dam in 1931.
- d. No errors

9. Choose the sentence that contains an error in punctuation or capitalization. If there are no errors, select Choice *D*.
- a. The student called her the 'best teacher ever' after the class was over.
- b. The sounds were coming from across the dark, gloomy valley.
- c. We built Jeremiah's house with clay and sticks.
- d. No errors

10. Choose the sentence that contains an error in punctuation or capitalization. If there are no errors, select Choice *D*.
- a. On Fridays, we always go out to eat.
- b. Gizelle went to the movie theater every tuesday in October.
- c. We sent an email to Dr. Branson expressing our congratulations.
- d. No errors

11. Choose the sentence that contains an error in punctuation or capitalization. If there are no errors, select Choice *D*.
- a. The doctor came in early every Wednesday.
- b. My best friend, Hattie Winter, visited me in December.
- c. We used lavender oil to take the itch away.
- d. No errors

12. Choose the sentence that contains an error in punctuation or capitalization. If there are no errors, select Choice *D*.
- a. Buster a yellow lab was the newest addition to our family.
- b. Brittany's sister, Melissa, lived with us for two years.
- c. Her voice was as pretty as a sparrow's.
- d. No errors

Usage

13. Choose the sentence that contains an error in usage. If there are no errors, select Choice *D*.
- a. Marty finished the book in August.
- b. We went to the pool and swam four laps.
- c. Because there was lots of food at the picnic.
- d. No errors

243

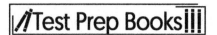

14. Choose the sentence that contains an error in usage. If there are no errors, select Choice *D*.
    a. We created another dish to serve on Saturday.
    b. The committee decided to count the votes.
    c. It rained that morning; they had to cancel the kayaking trip.
    d. No errors

15. Choose the sentence that contains an error in usage. If there are no errors, select Choice *D*.
    a. Their words was followed by a signing document.
    b. No one came to the theater that evening.
    c. Several cats were living in the abandoned house down the road.
    d. No errors

16. Choose the sentence that contains an error in usage. If there are no errors, select Choice *D*.
    a. According to the weather, it's going to snow tomorrow!
    b. Have you checked on the last post?
    c. Once my grades come out, I'll be able to breathe easier.
    d. No errors

17. Choose the sentence that contains an error in usage. If there are no errors, select Choice *D*.
    a. I looked forward to the springtime after the long, hard winter.
    b. Louise and me went to the movie together.
    c. I started painting again after I turned fifty.
    d. No errors

18. Choose the sentence that contains an error in usage. If there are no errors, select Choice *D*.
    a. We spotted two deers on our drive to the lake.
    b. My favorite activities are swimming, reading, and cycling.
    c. The plant began to show signs of nutrient deficiency.
    d. No errors

19. Choose the sentence that contains an error in usage. If there are no errors, select Choice *D*.
    a. I ate a salad with toasted almonds for lunch.
    b. "Are you sure about this?" Rachel asked.
    c. In spite of the overwhelming evidence they decided not to prosecute.
    d. No errors

20. Choose the sentence that contains an error in usage. If there are no errors, select Choice *D*.
    a. Mr. Henderson was a firefighter as well as a baseball coach.
    b. Despite her phone dropping in the water, it still worked the next day.
    c. Its a common misconception that the semicolon is used as a comma.
    d. No errors

21. Choose the sentence that contains an error in usage. If there are no errors, select Choice *D*.
    a. Bugs crawled all over us the night we went camping.
    b. "Let's look for Wyndam Road," Aisha said.
    c. We've restored the majority of power to homes in Cross Creek.
    d. No errors

244

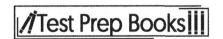

22. Choose the sentence that contains an error in usage. If there are no errors, select Choice D.
    a. The almonds were better than the cashews.
    b. We wanted something sweet so we got ice cream.
    c. Playing board games is our favorite pastime.
    d. No errors

23. Choose the sentence that contains an error in usage. If there are no errors, select Choice D.
    a. After her swim, Jeanine saw a blue kid's shovel.
    b. Pistachios are my favorite kind of nut, although they're expensive.
    c. One apple is better than two lemons.
    d. No errors

24. Choose the sentence that contains an error in usage. If there are no errors, select Choice D.
    a. There was a three-strike rule on absences.
    b. The television was repaired within five days.
    c. Before Oliver fed his dog that morning, he was not very happy.
    d. No errors

25. Choose the sentence that contains an error in usage. If there are no errors, select Choice D.
    a. The moon and the sun inspire me.
    b. We found three five-dollar bills on the way home.
    c. Before his vacation, he had to purchase appropriate clothing in order to stay warm.
    d. No errors

26. Choose the sentence that contains an error in usage. If there are no errors, select Choice D.
    a. Furthermore, I am going to Tokyo in the summer.
    b. I didn't do anything accept wash the dishes.
    c. Why didn't he say hello to me?
    d. No errors

27. Choose the sentence that contains an error in usage. If there are no errors, select Choice D.
    a. One thing I miss have been my friends from high school.
    b. Yellowstone National Park is in Wyoming and parts of Montana.
    c. I went to New York when I was in eleventh grade.
    d. No errors

28. Choose the sentence that contains an error in usage. If there are no errors, select Choice D.
    a. The cakes are in the oven.
    b. I voted for class president.
    c. The best dessert in the world.
    d. No errors

29. Choose the sentence that contains an error in usage. If there are no errors, select Choice D.
    a. They played dominoes until 2 a.m. that night.
    b. He purchased the swing set for twenty-five dollars.
    c. She wanted to start a business, join a local board, and ran for office.
    d. No errors

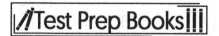

30. Choose the sentence that contains an error in usage. If there are no errors, select Choice *D*.
    a. We stopped at the local park and fed seven ducks.
    b. The time would come when he needed another shot.
    c. The taxi driver overcharged me for the ride.
    d. No errors

31. Choose the sentence that contains an error in usage. If there are no errors, select Choice *D*.
    a. What I didn't understand was how he lost all that weight.
    b. Sheila, and Derek flew to Hawaii last week.
    c. I ate seven bananas for breakfast.
    d. No errors

32. Choose the sentence that contains an error in usage. If there are no errors, select Choice *D*.
    a. I called to schedule an appointment, and talked to the receptionist.
    b. The lady at the supermarket bought treats and toys for her puppy.
    c. No one said that school would be easy.
    d. No errors

33. Choose the sentence that contains an error in usage. If there are no errors, select Choice *D*.
    a. She bought a movie pass last week.
    b. "That's too much!" exclaimed Richie.
    c. The table of cakes have fallen over.
    d. No errors

34. Choose the sentence that contains an error in usage. If there are no errors, select Choice *D*.
    a. My kids want a ferret for Christmas.
    b. The new mattress was way too flat to sleep on.
    c. Larisas car was taken into the shop yesterday.
    d. No errors

35. Choose the sentence that contains an error in usage. If there are no errors, select Choice *D*.
    a. Orange and purple are my favorite colors.
    b. We renovated the house last January.
    c. I fed the cat this morning.
    d. No errors

36. Choose the sentence that contains an error in usage. If there are no errors, select Choice *D*.
    a. He went swimming it was freezing outside.
    b. Their goals were accomplished early in life.
    c. The zoo was filled with apes and elephants.
    d. No errors

37. Choose the sentence that contains an error in usage. If there are no errors, select Choice *D*.
    a. The wildflowers grew in our backyard.
    b. She took cookies to class as a snack.
    c. Their was no turning back now.
    d. No errors

Spelling

38. Choose the sentence that contains an error in spelling. If there are no errors, select Choice *D*.
    a. The committee helped us with the voting process.
    b. I beleive you are correct in your assumptions.
    c. Her grandmother was very religious.
    d. No errors

39. Choose the sentence that contains an error in spelling. If there are no errors, select Choice *D*.
    a. The propoganda got quickly out of hand.
    b. Tomorrow we are going to the fair.
    c. The chocolate cake was irresistible.
    d. No errors

40. Choose the sentence that contains an error in spelling. If there are no errors, select Choice *D*.
    a. She got the gist of what I was trying to say.
    b. What happened last night?
    c. We reserved the pavilion for the party.
    d. No errors

41. Choose the sentence that contains an error in spelling. If there are no errors, select Choice *D*.
    a. To receive your mail, go to the post office.
    b. She was very successful in her career.
    c. They took posession of the car.
    d. No errors

42. Choose the sentence that contains an error in spelling. If there are no errors, select Choice *D*.
    a. The two were seperated within the hour.
    b. She had a tendency to leave work early.
    c. We all got matching tattoos.
    d. No errors

43. Choose the sentence that contains an error in spelling. If there are no errors, select Choice *D*.
    a. He had a very low threshhold for pain.
    b. It was necessary to make an A on the paper.
    c. She disappeared into the doorway.
    d. No errors

44. Choose the sentence that contains an error in spelling. If there are no errors, select Choice *D*.
    a. The embarrassing assignment was over.
    b. We should take care of the enviroment.
    c. There were finally two cars instead of one.
    d. No errors

45. Choose the sentence that contains an error in spelling. If there are no errors, select Choice *D*.
    a. The beginning of school is always the best.
    b. I was completely surprised by the present!
    c. We had a dilemma at the nursery this morning.
    d. No errors

46. Choose the sentence that contains an error in spelling. If there are no errors, select Choice *D*.
    a.   We dared her to go into the cemetery.
    b.   I definitely ate too much that night.
    c.   I have more independence with a car.
    d.   No errors

47. Choose the sentence that contains an error in spelling. If there are no errors, select Choice *D*.
    a.   My preferred communication is via the phone.
    b.   She interrupted the phone call with a laugh.
    c.   The gaurd watched her step into the store.
    d.   No errors

Composition

48. Choose the best word or words to complete the sentence.

    Nikki purchased the beef and rice, _____ Elaina purchased the tofu and noodles.

    a.   whereas
    b.   in addition
    c.   consequently
    d.   therefore

49. Choose the best word or words to complete the sentence.

    We bought a cake, _____ we set up a bubble machine for the party.

    a.   therefore
    b.   but
    c.   and
    d.   however

50. Choose the best word or words to complete the sentence.

    Callie found two dollars on the ground; _____, she is going to buy a piece of candy.

    a.   therefore
    b.   however
    c.   furthermore
    d.   whereas

51. Choose the best word or words to complete the sentence.

    Liam went to the basketball game, _____ he had an exam to study for.

    a.   in addition
    b.   consequently
    c.   and
    d.   even though

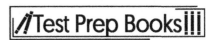

52. Choose the best word or words to complete the sentence.

Victor ran a mile for his workout; _____, he did one hour of resistance training.

a. however
b. nonetheless
c. though
d. in addition

53. Choose the best word or words to complete the sentence.

Neville wanted to become a scientist; _____, he wanted to study sociology.

a. but
b. also
c. consequently
d. therefore

54. Choose the best word or words to complete the sentence.

Casey tried to go to school in the morning, _____ her car wouldn't start.

a. therefore
b. and
c. but
d. whereas

55. Choose the best word or words to complete the sentence.

Lauren hated getting out in the evening; _____, she went to the grocery store at 5 p.m.

a. therefore
b. and
c. nevertheless
d. also

56. Choose the best word or words to complete the sentence.

Jamal submitted his online exam, _____ went to his night class.

a. then
b. but
c. however
d. consequently

57. Choose the best word or words to complete the sentence.

Boris got his resume together and sent it out; _____, he landed a job a week later.

a. but
b. and
c. whereas
d. consequently

Answer Explanations

Verbal Skills

Verbal Analogies

1. A: The best fit here is wheel is to truck as foot is to body. *Wheels* are the part of the truck that make contact with the ground to roll the vehicle forward. *Feet* are the part of the body that walk on the ground during locomotion.

2. B: *Wires* are the medium that carry *electricity*, allowing the current to flow in a circuit. *Pipes* carry *water* in a similar fashion. So the best choice is B. Choices A, C, and D contain words that are related to one another but not in the same way as wires and electricity.

3. C: *Cows* produce milk, so the question is looking for another pair that has a producer and their product. Horses don't produce cows, Choice A, and glasses don't produce milk, Choice D. The correct choice is C: bee is to honey. The tricky one here is Choice B, egg is to chicken, because it has the correct words but the wrong order; therefore, it reverses the relationship.

4. C: The first part of the analogy (web is to spider) describes the home (web) and who lives in it (spider), so the question is looking for what animal lives in a den. The best choice is C, *fox. Living room*, Choice A, is a synonym for a den.

5. A: *Sad* and *blue* are synonyms because they both describe the same type of mood. The word *blue* in this case is not referring to the color. Therefore, although Choice B, *yellow*, is sometimes considered a "happy" color, the question isn't referring to blue as a color. *Yellow* and *happy* are not synonyms. Someone who is happy may laugh or smile, Choices C and D. However, these words are not synonyms for happy. The best choice is *glad*.

6. D: The key to answering this question correctly is to recognize the relationship between *door* and *store. Door* and *store* are words that rhyme. You might be thinking that stores have doors. However, after seeing the other word choices and the given word *deal*, you should notice that none of the other words have this relationship. Instead, the answer should rhyme with *deal. Wheel* and *deal*, although spelled differently, are rhyming words. Therefore, the correct answer is Choice D.

7. A: This is a consumer/food analogy. The theme of this analogy is pairing a specific animal to their food source. Falcons prey on mice. Giraffes are herbivores and only eat one of the choices: leaves. Choice D, *grasslands*, describes a type of landscape, not a food source for animals.

8. A: The relationship in the first half of the analogy is that clocks are used to measure time. The second half of the analogy should have a tool that is used to measure something followed by what it measures. Rulers can be used to measure length. So Choice A is the best choice. Remember that the key to solving analogies is to be a good detective. Some of the other answer choices are related to clocks and time, but not to the relationship *between* clocks and time.

9. A: *Slippery* is an adjective that describes the surface of ice. The answer is best filled by a word that describes rugs, such as *soft*, Choice A. *Carpet*, Choice B, is a synonym for a rug rather than an adjective that describes rugs. Therefore, it is an incorrect choice. Rugs cover the floor, Choice C, so again, this is not an adjective for a rug and not the correct answer. Hard, Choice D, is an adjective, but the opposite of describing a rug.

10. C: A calf is a baby cow, and a foal is a baby horse. Choice C is the only answer choice that makes sense.

Synonyms

11. C: To *deduce* something is to figure it out using reason. While you can explain something you've deduced, explain is not a synonym for deduce.

12. B: To *elucidate* is to figuratively shine a light on a previously unknown or confusing subject. This Latin root, "lux" meaning "light," prominently figures into the solution. *Enlighten* means to educate or bring to light.

13. D: Looking at the Latin word "veritas," meaning "truth," will yield a clue as to the meaning of verify. To *verify* is the act of finding or assessing the truthfulness of something. This usually means amassing evidence to substantiate a claim. *Substantiate,* of course, means to provide evidence to prove a point.

14. A: If someone is *inspired*, they are motivated to do something. Someone who is an inspiration motivates others to follow their example.

15. D: *Mendacious* describes dishonesty or lying in several ways. This is another word of classical lineage. *Mendacio* in Latin means "liar." While *liar* lacks the Latin root, the meanings fit.

16. C: *Nomadic* tribes are those who, throughout history and even today, prefer to wander their lands instead of settling in any specific place. *Wanderer* best describes these people.

17. A: *Malevolent* literally means bad or evil-minded. The clue is also in the Latin root "mal-," which translates to bad.

18. D: *Perplexed* means baffled or puzzled, which are synonymous with *confused*.

19. D: *Lyrical* is used to refer to something being poetic or song-like, characterized by showing enormous imagination and description. While the context of lyrical can be playful or even whimsical, the best choice is *expressive*, since whatever emotion *lyrical* may be used to convey in its context will be expressive in nature.

20. C: *Brevity* literally means brief or concise. Note the similar beginnings of brevity and brief—from the Latin "brevis," meaning brief.

21. A: *Irate* means being in a state of anger. Clearly this is a negative word that can be paired with another word in kind. The closest word to match this is obviously *anger*. Research would also reveal that irate comes from the Latin "ira," which means anger.

22. C: *Lavish* is a synonym for *luxurious*. Both words describe elaborate, elegant lifestyles and/or settings.

23. C: *Retort* is a verb that means "to answer back," usually in a sharp manner. This term embodies the idea of a response, emphasized by the "re-" prefix meaning "back, again." Conversation and jest, even though both involve speaking with someone, do not embody the idea of a response, which is integral to a retort. *Counter*, however, means to respond in opposition when used as a verb.

24. A: *Subliminal* and *subconscious* share the Latin prefix "sub-," meaning under or below, or more commonly used when talking about messages the sender doesn't want the receiver to consciously take note of. The word *subliminal* means beneath the consciousness. Thus, *subconscious* is the perfect match.

25. C: Although *incite* usually has negative connotations, leaders can incite their followers to benevolent actions as well. In both cases, people rally to support a cause.

Answer Explanations

Logic

26. B: This answer is false. If squirrels are active during the day, and nocturnal animals are active during the night, then squirrels are *not* considered to be nocturnal animals.

27. B: This answer is false. Let's draw it out on a sheet of paper. Katie is our fastest runner all the way to the right. Behind Katie is Celia, who is slower. Behind Celia is John, who is slower than Celia. We have in order Katie, Celia then John. The third statement tells us, now, that John is faster than Katie. This can't be true based on the first two statements, given that John is slower than Celia who is slower than Katie. The third statement is false.

28. C: If the first two statements are true, the third statement isn't necessarily true. We are uncertain whether chocolate is better than strawberry given the first two statements. We know for sure that mint is better than both chocolate and strawberry, given the first two statements. The third tells us that chocolate is better than strawberry, but since we are only going off the first two statements as true, they don't tell us whether or not strawberry or chocolate is better than the other. This question is uncertain.

29. C: The third statement is uncertain. This question is pretty straightforward. We know that the first two statements are true because the question tells us that they are. So, cup A has orange juice and cup B has lemonade. This tells us nothing about cup C, so the third statement is uncertain.

30. A: The third statement must be true. We can see that all literature is important. If some poems are literature, then those poems must be considered important, since all literature is important.

31. A: The third statement must be true. Draw the boxes out on a piece of paper if this helps you determine the correct answer. We know for sure that blue boxes are heavier than red boxes. And if red boxes are heavier than green boxes, then blue boxes must be heavier than both green and red boxes. Therefore, "green boxes are not as heavy as blue boxes" must be true.

32. A: The third statement is true. We know from the second statement that all goldfish have gold specks, no matter what. We also know that some goldfish are red. Some of those red goldfish *must have gold specks*. Therefore, the third statement is true: Some goldfish are red with gold specks. Remember that the statements have nothing to do with the truth in reality; the first two statements are true no matter what the reality of the statement is.

33. A: The third statement is true. Whether or not you believe baseball is entertaining or not is irrelevant to the question. These questions are logic-based only, so we are working with two statements that we must take as absolute fact. We know that baseball is a sport, and that no sports are entertaining. Given this logic, we must assume that baseball is not entertaining.

34. B: The third statement is false. If all shampoos contain parabens, which are synthetic ingredients, then *all* shampoos must contain synthetic ingredients.

35. C: We're not sure, given the first two statements, that "no comedians are funny." We only know that Jordan is a comedian, and that Jordan is not funny.

Verbal Classifications

36. A: Canyons, gorges, and ravines are all types of narrow valleys or clefts. The word *mountain* does not belong here because mountains have peaks and rise above the surrounding earth, rather than dipping into the ground.

37. D: *Lackluster* is the word that does not belong here. Lackluster means dull, while the other words (*bright*, *dazzling*, and *luminous*) denote brilliance or brightness in appearance.

38. B: The word *vigorous* does not belong with the others. *Apathetic, lethargic,* and *indifferent* all relate to being lazy or sluggish.

39. B: *Morose* does not belong with the other words because it denotes sadness and depression. The words *exuberant, festive,* and *upbeat* all have to do with being joyous or happy.

40. C: *Assignment* is the word that does not belong with the others. The words *vacation, sabbatical,* and *intermission* all have to do with taking a leave or a break from work or assignment.

41. D: The word *declaration* means an assertion of belief and is unlike the other answer choices. *Origin, source,* and *derivation* all have to do with the cause or beginning of something.

42. A: *Amplify* means to increase in size and effect, so it is unlike the others. *Development, evolution,* and *migration* all have to do with movement toward something.

43. C: *Penguin* does not belong in the classification with the others. *Guppy, trout,* and *swordfish* are all types of fish.

44. D: The word *injury* does not belong. *Antibiotic, prescription,* and *pharmaceutical* all have to do with medications of some sort.

45. A: *Blandishment* means flattery, so this word is unlike the others. *Fulfillment, gratification,* and *contentment* all have to do with satisfaction of some kind.

46. B: *Office* is the odd word out here. *Tent, house,* and *camper* are all places where people live in permanently or temporarily and sleep inside. This one is a bit tricky, since all of these are structures, but three of them have more to do with living inside rather than working inside.

47. C: *Tree* is the odd one out here because it does not give off any kind of light. *Lamp, sun,* and *firecracker* are all sources of light.

48. C: The word *moss* does not fit in with this selection. *Cedar, maple,* and *mahogany* are all types of wood.

49. D: *Cooperation* does not belong with the other words because it means agreement or acceptance. The words *distinguished, exceptional,* and *phenomenal* mean excellent or superior in some way.

50. A: *Valley* does not belong with the other words because it is the only word that doesn't pertain to water. *Stream, river,* and *ocean* all have to do with water.

51. D: The word that does not belong here is *editor* because it is the only profession that doesn't work outside. *Farmer, ranger,* and *lifeguard* spend many of their hours working outside.

Antonyms

52. B: *Integral* is the opposite of *nonessential.* Integral means necessary. *Component* is a synonym of integral so Choice *A* is incorrect. *Parched* means thirsty, so Choice *C* is incorrect. *Tactful* means polite, so Choice *D* is incorrect.

53. A: *Tangible* means the opposite of *abstract. Spurious* means fake or counterfeit, so Choice *B* is incorrect. *Sallow* means sick, so Choice *C* is incorrect. *Radical* means extremist or fanatical, so Choice *D* is incorrect.

54. D: *Abandon* means the opposite of *restraint,* because restraint denotes self-control, and abandonment denotes a lack of control. Choice *A, clamorous,* means noisy. Choice *B, pensive,* means thoughtful. Choice *C, wary,* means cautious.

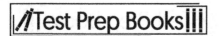

55. D: *Nonchalant* means the opposite of *enthusiastic*. Choice A, *elicit*, means to draw out. Choice B, *callous*, means unfeeling or harsh. Choice C, *banal*, means commonplace.

56. C: *Latent* means *hidden* so it is the opposite of *obvious*. Choice A, *impeccable*, means flawless or without suspicion. Choice B, *vanquish*, means to subdue or conquer. Choice D, *prosaic*, means ordinary.

57. B: *Macabre* means the opposite of *cheerful*. *Palpable* means apparent or clear, so Choice A is incorrect. Choice C is incorrect because *sanitation* is not the opposite of *macabre*; it has to do with cleanliness. Choice D is incorrect because *abrupt* means to be blunt or brief.

58. C: *Audacity* means bravery which is the opposite of timidity. *Oblivious,* Choice A, means unaware, so this is incorrect. *Refute* means to prove false, so Choice B is incorrect. Choice D, *reverence,* means a state of worship or high opinion of something, so this is also incorrect.

59. A: To be *superficial* is to be *inauthentic*, so it is the opposite of *authentic*. Choice B, *pretentious*, means conceited. Choice C, *transient*, means temporary or fleeting. Choice D, *intrepid*, means fearless.

60. D: *Subside* means to lessen or go down, so the opposite of this would be to *develop*. Choice A, *aloof,* means distant or unsympathetic. Choice B, *ruminate*, means to think about something. Choice C, *nomadic*, means to wander or roam.

Quantitative Skills

Number Series

1. B: The pattern in this series is that 3 is added to each number to form the subsequent number. So, for example, $4 + 3 = 7$, and $7 + 3 = 10$. Thus,

$$16 + 3 = 19$$

2. D: The pattern in this series is to double each number then subtract 1 to form the subsequent number. So, for example,

$$3 \times 2 - 1 = 5$$

$$9 \times 2 - 1 = 17$$

$$17 \times 2 - 1 = 33$$

3. A: The pattern in this series is that each integer is counting up, but the sign of the number flips with each subsequent number. Thus, after +5 is -6.

4. D: The pattern in this series is that each subsequent number is the sum of the prior two (much like the famous Fibonacci series: 1, 1, 2, 5, 8, 13, 21 ...). Thus, for the next number,

$$10 + 16 = 26$$

5. D: This one was slightly trickier. The pattern in this series is to divide by 2 to get the first next number, and then add 5 to get the next number after that. This pattern is then repeated for the next set of values. For example, we start at 18. To get the next number, we divide by 2, resulting in 9. Then, we add 5 to get the third number. The 14 is then divided by 2 to get 7. Then 5 is added back to get 12. To find the missing number, we are back at the dividing by 2 stage, so we are looking for the number 6.

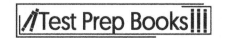

6. C: The pattern in this series is that each value in the series is 2 raised to the exponent of that number value in the series, usually denoted by n. For example, the first value in the series is 2. That is because $2^1 = 2$. The exponent of 1 was used because it is the first (1) number in the series. The second number is $2^2 = 4$; the third is $2^3 = 8$. So, the next value should be $2^6 = 64$.

7. B: The pattern in this series is that numerators increase by 2 and the denominators increase by 3 to form the subsequent fraction. In other words, the difference between subsequent numerators is 2 and the difference between subsequent denominators is 3.

8. C: The numerator in the sequence $\left\{\frac{(-1)^{n+1}}{n^2+5}\right\}_{n=0}^{\infty}$ indicates that the sign of each term changes from term to term. The first term is negative because $n = 0$ and $-1^{n+1} = -1^1 = -1$. Therefore, the second term is positive, the third term is negative, etc. The denominator is evaluated like a function for plugging in various n values. For example, the denominator of the first term, when $n = 0$, is $0^2 + 5 = 5$.

9. A: The pattern in this series is that the interval between subsequent values, which begins with 2 ($55 - 53 = 2$), increases by 2 and is subtracted each time (so the next value is found by subtracting 4, then subtracting 6, etc.). So, the next number is 10 less than 35, which is 25.

10. B: The pattern in this series is that the numbers are decreasing squares starting at 12 ($12^2 = 144$, $11^2 = 121$, $10^2 = 100$, $9^2 = 81$, $8^2 = 64$). Thus, the next number should be 7^2, which is 49.

11. A: The pattern in this series is to subtract three and then add ten. So, $14 - 3$ is 11. Then, for the next number, $11 + 10 = 21$. Then, for the next number, we are back at subtracting 3, so $21 - 3$ is 18. Then adding 10 gives us $18 + 10 = 28$. Finally, we are looking for the next number, which would be subtracting 3 in the pattern:

$$28 - 3 = 25$$

12. C: The numbers in this series are found by multiplying the previous number by -3. Therefore, the next number is:

$$405 \times (-3) = -1215$$

13. A: The numbers in this series are derived by dividing the previous value by 2. Therefore, the next number is:

$$3 \div 2 = 1.5$$

14. A: The pattern in this series is to subtract 0.5 to get the next number and then add 0.1 for the following interval in an alternating pattern. So $0.5 - 0.5$ is 0. Then, for the next number, $0 + 0.1 = 0.1$ Then, for the next number, we are back to subtracting 0.5, so $0.1 - 0.5$ is -0.04. Then, 0.1 is added, so we get -0.3. Finally, we are to subtract 0.5 to get the next number, which would yield -0.8.

15. C: The pattern in this series is that 6 is added to each number to form the subsequent number. So, for example, $3 + 6 = 9$, and $9 + 6 = 15$. Thus, $27 + 6 = 33$.

16. B: The pattern in this series is to multiply the previous number by 3 to get the next number. Thus, the missing value is 40.5. This can be checked by multiplying 40.5 by 3; indeed, it yields the last given value: 121.5.

17. D: The pattern in this series is that the next number is the sum of the previous two numbers. So the third term, 11, is the sum of the second term (6) and the first term (5). Thus, the subsequent missing term is the sum of 28 and 17, which is 45.

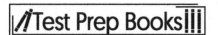

18. B: The pattern in this series is that the difference between subsequent numbers increases by 1 each time. In other words, the number subtracted from the previous value increases by 1 more each time. Looking at the numbers given,

$$30 - 1 = 29$$

$$29 - 2 = 27$$

$$27 - 3 = \_\_\_\_ (24)$$

$$24 - 4 = 20$$

$$20 - 5 = 15$$

Geometric Comparison

19. C: The value of g can be found using the formula for area of a rectangle ($A = l \times w$). So, $56 = g \times 4$, and $g = 14$in. To calculate the area (A) of a triangle, for II, the product of $\frac{1}{2}$, the base (b), and the height (h) is found

$$A = \frac{1}{2} \times b \times h$$

The area of the triangle indicated is 52 sq. inches, so:

$$52in^2 = \frac{1}{2} \times (x) \times (8in)$$

$$104 = 8x \rightarrow x = 13in$$

Therefore, II is less than I. For III, the value of the side length of a cube with a volume of 1728 cubic inches is calculated by taking the cube root of 1728, which is 12in. Therefore, III is the smallest of all three values, so I > II > III.

20. B: First, find the area of both figures. We can use the formula for the area of a triangle ($A = \frac{1}{2}bh$) to find the area of this triangle:

$$\frac{1}{2}(7) \times x = 3.5x \text{ square inches}$$

The area of the rectangle is $13 \times 8 = 104$ square inches. So, 7 times the area of the triangle, the quantity in I, would be 196 square inches, and 2 times the area of the rectangle, the quantity in II, would be 208 square inches. The area of the rectangle plus 3 times the area of the triangle is:

$$104 + 3 \times 28 = 188$$

This means that II > I > III.

21. A: The volume of the sphere is 288π cubic meters. Using the formula for sphere volume, we see that:

$$\frac{4}{3}\pi r^3 = 288\pi$$

256

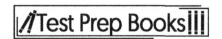

We solve this equation for r to obtain a radius of 6 meters. The formula for surface area is $4\pi r^2$, so:

$$SA = 4\pi 6^2 = 144\pi \text{ square meters}$$

Thus, all three quantities describe the same-sized sphere.

22. A: The triangle for which quantity I pertains can be labeled as a right triangle because it has a right angle measure in the corner. The Pythagorean Theorem can be used here to find the missing side lengths. The Pythagorean Theorem states that $a^2 + b^2 = c^2$, where a and b are side lengths and c is the hypotenuse. The hypotenuse, c, is equal to 35, and 1 side, a, is equal to 21. Plugging these values into the equation forms:

$$21^2 + b^2 = 35^2$$

Squaring both given numbers and subtracting them yields the equation $b^2 = 784$. Taking the square root of 784 gives a value of 28 for b. In the equation, b is the same as the missing side length x. For II, x (which we just found to be 28) would be the hypotenuse of the right triangle formed from the side length of 20 and the bisector implicated by the desired geometric quantity in II. Thus, $20^2 + b^2 = 28^2$, $b = 19.6$ (Note: you would not actually need to solve this because by definition, the length of the legs of a right triangle are shorter than the hypotenuse, and the hypotenuse is value I, so II is automatically less than I). For III, denote the width as w and the length as l. Then, $l = 3w + 5$. The perimeter is $2w + 2l = 90$. Substituting the first expression for l into the second equation yields:

$$2(3w + 5) + 2w = 90$$

$$6w + 10 + 2w = 90$$

$$8w = 80$$

$$w = 10$$

Putting this into the first equation, it yields:

$$l = 3(10) + 5 = 35$$

23. D: For I, because these are 2 parallel lines cut by a transversal, the angle with a measure of 45 degrees is equal to the measure of angle 6. Angle 6 and the angle labeled $5x + 35$ are supplementary to one another. The sum of these angles should be 180 degrees, so the following equation can be generated:

$$5x + 35 + 45 = 180$$

Solving for x, the sum of 35 and 45 is 80, which is then subtracted from 180 to yield 100 degrees. Dividing 100 by 5 gives the value of x, which is 20 degrees.

For II, the three angles lie on a straight line; therefore, the sum of all the angles must equal 180°. The values for angle x and angle y should be added together and subtracted from 180° to find the value for angle z as follows:

$$180 - \left(48° + 2(48°)\right) = 36°$$

Because the 65-degree angle and angle b sum to 180 degrees, the measurement of angle b is 115-degrees. Because they are corresponding angles, angle b is equal to angle f. Therefore, angle f measures 115-degrees.

24. C: The sum of all angles in a polygon with n sides is found by the expression $(n - 2) \times 180$. Since this polygon has 5 sides, the total degrees of the interior angles can be found using the equation:

$$(5-2) \times 180 = 540$$

Adding up each of the given angles yields a total of:

$$111 + 113 + 92 + 128 = 444 \; degrees$$

Taking the total of 540 degrees and subtracting the given sum of 444 degrees gives a missing value of 96 degrees for the measure of angle P. To find the measure of an angle in a regular pentagon, the 540 degrees is divided by 5, which is 108 degrees. For III, to calculate the measure of an angle on a regular hexagon, we first calculate the sum of the angles as we did for the pentagon, adding 1 to the n we used:

$$(n-2) \times 180 = (6-2) \times 180 = 720 \; degrees$$

Then, this sum is divided by the number of angles in the hexagon (6), which yields 120 degrees per angle. Thus, III > II > I.

25. B: The figure is composed of three sides of a square and a semicircle. The sides of the square are simply added: $8 + 8 + 8 = 24$ inches. The circumference of a circle is found by the equation $C = 2\pi r$. The radius is 4 in, so the circumference of the circle (using 3.14 for π) is 25.12 in, which is the value for II. Only half of the circle makes up the outer border of the entire figure (part of the perimeter) so half of 25.12 in is 12.56 in. Therefore, the total perimeter of the figure is: 24 in + 12.56 in = 36.56 in, so this is the value of I. The perimeter of the square is $4 \times 8 = 32$ in, but we have to subtract the radius of the circle (4 in), which yields 28 inches. Therefore, II < III < I.

26. D: The formula for the volume of a cylinder is $\pi r^2 h$, where r is the radius and h is the height. The diameter is twice the radius, so the barrels have a radius of 1 foot. That means each barrel has a volume of:

$$\pi \times 1^2 \times 3 = 3\pi \; cubic \; feet$$

Since there are three of them, the total is $3 \times 3\pi = 9\pi$ cubic feet. Using 3.14 for π gives us 28.26 cubic feet. The volume of the rectangular prism indicated in II is:

$$V = l \times w \times h$$

$$3 \times 2.5 \times 4 = 30 \; cubic \; feet$$

Finally, the formula used to calculate the volume of a cone is $\frac{1}{3}\pi r^2 h$. Essentially, the area of the base of the cone is multiplied by the cone's height and divided by three. The traffic cones in III have a radius of 1 foot and a height of 3 feet. The volume is calculated by utilizing the formula:

$$\frac{1}{3}\pi 1^2 \times 3 = \pi$$

After substituting 3.14 for π, the volume of 1 cone is 3.14 ft³. The volume of the 8 cones is:

$$8 \times 3.14 = 25.12 \; ft^3$$

This means that II > I > III.

27. A: The measure of two complementary angles sums up to 90 degrees, so $90 - 54 = 36$. Therefore, the complementary angle is 36 degrees. The measure of two angles that are supplementary sum to 180 degrees, so:

$$180 - 54 = 126 \; degrees$$

Lastly, a right angle is 90 degrees; thus, II > III > I.

258

Non-Geometric Comparison

28. C: The value of I is 9 because it is the square root of 81. The equation that produces this series is $2x + 1$. This gives $2(4) + 1 = 9, 2(9) + 1 = 19$, and so on. This means that the value of h in the series is 9, so the value of I and II are equal. III is 2 raised to the third power or $2 \times 2 \times 2$, which is 8, so this is less than I and II.

29. D: The first step in solving the equation in I is to collect like terms on the left side of the equation. This yields the new equation:

$$-4 + 8x = 8 - 10x$$

The next step is to move the x terms to one side by adding $10x$ to both sides, making the equation:

$$-4 + 18x = 8$$

Then the -4 can be moved to the right side of the equation to form $18x = 12$. Dividing both sides of the equation by 18 gives a value of 0.67, or $\frac{2}{3}$.

For the equation in II, we need to solve for b: $4b - 12 = -2b, 6b - 12 = 0, 6b = 12, b = 2$.

For III, a common denominator needs to be found:

$$\frac{4}{5} + \frac{2}{3} = \frac{12}{15} + \frac{10}{15} = \frac{22}{15} c = 3$$

$$22c = 45$$

So, $c = \frac{45}{22}$ or $2\frac{1}{22}$. Therefore, III is slightly greater than II, which is greater than I.

30. C: To solve any of these equations correctly, keep in mind the order of operations with the mnemonic PEMDAS (Please Excuse My Dear Aunt Sally). This stands for Parentheses, Exponents, Multiplication & Division, Addition & Subtraction. Let's start with I. Taking it step by step, start with the parentheses:

$$4 \times 7 + (4)^2 \div 2$$

Then, apply the exponent:

$$4 \times 7 + 16 \div 2$$

Multiplication and division are both performed next:

$$28 + 8 = 36$$

Now for II:

Parentheses:

$$7^2 - 3 \times (4 + 2) + 15 \div 5$$

$$7^2 - 3 \times (6) + 15 \div 5$$

Exponents:

$$49 - 3 \times 6 + 15 \div 5$$

Multiplication & division (from left to right):

$$49 - 18 + 3$$

Addition & subtraction (from left to right):

$$49 - 18 + 3 = 34$$

Lastly, we will again apply the order of operations for III:

$$9 \times 9 \div 9 + 9 - 9 \div 9$$

$$81 \div 9 + 9 - 9 \div 9$$

$$9 + 9 - 1$$

$$18 - 1$$

$$17$$

Thus, I > II > III.

31. C: For I, to find the fraction of the bill that the first three people pay, the fractions need to be added, which means finding the common denominator.

The common denominator will be 12:

$$\frac{1}{6} + \frac{1}{4} + \frac{1}{3} = \frac{2}{12} + \frac{3}{12} + \frac{4}{12} = \frac{9}{12} = \frac{3}{4}$$

The remainder of the bill is $1 - \frac{3}{4} = \frac{1}{4}$.

For II, the total fraction taken up by green and red shirts will be:

$$\frac{1}{3} + \frac{2}{5} = \frac{5}{15} + \frac{6}{15} = \frac{11}{15}$$

The remaining fraction is:

$$1 - \frac{11}{15} = \frac{15}{15} - \frac{11}{15} = \frac{4}{15}$$

For III, these numbers first need to be converted to improper fractions: $\frac{11}{3} - \frac{14}{5}$. Next, 15 is used as a common denominator:

$$\frac{11}{3} - \frac{14}{5} = \frac{55}{15} - \frac{42}{15} = \frac{13}{15}$$

Normally, to compare the three fractions found in I, II, and III, a common denominator would be necessary. However, II and III already have the same denominator, and it's easy to see that I is a significantly smaller value.

32. B: In I, to solve for x, multiply both sides by x to get $x + 2 = 2x$, which simplifies to $-x = -2$, or $x = 2$.

260

To solve for t, first, subtract 4 from each side. This yields $6t = 12$. Now, divide both sides by 6 to obtain $t = 2$.

Lastly, if $2a^2 - 4 = 14$, then $2a^2 = 18$, so $a^2 = 9$, and $a = 3$, because a is positive.

Therefore, III is greater than II and I, which are equal.

33. A: The variable y is directly proportional to x, which means that whenever x is multiplied by a number, y is multiplied by that same number. When x changes from 5 to 20, it is multiplied by 4, so the original y value must also be multiplied by 4. That means $y = 3 \times 4 = 12$.

With II, the average is calculated by adding all six numbers, then dividing by 6. The first five numbers have a sum of 25. This scenario can be expressed by the equation $\frac{25+n}{6} = 6$, where n is the unknown number. After multiplying both sides by 6, we get $25 + n = 36$, which means $n = 11$.

With III, if 60% of 50 workers are women, then there are 30 women working in the office. If half of them are wearing skirts, then that means 15 women wear skirts. Since nobody else wears skirts, this means there are 15 people wearing skirts.

34. D: If Shawna has used $\frac{1}{3}$ of the paint, she has $\frac{2}{3}$ remaining. The mixed fraction can be converted because $2\frac{1}{2}$ gallons is the same as $\frac{5}{2}$ gallons. The calculation is:

$$\frac{2}{3} \times \frac{5}{2} = \frac{10}{6} = \frac{5}{3} = 1\frac{2}{3} \text{ gallons}$$

For II:

$$\frac{1}{3} + \frac{1}{5} + \frac{3}{4} = \frac{20}{60} + \frac{12}{60} + \frac{45}{60} = \frac{77}{60} \text{ gal}$$

For III, $\frac{2}{5}$ of 4 gallons $= \frac{2}{5} \times \frac{4}{1} = \frac{8}{5}$ gallons.

Finally, to compare the fractions, a common denominator must be applied. For I, $\frac{5}{3} = \frac{100}{60}$. II is already in the correct form $(\frac{77}{60})$, and III is $\frac{8}{5} = \frac{96}{60}$. This means that I > III > II.

35. B: Each value can be calculated so that they can be compared to find which one is the greatest. The mean is equal to:

$$\frac{26 + 27 + 27 + 29 + 30 + 32 + 33 + 33 + 33 + 35}{10} = 30.5$$

The median is equal to:

$$\frac{30 + 32}{2} = 31$$

The mode is equal to 33 because that number occurs three times in the data set. Therefore, the mode is the greatest value of the answer choices.

261

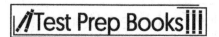

Number Manipulation

36. B: The first step is to make all exponents positive by moving the terms with negative exponents to the opposite side of the fraction. This expression becomes:

$$\frac{4b^3b^2}{a^1a^4} \times \frac{3a}{b}$$

Then the rules for exponents can be used to simplify. Multiplying the same bases means the exponents can be added. Dividing the same bases means the exponents are subtracted. Thus, after multiplying the exponents in the first fraction, the expression becomes:

$$\frac{4b^5}{a^5} \times \frac{3a}{b}$$

Therefore, we can first multiply to get:

$$\frac{12ab^5}{a^5b}$$

Then, simplifying yields:

$$12\frac{b^4}{a^4}$$

37. B: There are two zeros for the function: $x = 0, -2$. The zeros can be found several ways, but this particular equation can be factored into:

$$f(x) = x(x^2 + 4x + 4) = x(x + 2)(x + 2)$$

By setting each factor equal to zero and solving for x, there are two solutions: $x = 0$ and $x = -2$. On a graph, these zeros can be seen where the line crosses the x-axis.

38. B: To expand a squared binomial, it's necessary to use the first, outer, inner, last (FOIL) method.

$$(2x - 4y)^2$$

$$(2x)(2x) + (2x)(-4y) + (-4y)(2x) + (-4y)(-4y)$$

$$4x^2 - 8xy - 8xy + 16y^2$$

$$4x^2 - 16xy + 16y^2$$

39. A: The common denominator here will be $4x$. Rewrite these fractions as:

$$\frac{3}{x} + \frac{5u}{2x} - \frac{u}{4} = \frac{12}{4x} + \frac{10u}{4x} - \frac{ux}{4x} = \frac{12x + 10u - ux}{4x}$$

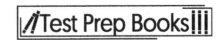

40. A: Finding the product means distributing one polynomial onto the other. Each term in the first polynomial must be multiplied by each term in the second polynomial. Then, like terms can be collected. Multiplying the factors yields the expression:

$$20x^3 + 4x^2 + 24x - 40x^2 - 8x - 48$$

Collecting like terms means adding the x^2 terms and adding the x terms. The final answer after simplifying the expression is:

$$20x^3 - 36x^2 + 16x - 48$$

41. D: Finding the zeros for a function by factoring is done by setting the equation equal to zero, then completely factoring. Since there is a common x for each term in the provided equation, that should be factored out first to get $x(x^2 - 3x - 4)$. Then, the quadratic that is left can be factored into two binomials, which are $(x + 1)(x - 4)$. This gives the factored equation $0 = x(x + 1)(x - 4)$.

42. D: Dividing rational expressions follows the same rule as dividing fractions. The division is changed to multiplication by the reciprocal of the second fraction. This turns the expression into:

$$\frac{5x^3}{3x^2y} \times \frac{3y^9}{25}$$

This can be simplified by finding common factors in the numerators and denominators of the two fractions.

$$\frac{x^3}{x^2y} \times \frac{y^9}{5}$$

Multiplying across creates:

$$\frac{x^3 y^9}{5x^2 y}$$

Simplifying leads to the final expression of:

$$\frac{xy^8}{5}$$

43. B: We can try to solve the equation by factoring the numerator into $(x + 6)(x - 5)$. Since the factor $(x - 5)$ is on the top and bottom, it cancels out. This leaves the equation $x + 6 = 11$. Solving the equation gives the answer $x = 5$. When this value is plugged into the equation, it yields a zero in the denominator of the fraction. Since this is undefined, there is no solution.

44. D: This problem can be solved by using unit conversion. The initial units are miles per minute. The final units need to be feet per second. Converting miles to feet uses the equivalence statement 1 mi = 5,280 ft. Converting minutes to seconds uses the equivalence statement 1 min = 60 s. Setting up the ratios to convert the units is shown in the following equation:

$$\frac{72 \text{ mi}}{90 \text{ min}} \times \frac{1 \text{ min}}{60 \text{ s}} \times \frac{5{,}280 \text{ ft}}{1 \text{ mi}} = 70.4 \frac{\text{ft}}{\text{s}}$$

The initial units cancel out, and the new units are left.

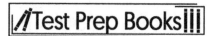

45. B: The formula can be manipulated by dividing both the length, l, and the width, w, on both sides. The length and width will cancel on the right, leaving height, h, by itself.

46. D: This problem can be solved by setting up a proportion involving the given information and the unknown value. The proportion is:

$$\frac{21 \text{ pages}}{4 \text{ nights}} = \frac{140 \text{ pages}}{x \text{ nights}}$$

We can cross-multiply to get $21x = 4 \times 140$. Solving this, we find $x \approx 26.67$. Since this is not an integer, we round up to 27 nights because 26 nights would not give Sarah enough time to finish.

47. D: The slope from this equation is 50, and it is interpreted as the cost per gigabyte used. Since the g-value represents the number of gigabytes and the equation is set equal to the cost in dollars, the slope relates these two values. For every gigabyte used on the phone, the bill goes up 50 dollars.

48. B: The y-intercept of an equation is found where the x-value is zero. Plugging zero into the equation for x, the first two terms cancel out, leaving -4:

$$0^2 + 3(0) - 4 = -4$$

49. A: The area of floor that he mops equals his rate of mopping multiplied by the amount of time he works: $a = rt$. (This is similar to the distance formula, $d = rt$.) On Monday, his rate was p, and his time was 4 hours, so we can use our formula to find that the floor's area is $a = p \times 4$, or $4p$. On Tuesday, the area of the floor remains the same, but the time is now $t = 3$, and the unknown rate r is what we're trying to find, so our area formula tells us that $4p = r \times 3$. Solving this equation for r, we find $r = \left(\frac{4}{3}\right)p$.

50. C: $40N$ would be 4,000% of N. All of the other coefficients are equivalent to $\frac{40}{100}$ or 40%.

51. B: Instead of multiplying these out, we can estimate the product by using $18 \times 10 = 180$.

52. B: Solve for n:

$$\frac{5}{2} \div \frac{1}{3} = \frac{5}{2} \times \frac{3}{1} = \frac{15}{2} = 7.5$$

Since $n = 7.5$, it falls between 7 and 9. Therefore, Choice B is the correct answer.

Reading

Comprehension

1. B: The passage begins by giving the reader information about traditional birthing situations. Then, we are told that Mr. and Mrs. Button decide to go against tradition to have their baby in a hospital. The next few paragraphs are dedicated to letting the reader know how Mr. Button dresses and goes to the hospital to welcome his new baby. There is a doctor in this excerpt, as Choice C indicates, and clothes are discussed, as Choice D indicates. However, Mr. Button is not going to the doctor's office, nor is he about to go shopping for new clothes.

2. A: We are told in the fourth paragraph that Mr. Button "arose nervously." We also see him running without caution to the doctor to find out about his wife and baby—this indicates his excitement. We also see him stuttering in a nervous yet excited fashion as he asks the doctor if it's a boy or girl. Though the doctor may seem a bit abrupt at

the end, indicating a bit of anger or shame, neither of these choices is the overwhelming tone of the entire passage. Despite the circumstances, joy and gratitude are not the main tone in the passage.

3. C: The morning is dedicated to the birth of the Buttons' child. Choice A, *numbed*, Choice B, *chained*, and Choice D, *moved*, all could grammatically fit in the sentence. However, they do not match the excerpt's use of *consecrated* the way *dedicated* does.

4. D: The author describes a visual image—the doctor rubbing his hands together—first and foremost. The author may be trying to make a comment about the profession; however, the author does not "explain the details of the doctor's profession" as Choice B suggests.

5. D: We know we are being introduced to the setting because we are given the year in the very first paragraph, along with the season: "one day in the summer of 1860." This is a classic structure for an introduction of the setting. In the third paragraph we also get a long explanation of Mr. Button, who is related to him, and what his life is like.

6. B: "Talk sense!" is an example of an imperative sentence. An imperative sentence gives a command. The doctor is commanding Mr. Button to talk sense. Choice A is an example of an exclamatory sentence, which expresses excitement. Choice C is an example of an interrogative sentence—these types of sentences ask questions. Choice D is an example of a declarative sentence. This means that the character is simply making a statement.

7. C: The point of view is told in third person omniscient. We know this because the story starts out with us knowing something that the character does not know: that her husband has died. Mrs. Mallard eventually comes to know this, but we as readers know this information before it is broken to her. In third person limited, Choice D, we would only see and know what Mrs. Mallard herself knew, and we would find out the news of her husband's death when she found out the news, not before.

8. A: The irony in this story is called situational irony, which means the situation that takes place is different than what the audience anticipated. At the beginning of the story, we see Mrs. Mallard react with a burst of grief to her husband's death. However, once she's alone, she begins to contemplate her future and says the word "free" over and over. This is quite a different reaction from Mrs. Mallard than what readers expected from the beginning of the story.

9. B: The word *elusive* most closely means *indefinable*. *Elusive* means "difficult to find, catch, or achieve". *Horrible*, Choice A, means "causing horror or shock", which doesn't match the word *elusive*. Choice C and D are also not good matches for the word *elusive*. *Indefinable* means "not able to be defined or described exactly", so Choice B is the best option.

10. D: A summary is a brief explanation of the main point of a story. The story mostly focuses on Mrs. Mallard and her reaction to her husband's death, especially in the room when she's alone and contemplating the present and future.

11. D: The interesting thing about this story is that feelings that are confused, joyful, and depressive all play a unique and almost equal part in this story. There is no one right answer here because the author seems to display all of these emotions through the character of Mrs. Mallard. She displays feelings of depression in her grief at the beginning; then, when she receives feelings of joy, she feels moments of confusion. We as readers cannot help but go through these feelings with the character. Thus, the author creates a tone of depression, joy, and confusion, all in one story.

12. C: If you don't know the meaning of "tumultuously," look at the surrounding context to figure it out. In the next few sentences, we see Mrs. Mallard striving to "beat back" the "thing that was approaching to possess her." We see

265

a fearful and almost violent reaction to the emotion that she's having. Thus, her chest would rise and fall tumultuously, or violently.

13. D: Outspending other countries on education could have other benefits, but there is no reference to this in the passage, so Choice *A* is incorrect. Choice *B* is incorrect because the author does not mention corruption. Choice *C* is incorrect because there is nothing in the passage stating that the tests are not genuinely representative. Choice *D* is accurate because spending more money has not brought success. The United States already spends the most money, and the country is not excelling on these tests. Choice *D* is the correct answer.

14. B: The thesis is a statement that contains the author's topic and main idea. The main purpose of this article is to use historical evidence to provide counterarguments to anti-Stratfordians. Choice *A* is simply a definition; Choice *C* is a supporting detail, not a main idea; and Choice *D* represents an idea of anti-Stratfordians, not the author's opinion.

15. C: This question requires readers to be familiar with different types of rhetorical devices. A rhetorical question is a question that is asked not to obtain an answer but to encourage readers to more deeply consider an issue.

16. B: This question asks readers to refer to the organizational structure of the article and demonstrate understanding of how the author provides details to support their argument. This particular detail can be found in the second paragraph where the author says, "even though he did not attend university, grade-school education in Shakespeare's time was actually quite rigorous."

17. A: The best choices provided for the meaning of "bustling" is "busy." This is a vocabulary question that can be answered using context clues. Other sentences in the paragraph describe London as "the most populous city in England" filled with "crowds of people," giving an image of a busy city full of people. Choice *B* is incorrect because London was in Shakespeare's home country, not a foreign one. Choice *C* is not mentioned in the passage. Choice *D* is not a good answer choice because the passage describes how London was a popular and important city, not an undeveloped one.

18. D: The purpose is to define and describe instances of spinoff technology. This is an example of a purpose question—*why* did the author write this? The article contains facts, definitions, and other objective information without telling a story or arguing an opinion. In this case, the purpose of the article is to inform the reader. Choices *A* and *B* are incorrect because they argue for an opinion or present a position. Choice *C* is incorrect because the focus of the article is spinoff technology, not the history of space technology.

19. A: This organization question asks readers to analyze the structure of the essay. The topic of the essay is spinoff technology; the first paragraph gives a general definition of the concept, while the following two paragraphs offer more detailed examples to help illustrate this idea.

20. C: This reading comprehension question can be answered based on the second paragraph—scientists were concerned about astronauts' nutrition and began researching useful nutritional supplements (such as algae) in their quest to find ways to add health benefits to food. Choice *A* in particular is not true because it reverses the order of discovery. First NASA identified the algae for astronauts to use and then it was further developed for use in baby food, not the other way around. Choices *B* and *D* are not uses of algae discussed in the article.

21. B: Even for readers who have never encountered the word *neurological* before, the passage does provide context clues. The sentence following the statement about neurological benefits says algae has "potential to boost brain health." From this context, readers should be able to infer that *neurological* is related to the brain.

22. D: This purpose question requires readers to understand the relevance of the given detail. In this case, the author mentions "costly and crucial equipment" before mentioning space suit visors, which are given as an example of something that is very valuable. Choice *A* is not correct because fashion is only related to sunglasses, not to NASA

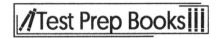

equipment. Choice *B* can be eliminated because it is simply not mentioned in the passage. While Choice *C* seems like it could be a true statement, it is also not relevant to what is being explained by the author.

23. C: The article gives several examples of how businesses have been able to capitalize on NASA research, so it is unlikely that the author would agree with this statement. Evidence for the other answer choices can be found in the article. For Choice *A*, the author mentions that "many consumers are unaware that products they are buying are based on NASA research"; Choice *B* is a general definition of spinoff technology; and Choice *D* is mentioned in the final paragraph.

24. B: "Four score and seven years ago" is eighty-seven years, because the word "score" means "twenty."

25. C: The setting of this text is a battlefield in Gettysburg, Pennsylvania. Choices *A*, *B*, and *D* are incorrect because the text specifies that they "met on a great battlefield of that war."

26. D: Abraham Lincoln is a former president of the United States, so the correct answer is *D*, "The American Civil War." Though the U.S. was involved in World War I and II, Choices *A* and *C* are incorrect because they occurred long after the Gettysburg address. Choice *B* is incorrect, as the War of Spanish Succession involved Spain, Italy, Germany, and the Netherlands, and not the United States.

27. A: The speaker is trying to convey that the audience should perpetuate the ideals of freedom that the soldiers died fighting for. The speech calls on the audience to consider the soldiers who died on the battlefield and to perpetuate the ideals of freedom so that their deaths would not be in vain. Choice *B* is incorrect because, although they are there to "dedicate a portion of that field," there is no mention in the text of an annual memorial service. Choice *C* is incorrect because there is no aggressive language in the text, only reverence for the dead. Choice *D* is incorrect because forgetting the lives that were lost is the opposite of what Lincoln is suggesting.

28. A: Choice *A* is correct because Lincoln's intention was to memorialize the soldiers who had fallen as a result of war as well as celebrate those who had put their lives in danger for the sake of their country. Choices *B* and *C* are incorrect because Lincoln's speech was supposed to foster a sense of pride among the members of the audience while connecting them to the soldiers' experiences. Choice *D* is incorrect because Lincoln is saying that the sacrifice of the soldiers is more significant than a dedication ceremony, but he doesn't suggest that the ceremony is inappropriate.

29. C: The passage mentions teaching, Choice *A*, but it does not fit the format of a how-to document. A how-to document is a set of instructions for the reader to follow. Choice *B* is incorrect; the writer of the letter is not writing as a consumer of products, but is applying for a certain position within the company. Choice *D* is also incorrect, as the writer of the letter is not yet an employee, and therefore is incapable of writing the company's memo.

30. B: The writer of the letter has a master's degree in English. Choice *A* is incorrect because the writer of the letter is applying to be a writer/producer at Shadow Heat—they aren't currently a writer/producer there. Choice *C* is also incorrect because the passage states that the writer has nine years' experience in higher education, not ten. Choice *D* is incorrect because the position is listed in the very first sentence: writer/producer, not website designer.

31. D: Although Washington was from a wealthy background, the passage does not say that his wealth led to his republican ideals, so Choice *A* is not supported. Choice *B* also does not follow from the passage. Washington's warning against meddling in foreign affairs does not mean that he would oppose wars of every kind, so Choice *B* is wrong. Choice *C* is also unjustified since the author does not indicate that Alexander Hamilton's assistance was absolutely necessary. Choice *D* is correct because the passage states that Washington's farewell address clearly opposes political parties and partisanship. The author then notes that presidential elections often hit a fever pitch of partisanship. Thus, it follows that George Washington would probably not approve of modern political parties and their involvement in presidential elections.

 Answer Explanations

32. A: The author finishes the passage by applying Washington's farewell address to modern politics, so the purpose probably includes this application. The other descriptions also fit the passage to some degree, but they do not describe the author's main purpose, which is revealed in the final paragraph.

33. D: Choice *A* is wrong because the last paragraph is not appropriate for a history textbook. Choice *B* is false because the piece is not a notice or announcement of Washington's death. Choice *C* is false because it is not fiction, but a historical writing. Choice *D* is correct. The passage is most likely to appear in a newspaper editorial because it cites information that is relevant and applicable to the present day, a popular subject in editorials.

34. D: The passage does not proceed in chronological order since it begins by pointing out Christopher Columbus's explorations in America, so Choice *A* does not work. Although the author compares and contrasts Erikson with Columbus, this is not the main way the information is presented; therefore, Choice B does not work. Choice C is also incorrect because there is no mention of or reference to cause and effect in the passage. However, the passage does offer a conclusion (Leif Erikson deserves more credit) and premises (first European to set foot in the New World and first to contact the natives) to substantiate Erikson's historical importance. Thus, Choice *D* is correct.

35. C: Choice *A* is wrong because it describes facts: Leif Erikson was the son of Erik the Red and historians debate Leif's date of birth. These are not opinions. Choice *B* is wrong; Erikson calling the land Vinland is a verifiable fact, as is Choice *D*, because he did contact the natives almost 500 years before Columbus. Choice *C* is the correct answer because it is the author's opinion that Erikson deserves more credit. Another person could argue that Columbus or another explorer deserves more credit, which makes it an opinion rather than a historical fact.

36. B: Choice *A* is wrong because the author aims to go beyond describing Erikson as merely a legendary Viking. Choice *C* is wrong because the author does not focus on Erikson's motivations, let alone name the spreading of Christianity as his primary objective. Although it's true that Erikson contacted the natives 500 years before Columbus, Choice *D* is wrong because it isn't the author's main conclusion, it is simply a fact used to support the main conclusion. Choice *B* is correct because it accurately identifies the author's statement that Erikson deserves more credit than he has received for being the first European to explore the New World.

37. B: Choice *A* is wrong because the author is not in any way trying to entertain the reader. Choice *D* is wrong because he goes beyond merely a suggestion; "suggest" is too vague. Although the author is certainly trying to alert the readers (make them aware) of Leif Erikson's underappreciated and unheralded accomplishments, the nature of the writing does not indicate the author would be satisfied with the reader merely knowing of Erikson's exploration, Choice *C*. Rather, the author would want the reader to be informed about it, which is more substantial, Choice *B*.

38. D: Choice *A* is wrong because the author never addresses the Vikings' state of mind or emotions. Choice *B* is wrong because the author does not elaborate on Erikson's exile and whether he would have become an explorer if not for his banishment. Choice *C* is wrong because there is not enough information to support this premise. It is unclear whether Erikson informed the King of Norway of his findings. Although it is true that the king did not send a follow-up expedition, he could have simply chosen not to expend the resources after receiving Erikson's news. It is not possible to logically infer whether Erikson told him. Choice *D* is correct because the uncertainty about Leif Erikson's birth year is an example of how historians have trouble pinning down important details in Viking history.

39. B: Narrative, Choice *A*, means a written account of connected events. Think of narrative writing as a story. Choice *C*, expository writing, generally seeks to explain or describe some phenomenon, whereas Choice *D*, technical writing, includes directions, instructions, and/or explanations. This passage is persuasive writing, which hopes to change someone's beliefs based on an appeal to reason or emotion. The author is aiming to convince the reader that smoking is terrible. They use health, price, and beauty in their argument against smoking, so Choice *B*, persuasive, is the correct answer.

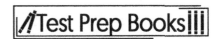

40. B: The author is opposed to tobacco. The author cites disease and deaths associated with smoking, and points to the monetary expense and aesthetic costs. Choice *A* is wrong because alternatives to smoking are not addressed in the passage. Choice *C* is wrong because it does not summarize the passage but rather is just a premise. Choice *D* is wrong because, while these statistics are a premise in the argument, they do not represent a summary of the piece. Choice *B* is the correct answer because it states the three critiques offered against tobacco and expresses the author's conclusion.

Vocabulary

41. C: Jackson wanted to relieve his *parched* throat. *Parched* is the correct answer because it means *thirsty*. Choice *A*, humid, means moist, and usually refers to the weather. Choice *B*, scorched, means blackened or baked, and doesn't fit in this context. While Jackson's throat could have been dusty, Choice *D*, from playing baseball, one usually doesn't need to relieve a dusty throat, but instead clean it.

42. A: The two friends became closer. For this question, it's important to look at the context of the sentence. The second sentence says the friends shared good memories on the trip, which would not make the friends distant or irritable, Choices *B* and *D*. Choice *C* does not grammatically fit within the sentence: "became suffering" is incorrect usage. Therefore, Choice *A* is correct.

43. B: She promised her fans the sequel would be just as exciting as the first. Choice *A*, *denied*, is the opposite of the word *promised* and does not fit with the word *excited*. Choice *C*, *invigorated*, means energized, and might fit the tone of the sentence with the word *excited.* However, *promised* is the better word to use here. Choice *D*, *germinated*, means to grow.

44. C: My hands started shaking and my heart stopped. Usually when someone is afraid or nervous, their hands start to shake. Choice *A*, *dancing*, does not make sense in the context of the sentence. Choice *B*, *glowing,* is incorrect; hands usually do not glow when one is afraid of something. Choice *D*, *throbbing,* is closer than *A* or *B*, but Choice *C*, *shaking*, is a better answer than *throbbing.*

45. B: Gabriel would usually go to the library and study after school. This is the best answer choice because the typical place for someone to go and study would be the library. The park is incorrect because Leo was already playing basketball in the park, and the sentence tells us "Unlike Leo." Usually people don't go to the mall or the arcade to study.

46. A: The runners sprinted toward the finish line. Choice *B* is incorrect; runners who begin a race usually don't skip toward the finish line. Choice *C* does not fit within the context of the sentence, as normally runners would be *sprinting* and not *rejoicing* toward a finish line. Choice *D*, *herded,* means to gather around something; usually *herded* is used for animals and not for runners.

47. D: Lashonda *vowed* to write it before it was due. *Vowed* means to promise something. In this case, LaShonda vowed to write her paper early so that she would get an *A* on her paper. Choice *A*, refused, is incorrect because if she refused to write the paper two weeks before it was due, she probably wouldn't get an *A* on it. Choice *B*, procrastinated, means to put off, so this is incorrect. Choice *C*, located, doesn't make sense in this context.

48. D: They went to the bank to deposit a check. When people go to the bank with a check, they usually don't *celebrate* it, Choice *A*, but do something more practical with it, like deposit it. Choice *B*, *neutralize*, means to counteract something, and is incorrect in this sentence. Choice *C, eliminate*, means to get rid of something, and is also incorrect here.

49. B: The sale at the grocery store inspired my dad to buy four avocados instead of two. The word *inspired* means encouraged or stimulated. Sales are usually seen as a positive experience, so the sale *inspired* the dad to buy more avocados. The rest of the words (*intimidated, dismayed,* and *berated*) have negative connotations and therefore do not fit within the context of the sentence.

50. A: In order to increase the quality of her health. This word makes the most sense within the context of the sentence. Becoming healthier is a direct effect of consuming fruits and vegetables, so *quality* is the best choice here.

51. C: When Lindsay asked me to attend her party. Choice *A*, *acclaim*, is an expression of approval, and is not the right fit here. Choice *B*, *astound*, means to amaze. Usually we don't hear of people "amazing" other people's parties. This is not the best choice. Choice *D*, *amend*, means to improve or correct. Again, this is not the best choice for the context; the speaker is wondering what gift to bring Lindsay, and is not thinking about ways to correct the party.

52. A: Until she activated the fire alarm by burning the casserole in the oven. Choice *B*, *offended*, is the wrong choice here. You can offend a person because they have emotions, but you cannot offend a fire alarm. Choice *C*, *unplugged*, is also incorrect. You cannot unplug a fire alarm by burning a casserole. Choice *D*, *disbanded,* is the opposite of *activated* and is incorrect in this context.

53. D: Before she arrived at the dreaded dentist's office. Choice *A*, *refreshing*, is not an adjective used to describe a dentist's office, especially when the patient is about to take care of a cavity. Choice *B*, *creative*, also does not fit within the context of the sentence. Choice *C*, *rapturous*, means ecstatic or happy, and is the opposite sentiment of what we are looking for.

54. B: Told us that the bird was indigenous to the southeast part of the United States. *Indigenous* means native to a certain area, so Choice *B* is the best answer here. Choice *A*, *entertaining*, does not make sense within this context. Choice *C*, *impudent,* means bold or shameless. Choice *D*, *monotonous*, means remaining the same or dull. These latter two answer choices are not the best fit for this context.

55. C: The correct word here is *route*, which means course or road.

56. D: Their bodies slithered out of our hands and back into the water. Choices *A* and *C*, *exploded* and *thundered*, are too extreme for the context. *Deteriorated*, Choice *B*, means to have crumbled or disintegrated, which is not something an eel's body is likely to do on its own. Choice *D* is the best answer for this sentence.

57. A: My mom requested the eggplant with no cheese. *Directed*, Choice *B*, means to supervise or conduct, and does not make sense in the context of the sentence. Choice *C*, *mourned*, means to grieve over, and is also incorrect. Choice *D*, *endorsed*, means to approve or support something. Pay attention to words like *even though* that suggest a contrast of surprising facts.

58. A: The correct answer choice is *A*, admittance, which means the right to enter. Choice *B*, annex, is incorrect. Annex means an extension or something added. Choice *C*, disjunction, is incorrect because it means separation. Choice *D* is incorrect because *occult* is an adjective and means secret or mysterious.

59. C: Diligent is the correct answer because it means hard-working, and someone would be *hard-working* if they saved money to go on a trip. Choice *A*, *delirious*, means mentally unbalanced, so this is incorrect. *Superfluous* means extra or unnecessary, so Choice *B* is incorrect. *Reticent* means secret or quiet, so Choice *D* is also not the best answer choice.

60. D: Friendships can grow distant, Choice *D*. Choice *A*, *elegant*, is incorrect, because it means beautiful or tasteful. Choices *B* and *C*, *loquacious* (talkative) and *mingling* (to mix), is something that happens to friendships when they are going well. However, since we know that the context makes it difficult for the friendship to flourish, Choice *D* is the best answer.

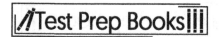

61. B: *Convalescence* is the correct word here because convalescence means the time of recovery after an illness. Choice *A*, *transaction*, is a process used in business and is not correct in this context. Choice *B*, *reverberation*, means a reechoed sound, so this is incorrect. Choice *D*, *consciousness*, is incorrect. It doesn't make sense for consciousness to be "a long one."

62. B: The best answer here is *hastily*, because it means hurriedly, and the luckiest thing would be if the deer got out of the way hurriedly. Choice *A*, *wistfully*, means sadly, so this is incorrect. Choice *C*, *vivaciously*, means spirited or animated, and while deer could jump this way, this answer doesn't really fit with the tone of getting out of a truck's way. Choice *D* is incorrect because again, while some deer might jump *augustly*, meaning to inspire reverence, this is not the best answer in context.

Mathematics

1. A: Compare each number after the decimal point to figure out which overall number is greatest. In Choices *A* (1.43785) and *C* (1.43592), both have the same tenths place (4) and hundredths place (3). However, the thousandths place is greater in Choice *A* (7), so *A* has the greatest value overall.

2. D: By rearranging and grouping the factors in Choice *D*, we can notice that $3 \times 3 \times 4 \times 2 = (3 \times 2) \times (4 \times 3) = 6 \times 12$, which is what we were looking for.

3. C: The total percentage of a pie chart equals 100%. We can see that CD sales make up less than half of the chart (50%) but more than a quarter (25%), and the only answer choice that meets these criteria is Choice *C*, 40%.

4. B: Since $850 is the price after a 20% discount, $850 represents 80% of the original price. To determine the original price, set up a proportion with the ratio of the sale price (850) to the original price (unknown) equal to the ratio of sale percentage (where x represents the unknown original price):

$$\frac{850}{x} = \frac{80}{100}$$

To solve a proportion, cross multiply and set the products equal to each other:

$$(850)(100) = (80)(x)$$

Multiplying each side results in the equation:

$$85,000 = 80x$$

To solve for x, divide both sides by 80:

$$\frac{85,000}{80} = \frac{80x}{80}$$

$$x = 1,062.5$$

Remember that x represents the original price. Subtracting the sale price from the original price ($1,062.50 − $850) indicates that Frank saved $212.50.

5. C: An x-intercept is the point where the graph crosses the x-axis. At this point, the value of y is 0. To determine if an equation has an x-intercept of −2, substitute −2 for x, and calculate the value of y. If the value of −2 for x corresponds with a y-value of 0, then the equation has an x-intercept of −2. The only answer choice that produces this result is Choice *C*.

$$0 = (-2)^2 + 5(-2) + 6$$

6. C: In this scenario, the variables are the number of sales and Karen's weekly pay. The weekly pay depends on the number of sales. Therefore, weekly pay is the dependent variable (y), and the number of sales is the independent variable (x). All four answer choices are in slope-intercept form, $y = mx + b$, so we just need to find m (the slope) and b (the y-intercept). We can calculate both by picking any two points, for example, (2, 380) and (4, 460).

The slope is given by $m = \frac{y_2 - y_1}{x_2 - x_1}$, so $m = \frac{460-380}{4-2} = 40$. This gives us the equation $y = 40x + b$. Now we can plug in the x and y values from our first point to find b. Since $380 = 40(2) + b$, we find $b = 300$. This means the equation is $y = 40x + 300$.

7. D: The total faculty is:

$$15 + 20 = 35$$

So, the ratio is $35 : 200$. Then, divide both of these numbers by 5, since 5 is a common factor to both, with a result of $7 : 40$.

8. C: The first step in solving this problem is expressing the result in fraction form. Multiplication and division are typically performed in order from left to right, but they can be performed in any order. For this problem, let's start with the division operation between the last two fractions. When dividing one fraction by another, invert—or flip—the second fraction and then multiply the numerators and denominators.

$$\frac{7}{10} \times \frac{2}{1} = \frac{14}{10}$$

Next, multiply the first fraction by this value:

$$\frac{3}{5} \times \frac{14}{10} = \frac{42}{50}$$

Decimals are expressions of 1 or 100%, so multiply both the numerator and denominator by 2 to get the fraction into the form 100.

$$\frac{42}{50} \times \frac{2}{2} = \frac{84}{100}$$

In decimal form, this would be expressed as 0.84.

9. C: To find what 85% of 20 questions is, multiply 20 by .85:

$$20 \ x \ .85 \ = \ 17 \ questions$$

10. B: The power of 10 by which a digit is multiplied corresponds with the number of zeros following the digit when expressing its value in standard form. Therefore:

$$(1 \times 10^4) + (3 \times 10^3) + (7 \times 10^1) + (8 \times 10^0)$$

$$10{,}000 + 3{,}000 + 70 + 8 = 13{,}078$$

11. B: Using the conversion rate, multiply the projected weight loss of 25 lb by $0.45 \frac{\text{kg}}{\text{lb}}$ to get the amount in kilograms (11.25 kg).

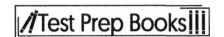

12. D: First, subtract $1,437 from $2,334.50 to find Johnny's monthly savings; this equals $897.50. Then, multiply this amount by 3 to find out how much he will have (in 3 months) before he pays for his vacation; this equals $2,692.50. Finally, subtract the cost of the vacation ($1,750) from this amount to find how much Johnny will have left: $942.50.

13. B: Dividing by 98 can be approximated by dividing by 100, which would mean shifting the decimal point of the numerator to the left by 2. The result is 4.2, which rounds to 4.

14. A: Parallel lines have the same slope. The slope of the given equation is 3. The slope of Choice C can be seen to be $\frac{1}{3}$ by dividing both sides by 3. The other choices are in standard form $Ax + By = C$, for which the slope is given by $\frac{-A}{B}$. For Choice A, the equation can be written as $6x - 2y = -2$. Therefore, the slope is:

$$\frac{-A}{B} = \frac{-6}{-2} = 3$$

This is the same as the given equation. The slope of Choice B is:

$$\frac{-A}{B} = \frac{-4}{-1} = 4$$

The slope of Choice B is 4. The slope of Choice D is:

$$\frac{-A}{B} = \frac{-2}{-2} = 1$$

The slope of Choice D is 1. Therefore, the only equation with a parallel slope of 3 is $6x - 2y = -2$.

15. C: The formula for the perimeter of a rectangle is $P = 2L + 2W$, where P is the perimeter, L is the length, and W is the width. The first step is to substitute all of the data into the formula:

$$36 = 2(12) + 2W$$

Simplify by multiplying 2×12:

$$36 = 24 + 2W$$

Simplifying this further by subtracting 24 on each side, which gives:

$$36 - 24 = 24 - 24 + 2W$$

$$12 = 2W$$

Divide by 2:

$$6 = W$$

The width is 6 cm. Remember to test this answer by substituting this value into the original formula:

$$36 = 2(12) + 2(6)$$

273

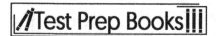

16. D: To find the average of a set of values, add the values together and then divide by the total number of values. In this case, include the unknown value, x, of what Dwayne needs to score on his next test. The average must equal 90. Set up the equation and solve.

First, combine like terms:

$$\frac{78 + 92 + 83 + 97 + x}{5} = 90$$

$$\frac{350 + x}{5} = 90$$

Next, multiply both sides by 5:

$$(5)(\frac{350 + x}{5}) = (90)(5)$$

$$350 + x = 450$$

Lastly, subtract 350 from both sides:

$$350 + x - 350 = 450 - 350$$

$$x = 100$$

17. D: For an even number of total values, the median is calculated by finding the mean, or average, of the two middle values once all values have been arranged in ascending order from least to greatest. In this case, $\frac{83+92}{2}$ would equal the median 87.5, Choice D. Choice A is the lowest two values divided by 2, $\frac{78+83}{2} = 80.5$. Choice B is the first and third values divided by 2, $\frac{78+92}{2} = 85$. Choice C is the second and fourth values divided by 2, $\frac{83+97}{2}=90$.

18. C: Follow the order of operations in order to solve this problem. Evaluate inside the parentheses first, being sure to follow the order of operations inside the parentheses as well. First, simplify the square roots:

$$(6 \times 4) - 3^2$$

Then, multiply inside the parentheses:

$$24 - 3^2$$

Next, simplify the exponent:

$$24 - 9$$

Finally, subtract to get 15, Choice C.

19. D: Three girls for every two boys can be expressed as a ratio: 3:2. This can be visualized as splitting the school into five groups: three girl groups and two boy groups. The number of students that are in each group can be found by dividing the total number of students by five:

$$\frac{650 \text{ students}}{5 \text{ groups}} = \frac{130 \text{ students}}{\text{group}}$$

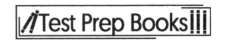

To find the total number of girls, multiply the number of students per group (130) by the number of girl groups in the school (3). This equals 390, Choice *D*.

20. D: The total amount the company pays, y, equals the cost of the building ($50,000) plus the cost of the saws. Since the saws cost $40 each, the overall cost of the saws is $40 times x, where x is the number of saws. Putting all this together, we have $y = 50,000 + 40x$, which is equivalent to Choice *D*.

21. C: Kimberley worked 4.5 hours at the rate of $10 / h and 1 hour at the rate of $12 / h. The problem states that her time is rounded to the nearest hour, so the 4.5 hours would round up to 5 hours at the rate of $10 / h.

$$(5 \text{ h}) \times \left(\frac{\$10}{h}\right) + (1 \text{ h}) \times \left(\frac{\$12}{h}\right) = \$50 + \$12 = \$62$$

22. D:

$9x + x - 7 = 16 + 2x$	Combine $9x$ and x.
$10x - 7 = 16 + 2x$	
$10x - 7 + 7 = 16 + 2x + 7$	Add 7 to both sides to remove the −7.
$10x = 23 + 2x$	
$10x - 2x = 23 + 2x - 2x$	Subtract $2x$ from both sides to move it to the other side of the equation.
$8x = 23$	
$\dfrac{8x}{8} = \dfrac{23}{8}$	Divide by 8 to get x by itself.
$x = \dfrac{23}{8}$	

23. C: For each fraction, we can divide the numerator by the denominator to find a decimal value. $\frac{4}{5} = 0.8$, $\frac{2}{3} \approx 0.67$, and $\frac{91}{100} = 0.91$. Ordering these from least to greatest gives us 0.67, 0.8, 0.85, and 0.91, which matches Choice *C*.

24. B: First, calculate the difference between the larger value and the smaller value:

$$378 - 252 = 126$$

To calculate this difference as a percentage of the original value, and thus calculate the percentage *increase*, divide 126 by 252 to get 0.5, then multiply by 100 to reach the percentage 50%, Choice *B*.

25. C: There are 34 girls who are potty-trained out of a total of 52 girls:

$$34 \div 52 \approx 0.65 = 65\%$$

26. A: First, simplify the larger fraction by separating it into two. When dividing one fraction by another, remember to invert the second fraction and multiply, like so:

275

$$\frac{5}{7} \times \frac{11}{9}$$

The resulting fraction $\frac{55}{63}$ cannot be simplified further, so this is the answer to the problem.

27. A: To calculate the range in a set of data, subtract the lowest value from the highest value. In this graph, the range of Mr. Lennon's students is 4, which can be be seen physically in the graph as having the smallest difference compared with the other teachers between the highest value and the lowest value.

28. C: The number of days can be found by taking the total amount Bernard needs to make and dividing it by the amount he earns per day:

$$\frac{300}{80} = \frac{30}{8} = \frac{15}{4} = 3.75$$

Bernard will need to work four days since he is only working full days and three days is not enough time.

29. D: To calculate the circumference of a circle, use the formula $2\pi r$, where r equals the radius (half of the diameter) of the circle and $\pi \approx 3.14$. Substitute the given information to get:

$$2 \times 3.14 \times 5 = 31.4$$

30. A: Mean. An outlier is a data value that's either far above or below the majority of values in a sample set. The mean is the average of all values in the set. In a small sample, a very high or low number could greatly change the average. The median is the middle value when arranged from lowest to highest. Outliers would have no more of an effect on the median than any other value. The mode is the value that repeats most often in a set. Assuming that the same outlier doesn't repeat, outliers would have no effect on the mode of a sample set.

31. A: This kind of line indicates a positive relationship. A negative relationship would match a line traveling from the upper left of the graph to the lower right. Exponential and logarithmic functions aren't linear—their graphs do not make a straight line.

32. A: The conversion can be obtained by setting up and evaluating the following expression:

$$4{,}382 \text{ ft} \times \frac{0.3048 \text{ m}}{1 \text{ ft}} \times \frac{1 \text{ km}}{1{,}000 \text{ m}} = 1.336 \text{ km}$$

33. D: Solve a linear inequality in a similar way to solving a linear equation. First, start by distributing the -3 on the left side of the inequality.

$$-3x - 12 \geq x + 8$$

Then, add 12 to both sides.

$$-3x \geq x + 20$$

Next, subtract x from both sides.

$$-4x \geq 20$$

Finally, divide both sides of the inequality by -4. Don't forget to flip the inequality sign because you are dividing by a negative number.

$$x \leq -5$$

34. A: Putting the scores in order from least to greatest, we have 60, 75, 80, and 85, as well as one unknown. The median is 80, so 80 must be the middle data point out of these five. Therefore, the unknown data point must be the fourth or fifth data point, meaning it must be greater than or equal to 80. The only answer that fails to meet this condition is 60.

35. A: Let the unknown score be x. The average will be:

$$\frac{5 \times 50 + 4 \times 70 + x}{10} = \frac{530 + x}{10} = 55$$

Multiply both sides by 10 to get $530 + x = 550$, or $x = 20$.

36. C: The scenario involves data consisting of two variables: month and stock value. Box plots display data consisting of values for one variable. Therefore, a box plot is not an appropriate choice. Both line plots and circle graphs are used to display frequencies within categorical data. Neither can be used for the given scenario. Line graphs display two numerical variables on a coordinate grid and show trends among the variables.

37. B: Start with the original equation, then simplify:

$$4\frac{1}{3} + 3\frac{3}{4} = 4 + 3 + \frac{1}{3} + \frac{3}{4} = 7 + \frac{1}{3} + \frac{3}{4}$$

Adding the fractions gives:

$$\frac{1}{3} + \frac{3}{4} = \frac{4}{12} + \frac{9}{12} = \frac{13}{12} = 1 + \frac{1}{12}$$

Finally:

$$7 + \frac{1}{3} + \frac{3}{4} = 7 + 1 + \frac{1}{12} = 8\frac{1}{12}$$

38. D: The probability of picking the winner of the race is $\frac{1}{4}$ or:

$$\left(\frac{\text{number of favorable outcomes}}{\text{number of total outcomes}}\right)$$

Assuming the winner was picked on the first selection, three horses remain from which to choose the runner-up (these are dependent events). Therefore, the probability of picking the runner-up is $\frac{1}{3}$. To determine the probability that multiple events all happen, multiply the probabilities of the events:

$$\frac{1}{4} \times \frac{1}{3} = \frac{1}{12}$$

39. A: The core of the pattern consists of 4 items: ▲○○□. Therefore, the core repeats in multiples of 4, with the pattern starting over on the next step. The highest multiple of 4 that's below 42 is 40. Step 40 is the end of the core (□), so step 41 will start the core over (▲) and step 42 is ○.

40. D: This system of equations involves one quadratic equation and one linear equation. One way to solve this is through substitution.

Solving for y in the second equation yields:

$$y = x + 2$$

Plugging this equation in for the y of the quadratic equation yields:

$$x^2 - 2x + x + 2 = 8$$

Simplify the equation:

$$x^2 - x + 2 = 8$$

Set this equal to zero and factor:

$$x^2 - x - 6 = 0 = (x - 3)(x + 2)$$

Solving these two factors for x gives the zeros:

$$x = 3, -2$$

To find the y-value for the point, plug in each number to either original equation. Solving each one for y yields the points $(3, 5)$ and $(-2, 0)$.

41. D: Parallel lines will never intersect. Therefore, the lines are not parallel. Perpendicular lines intersect to form a right angle (90°). Although the lines intersect, they do not form a right angle, which is usually indicated with a box at the intersection point. Therefore, the lines are not perpendicular.

42. C: Nothing is added to x and y since the center is 0 and 5^2 is 25. Choice *A* is not the correct answer because you do not subtract the radius from x and y. Choice *B* is not the correct answer because you must square the radius on the right side of the equation. Choice *D* is not the correct answer because you do not add the radius to x and y in the equation.

43. D: To convert a fraction to a percent, we can first convert the fraction to a decimal. To do so, divide the numerator by the denominator: $4 \div 5 = 0.8$. To convert a decimal to a percent, multiply by 100:

$$0.8 \times 100 = 80\%$$

44. B: The total trip time is:

$$1 + 3.5 + 0.5 = 5 \ hours$$

The total time driving is:

$$1 + 0.5 = 1.5 \ hours$$

So, the fraction of time spent driving is $\frac{1.5}{5}$ or $\frac{3}{10}$. To convert this to a percentage, multiply the top and bottom by 10 to make the denominator 100. We find $\frac{3}{10} \times \frac{10}{10} = \frac{30}{10}$. Since the denominator is 100, the numerator is our percentage: 30%.

45. D: This problem can be solved using basic arithmetic. Xavier starts with 20 apples, then gives his sister half, so 20 divided by 2:

$$\frac{20}{2} = 10$$

He then gives his neighbor six apples, so 6 is subtracted from 10.

$$10 - 6 = 4$$

Finally, he uses $\frac{3}{4}$ of his remaining apples to make a pie. Since $\frac{3}{4}$ of 4 is 3, he uses 3 apples, so 3 is subtracted from 4.

$$4 - 3 = 1$$

46. A: The hundredths place value is located two digits to the right of the decimal point (the digit 9 in the original number). To decide whether to round up or keep the digit, examine the digit to the right, and if it is 5 or greater, round up. In this case, the digit to the right is 6, so the hundredths place is rounded up. When rounding up, if the digit to be increased is a 9, the digit to its left is increased by one and the digit in the desired place value is made a zero. Therefore, the number is rounded to 847.90.

47. B: Fractions must have like denominators to be added. The common denominator is the least common multiple (LCM) of the two original denominators. In this case, the LCM is 15, so both fractions should be changed to equivalent fractions with a denominator of 15. Multiply the bottom of each fraction by whatever number is needed to produce 15, and multiply the top of each fraction by that same number:

$$\frac{1 \times 5}{3 \times 5} = \frac{5}{15} \ and \ \frac{2 \times 3}{5 \times 3} = \frac{6}{15}$$

Now, add the numerators and keep the denominator the same:

$$\frac{5}{15} + \frac{6}{15} = \frac{11}{15}$$

48. C: The sample space is made up of:

$$8 + 7 + 6 + 5 = 26 \text{ balls}$$

The probability of pulling each individual ball is $\frac{1}{26}$. Since there are 7 yellow balls, the probability of pulling a yellow ball is $\frac{7}{26}$.

49. A: Flip the second fraction and multiply.

$$\frac{4}{13} \times \frac{169}{27}$$

Simplify the fractions before multiplying to make the numbers simpler to work with.

$$\frac{4}{1} \times \frac{13}{27}$$

Multiply across the top and across the bottom.

$$\frac{4 \times 13}{1 \times 27} = \frac{52}{27}$$

The numerator and denominator do not have any factors in common, so this fraction cannot be reduced.

50. A: Divide 54 by 15:

$$
\begin{array}{r}
3 \\
15\overline{)54} \\
-45 \\
\hline
9
\end{array}
$$

The result is 3 with a remainder of 9, which is equivalent to $3\frac{9}{15}$. Reduce the fraction $\frac{9}{15}$ for the final answer, $3\frac{3}{5}$.

51. A: Using the order of operations, multiplication and division are computed first from left to right. Multiplication is on the left; therefore, multiplication should be performed first.

52. A: The formula for the area of a circle is A=πr^2. Here, $r = 9$, so we calculate $A = \pi(9^2) = 81\pi$.

53. D: The formula for finding the volume of a rectangular prism is $V = l \times w \times h$, where l is the length, w is the width, and h is the height. The volume of the original box is calculated:

$$V = 8 \text{ in} \times 14 \text{ in} \times 4 \text{ in} = 448 \text{ in}^3$$

The volume of the new box is calculated:

$$V = 16 \text{ in} \times 28 \text{ in} \times 8 \text{ in} = 3{,}584 \text{ in}^3$$

The volume of the new box divided by the volume of the old box equals 8.

54. D: Subtract the center from the x- and y-values of the equation and square the radius on the right side of the equation. Choice A is not the correct answer because it fails to square the radius. Choice B is not the correct answer because it incorrectly squares the x- and y-values of the center. Choice C is not the correct answer because it incorrectly adds the x- and y-values of the center rather than subtracting them.

55. A: We use the place value to the right of the thousandths place, which would be the ten-thousandths place. The value in the thousandths place is 7. The number in the place value to its right is greater than 4, so the 7 is bumped up to 8. Everything to its right is removed, which gives us 245.268.

56. C: The perimeter is found by calculating the sum of all sides of the polygon:

$$9 + 9 + 9 + 8 + 8 + s = 56$$

Let s be the missing side length. Therefore, $43 + s = 56$. The missing side length is 13 cm.

57. B: The area of a rectangle is $A = lw$. We don't know the length or width of this rectangle, but the area is 24, so we can say that $lw = 24$. Length and width are each multiplied by 3, so the area of our new rectangle is $3l \times 3w$, or $9lw$. Since we know that $lw = 24$, the area of the new rectangle is $9lw = 9 \times 24 = 216\ cm^2$.

58. C: Because area is a two-dimensional measurement, the dimensions are multiplied by a scale factor that is squared to determine the scale factor of the corresponding areas. The dimensions of the rectangle are multiplied by a scale factor of 3. Therefore, the area is multiplied by a scale factor of 3^2 (which is equal to 9):

59. D: Let a represent the number of apples and b the number of bananas. The total number of fruits is $a + b = 10$, and the total cost is $2a + 3b = 22$. To solve this pair of equations, we can multiply the first equation by –3:

$$-3(a + b) = -3(10)$$

$$-3a - 3b = -30$$

When we add this to the other equation, the b terms cancel out:

$$(-3a - 3b = -30) + (2a + 3b = 22)$$

$$= (-a = -8)$$

This simplifies to $a = 8$.

60. A: First, convert these numbers to improper fractions: $\frac{11}{3} - \frac{9}{5}$. Then, convert the fractions to have a common denominator of 15, subtract, and convert the answer back to a mixed number.

$$\frac{11}{3} - \frac{9}{5} = \frac{55}{15} - \frac{27}{15} = \frac{28}{15} = 1\frac{13}{15}$$

61. A: Setting up a proportion is the easiest way to represent this situation. The proportion is $\frac{20}{x} = \frac{40}{100}$, and cross-multiplication can be used to solve for x. Here, $40x = 2,000$, so $x = 50$.

62. A: Simplify this to:

$$(4x^2y^4)^{\frac{3}{2}} = 4^{\frac{3}{2}}(x^2)^{\frac{3}{2}}(y^4)^{\frac{3}{2}}$$

Now:

$$4^{\frac{3}{2}} = (\sqrt{4})^3 = 2^3 = 8$$

For the rest, recall that the exponents must be multiplied, so this yields:

$$8x^{2 \cdot \frac{3}{2}}y^{4 \cdot \frac{3}{2}} = 8x^3y^6$$

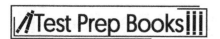
63. A: The slope is given by:

$$m = \frac{y_2 - y_1}{x_2 - x_1} = \frac{0 - 4}{0 - (-3)} = -\frac{4}{3}$$

64. C: We know that red cans are $1 each and blue cans are $2 each. Since the total cost is $16, we can say that $r \times 1 + b \times 2 = 16$, where r is the number of red cans and b is the number of blue cans. We can write this equation more simply as $r + 2b = 16$.

Because Jessica buys 10 cans total, we know that $r + b = 10$, so $b = 10 - r$. Substituting in $10 - r$ for b in the original equation, we get $r + 2(10 - r) = 16$. Simplifying and solving for r, we find:

$$r + 20 - 2r = 16$$

$$20 - r = 16$$

$$r = 4$$

Language

Punctuation and Capitalization

1. C: The correct answer choice is "Lets celebrate tomorrow." *Lets* is supposed to be short for "let us," and therefore needs an apostrophe between the *t* and the *s*: *Let's*.

2. A: The problematic choice is "It was true, Lyla ate the last cupcake." The comma creates a comma splice where a period or a semicolon should be since we have two independent clauses on either side of the comma.

3. D: Choices *A, B,* and *C* contain no errors in punctuation or capitalization.

4. C: Choice *C* is the correct answer because "Did you water the plants?" should have quotations around it. The other answer choices are correct as they are.

5. B: The words "great depression" should be capitalized to "Great Depression." Any kind of historical era must always be capitalized.

6. B: The problematic choice is *B*. Street names should always be capitalized. Therefore, the statement should say, "When I was a kid, we lived on Evergreen Road."

7. D: Choices *A, B,* and *C* contain no errors in punctuation or capitalization.

8. C: Choice *C* is the problematic answer; the whole phrase "Hoover Dam" should be capitalized, not just "Hoover."

9. A: Choice *A* is problematic; the phrase 'best teacher ever' should be in double quotes: "best teacher ever." Single quotes are used only when there is a quote inside a quote, like this: "What does the poem 'After Apple-Picking' mean?" asked Alexander.

10. B: Choice *B* is problematic because days of the week should always be capitalized: Monday, Tuesday, Wednesday, Thursday, Friday, Saturday, and Sunday.

11. D: Choices *A, B,* and *C* contain no errors in punctuation or capitalization.

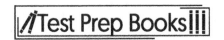

12. A: Choice *A* is problematic because the phrase "a yellow lab" should be separated by commas, since it's a descriptive phrase. It should read: "Buster, a yellow lab, was the newest addition to our family."

Usage

13. C: Choice *C* has an error in the sentence. "Because there was lots of food at the picnic" is considered a fragment. This fragment needs to be connected to an independent clause, like "We left satisfied because there was lots of food at the picnic."

14. D: Choices *A, B,* and *C* contain no errors in usage.

15. A: This error is marked by a subject/verb agreement. *Words* is plural, so the verb must be plural as well. The correct usage would be: "Their words were followed by a signing document."

16. D: Choices *A, B,* and *C* contain no errors in usage.

17. B: The choice with the error in usage is Choice *B*: "Louise and me went to the movie together." This should read: "Louise and I went to the movie together."

18. A: The error in Choice *A* is that "deers" is incorrect usage for the plural of "deer." The singular "deer" is also used for the plural "deer." "Deers" is not a word.

19. C: Choice *C* is incorrect because there is a comma missing after the introductory phrase. The sentence should say: "In spite of the overwhelming evidence, they decided not to prosecute."

20. C: Choice *C* has incorrect usage because "Its" should be "It's." We would say, "It is a common misconception," and the apostrophe is needed to denote that there are two words brought together as one, forming a contraction.

21. D: Choices *A, B,* and *C* contain no errors in usage.

22. B: Choice *B* has incorrect usage. In a compound sentence, the comma must go before the conjunction. The sentence should read like this: "We wanted something sweet, so we got ice cream." There are two independent clauses separated by a conjunction, so a comma is required here.

23. A: Choice *A* has the error in usage because we have a dangling modifier with the phrase "blue kid's shovel." The sentence indicates the kid is blue. We want the sentence to say that the shovel is blue. Therefore, it should be: "After her swim, Jeanine saw a kid's blue shovel."

24. C: In Choice *C* we are dealing with a vague pronoun reference. We're not sure if Oliver wasn't very happy or if the dog wasn't very happy. We would need to say, "Before feeding his dog that morning, Oliver was not very happy," or "Oliver's dog wasn't very happy that morning until he got fed."

25. D: Choices *A, B,* and *C* contain no errors in usage.

26. B: Choice *B* has a usage error in word choice. The word "accept" is mistaken for the word "except." "Except" means other than, while "accept" means to consent to something.

27. A: This choice has a faulty subject/verb agreement. Our subject here is "thing," not "friends," so the verb must also match the singular subject. The correct sentence should say, "One thing I miss has been my friends from high school."

28. C: This choice is correct because it contains a fragment. There is no verb in the phrase "The best dessert in the world," making it a fragment.

29. C: Choice C defies parallel structure. To make this sentence correct, it would look like this: "She wanted to start a business, join a local board, and run for office."

30. D: Choices A, B, and C contain no errors in usage.

31. B: Choice B has an error, because it contains a superfluous comma. To correct this sentence, take the comma out. It isn't needed.

32. A: The error is in Choice A. There is a comma in this sentence that doesn't belong. If there were two independent clauses, the comma would be correct, like this: "I called to schedule an appointment, and I talked to the receptionist." Or, we could say: "I called to schedule an appointment and talked to the receptionist."

33. C: Choice C has the error in usage. The word "table" is the subject of the sentence, not "cakes." Therefore, the verb must agree with "table." The correct sentence looks like this: "The table of cakes has fallen over."

34. C: There is a usage error in Choice C. The sentence lacks an apostrophe to show possession. It should look like the following: "Larisa's car was taken into the shop yesterday."

35. D: Choices A, B, and C contain no errors in usage.

36. A: The error is in Choice A because this is a run-on sentence. There should be a semicolon or a period after "swimming": "He went swimming; it was freezing outside."

37. C: Choice C has a usage error. The word "Their" should be "There." "Their" indicates a group of people.

Spelling

38. B: There is a spelling error in Choice B. The word "beleive" should be "believe." Remember the rule, "I before E except after C."

39. A: The misspelled word is Choice A, "propoganda." The correct spelling is "propaganda."

40. D: Choices A, B, and C contain no errors in spelling.

41. C: There is a spelling error in Choice C. The word "posession" is spelled "possession."

42. A: The spelling error in Choice A is "seperated." The correct spelling should be "separated."

43. A: The spelling error in Choice A is "threshhold." The correct spelling should be "threshold."

44. B: Choice B had the spelling error with the word "enviroment." The correct spelling is "environment."

45: D: Choices A, B, and C contain no errors in spelling.

46: D: Choices A, B, and C contain no errors in spelling.

47. C: The spelling error is in Choice C. The word "gaurd" should be spelled "guard."

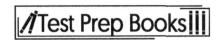

Composition

48. A: The correct answer is Choice *A*, whereas. Here we see a contrast in food choices; the word "whereas" indicates a contrast.

49. C: There is no cause and effect here or contrast. The correct answer is "and," because this is simply displaying steps taken in preparing for a party.

50. A: The correct answer is "therefore," because Callie's buying a piece of candy is a direct consequence of finding two dollars on the ground.

51. D: The correct answer is "Liam went to the basketball game, even though he had an exam to study for." "Even though" tells us "despite the fact" that Liam had an exam to study for, he did something else.

52. D: The correct answer is "Victor ran a mile for his workout; in addition, he did one hour of resistance training." The other answer choices do not indicate a continuation of the workout.

53. B: "Also" is the correct answer because it indicates a similarity. He wants to be a scientist *as well as* study sociology.

54. C: The word "but" indicates an opposition. So, we have Casey trying to go to school. But instead of this happening, her car did not start, causing the opposite to happen.

55. C: "Nevertheless" indicates an opposition. It's like saying, "Even though she hated it, she went anyway."

56. A: The correct transition word is "then." This constitutes that one thing happened after another thing. There is no cause and effect or contrast happening in this sentence.

57. D: This sentence displays a consequence; Boris got a job as a consequence of preparing his resume. Therefore, the word we are looking for is "consequently."

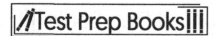
HSPT Practice Test #2

To keep the size of this book manageable, save paper, and provide a digital test-taking experience, the 2nd practice test can be found online. Scan the QR code or go to this link to access it:

testprepbooks.com/bonus/hspt

The first time you access the tests, you will need to register as a "new user" and verify your email address.

If you have any issues, please email support@testprepbooks.com.

Dear HSPT Test Taker,

Thank you for purchasing this study guide for your HSPT exam. We hope that we exceeded your expectations.

Our goal in creating this study guide was to cover all of the topics that you will see on the test. We also strove to make our practice questions as similar as possible to what you will encounter on test day. With that being said, if you found something that you feel was not up to your standards, please send us an email and let us know.

We would also like to let you know about other books in our catalog that may interest you.

SAT

This can be found on Amazon: amazon.com/dp/1637753381

ACT

amazon.com/dp/1637758596

ACCUPLACER

amazon.com/dp/1637756356

We have study guides in a wide variety of fields. If the one you are looking for isn't listed above, then try searching for it on Amazon or send us an email.

Thanks Again and Happy Testing!
Product Development Team
info@studyguideteam.com

FREE Test Taking Tips Video/DVD Offer

To better serve you, we created videos covering test taking tips that we want to give you for FREE. **These videos cover world-class tips that will help you succeed on your test.**

We just ask that you send us feedback about this product. Please let us know what you thought about it—whether good, bad, or indifferent.

To get your **FREE videos**, you can use the QR code below or email freevideos@studyguideteam.com with "Free Videos" in the subject line and the following information in the body of the email:

      a. The title of your product

      b. Your product rating on a scale of 1-5, with 5 being the highest

      c. Your feedback about the product

If you have any questions or concerns, please don't hesitate to contact us at info@studyguideteam.com.

Thank you!

Made in the USA
Las Vegas, NV
27 November 2024